The Tragedy of Liberalism

SUNY series in Social and Political Thought
Kenneth Baynes, editor

The Tragedy of Liberalism

~

An Alternative Defense of a Political Tradition

Bert van den Brink

STATE UNIVERSITY OF NEW YORK PRESS

Published by
State University of New York Press, Albany

Printed in the United States of America

For information, address State University of New York
Press, State University Plaza, Albany, N.Y., 12246

Production by Diane Ganeles
Marketing by Anne Valentine

Library of Congress Cataloging-in-Publication Data

Brink, Bert van den.
     The tragedy of liberalism : an alternative defense of a political
tradition / Bert van den Brink.
          p. cm. — (SUNY series in social and political thought)
     Includes bibliographical references and index.
     ISBN 0–7914–4669–7 (hc : acid-free). — ISBN 0–7914–4670–0
(pb : acid-free)
     1. Liberalism. I. Title. II. Series.
JC574.B75   2000
320.51'3—dc21
                                                            99–055786

10 9 8 7 6 5 4 3 2 1

To my parents,
my sisters,
and my brother

Contents

Preface

This book is about what I call liberalism's tragic predicament—
when the universalist and egalitarian doctrine of liberalism cannot
make sense of its own ideals without articulating a normative
framework that lets some conceptions of a valuable and good life appear to be more valid than others. In itself, this may seem to be an
unavoidable consequence for any normative political theory. However, many leading liberal theorists overlook or even deny the fact
that liberal ideals and practices can result in the morally problematic exclusion of, for instance, traditionalist and religious worldviews and social practices that seem to be of genuine value to some
people. It should be possible to show that liberalism's tragic predicament is both undeniable and of fundamental importance for an
understanding of the limits and scope of liberal ideals under ever-
changing social and cultural conditions. I argue that only those theories that recognize the fact that liberalism is a party to sometimes
irreconcilable conflicts—over, for instance, public justice, cultural
authenticity, and the definition of a good life—will arrive at an account of liberalism that may be expected to appeal to members of
contemporary pluralist societies.

   This book is an attempt both to develop a systematic thesis concerning the normative core and developmental potential of liberal
ideals and to come to terms with the many schools that exist within
contemporary liberal-democratic thought. As a consequence, it can
be read at two levels. First, as an investigative journey through
some of the most important strands of contemporary American and
European political philosophy, which include John Rawls's political

1

liberalism, Joseph Raz's liberal perfectionism, Jürgen Habermas's theory of deliberative democracy, Axel Honneth's social theory of struggles for recognition, and Will Kymlicka's multiculturalist liberalism. Second, the book can be read as a systematic argument concerning a tragic conflict of universalist and particularist sympathies that lies at the heart of liberalism.

In part 1, I introduce the concept of liberalism and ask how it should be defended under conditions of pluralism. Subsequently, I discuss various theses concerning liberalism's tragic predicament. Later, I develop an hypothesis that is tested in the subsequent parts of the book. This hypothesis might be understood as a detailed research question that has helped me to make sense of the loose ideas and intuitions phrased in the first paragraph.

Part 2 concerns two of the most influential contemporary liberal theories—Rawls's "political liberalism" and Raz's "liberal perfectionism." The aim is to argue for the correctness of the thesis that I have only hypothetically introduced in part 1. In many ways, these interpretations of liberalism turn out to presuppose each other's validity. Together, they sketch a picture of a political tradition with an irreconcilable and tragic tension. This emanates from the irreconcilability of two of liberalism's highest aims: on the one hand, the politically liberal aim for state neutrality toward various conceptions of the good life and, on the other, the necessity for liberalism to affirm—both in theory and in practice—the perfectionist values of personal autonomy and a pluralist social environment.

In part 3, I discuss Habermas's theory of "deliberative democracy." This doctrine holds out the promise that it is able to overcome the problems that confront political liberalism and liberal perfectionism. First, it presents a justificatory strategy for a liberal-democratic order that is more neutral toward competing conceptions of the good life than the politically liberal strategy. Second, it maintains that, contrary to liberal perfectionism, it is not founded on an ethically controversial affirmation of the values of personal autonomy and pluralism. Whereas, in a way, the former claim turns out to be correct, the latter is not. This will lead me to the conclusion that, although the deliberatively democratic approach can somewhat mitigate liberalism's tragic predicament, it cannot really overcome it.

In part 4, I pick up the loose threads from the preceding parts, which were mainly concerned with a conceptual analysis of normative theories. This analysis does not only show that liberalism is, already on a purely conceptual level, a tragic doctrine, but also that it is not enough to identify this fact. Therefore, the focus of the study shifts from purely conceptual questions of normative theory to questions of social theory and citizenship virtue. This aims to justify the heuristic role that tragic conflicts play in social struggles over the legitimate ordering of modern societies. To put it simply, I look at the tragic predicament of liberalism in ways that try to articulate to what extent liberal societies could actually benefit from—could become *more* liberal by—taking seriously the tragic conflicts that liberalism generates. First, I look at Christoph Menke's very perceptive typology of different kinds of tragic conflicts in liberal-democratic societies. Second, I adapt the vocabulary of Honneth's social theory that analyzes normative conflicts in terms of struggles for recognition. Both accounts turn out to be extremely helpful in developing an understanding of the normative potential of tragic conflicts that threaten to undermine liberalism's universalist and egalitarian aims. Finally, the chapter on citizenship virtue articulates a normative picture of liberal citizenship that makes it possible to understand what may be expected of those whose goal is to take the tragic predicament of liberalism seriously.

In the final part, I analyze liberal contributions to recent debates over multiculturalism. By doing so, I hope to have shown that the perspective on liberalism presented in this study is not just an exercise in academic philosophy, but has real value for liberal attempts to deal with the actual world we live in. I discuss the strategies for dealing with questions of multiculturalism that authors such as Charles Taylor, Jeremy Waldron, and Will Kymlicka have developed. I argue that the most convincing strategies implicitly acknowledge the tragedy of liberalism and that their convincing character is not just accidentally related to this fact.

This book developed from my doctoral dissertation. Many thanks are due to my supervisors at Utrecht University, the Netherlands, Willem van Reijen, Wibren van der Burg, and Peter Leisink, and to my friends and colleagues Maureen Sie and Marc Slors. The Faculty of the Social Sciences and the Department of Philosophy generously supported me throughout that period.

Over the years, Keimpe Algra, Albena Azmanova, Jan Bransen, Axel Honneth, Paulien Kleingeld, Christoph Menke, Anne Fritz Middelhoek, and Sean Sayers helped me considerably by discussing my evolving ideas. A special word of thanks is due to Joel Anderson, who was one of the reviewers of the manuscript for SUNY Press. Our discussions enabled me to fine-tune many of my arguments. I thank

Kenneth Baynes for his comments and support, and Zina Lawrence and Diane Ganeles of SUNY Press for their meticulous editing.

I also received advice from several members of the research program on "The Importance of Ideals in Law, Morality, and Politics" at the Faculty of Law of Tilburg University in the Netherlands. This program is supported by The Netherlands Organization for Scientific Research. Wibren van der Burg generously granted me the extra research time I needed. Sanne Taekema, Willem Witteveen, and Bertjan Wolthuis offered insightful comments. Rob Assmann and Karlijn van Blom assisted me in preparing the final document and Hildegard Penn did a great job of Americanizing the book.

∼

PART I

Liberalism, Pluralism, and Tragedy

Introduction

Contrary to what its title may at first sight suggest, this is not yet another study that aims to demonstrate the fact that liberalism is an indefensible political tradition. Rather, this study should be understood as a defense of liberalism. However, the title is meant to suggest that there is a problem with liberalism that has to be taken seriously by everyone who wants to gain knowledge of its limits and scope. This problem—that liberalism is a tragic doctrine—is too often neglected by liberal theorists.

By stating that liberalism is a tragic doctrine, I claim that it is characterized by conceptual tensions and practical moral conflicts that are (1) inescapable and even necessary, which (2) often seem and sometimes really are irreconcilable, and which (3) always involve experiences of moral loss.

(1) An example of a fundamental conceptual tension I will discuss is the tension between the ideal of the neutrality of the liberal state with respect to competing conceptions of the good life on the one hand and the "secularized" concept of the liberal public domain that accompanies this ideal on the other. Well-known examples of practical conflicts emanating from this tension are conflicts over abortion; euthanasia; genetic engineering; and the freedom to wear religious attire in schools, public institutions, and so forth. I will argue that, in a liberal society, these and similar conceptual tensions and practical conflicts are inescapable because they cannot be evaded. Furthermore, they are necessary in the stronger sense that

5

if we do not accept the reality of these tensions and conflicts, it becomes impossible to make sense of liberal ideals as such. In short, the conceptual tensions and practical conflicts I discuss emanate from fundamental normative assumptions without which liberalism's strategy to deal with the pluralist social world cannot successfully be defended and realized.

(2) The tensions and conflicts I will discuss are irreconcilable to the extent that liberalism is unable to transcend and to overcome them by means of the classic strategies of referring to uncontroversial principles of morality, practical reason, human nature, or conceptions of the good life. This does not mean, however, that it is impossible to distinguish between strategies of dealing with irreconcilable conflict. In later parts of the book, I will try to delineate some necessary conditions of promising strategies for dealing with irreconcilable practical conflicts in liberal society.

(3) My most important claim will be that these conceptual tensions and practical conflicts are tragic insofar as they confront liberalism with the dilemma that in trying to reach for its highest aim—letting the interests of all citizens in leading a good life matter equally[1]—it sometimes cannot but undermine this very aim. In reaching for its highest aim, liberalism inescapably and necessarily is biased against some conceptions of the good that in theory it aims to tolerate, especially those associated with cultural membership, orthodox religious belief, and traditional worldviews. This tragic circumstance involves an experience of moral loss not only for members of, for example, indigenous cultures and orthodox religious groups, but also for liberals who take seriously the aim of guaranteeing equal opportunity for all. This last point will eventually enable me to offer an account of liberalism's tragic predicament that does not result in resignation in the face of irreconcilable conceptual tensions and moral conflicts nor denies the fact that these tensions and conflicts should be taken seriously, but genuinely tries to learn from them. Indeed, my claim will be that the best liberal theories are those that are aware of their tragic predicament.

This first part of the book is meant to elucidate this abstract, controversial, and as yet unsubstantiated claim in general terms. For several reasons, I must ask the reader to have some patience with me. First, I will sometimes have to present the normative implications and the methodological foundations of various liberal theories in ways that do not always do justice to all their nuances. However, I hope to make up for this later parts. Second, I cannot immediately dive into the depths of the thesis that liberalism is a tragic doctrine. For in order to make clear what I am trying to say, I will first have to introduce the reader to some basic ideas characteristic of liberalism and to the important philosophical question of how liberalism is best defended in a pluralist age. Only after I have done this will I be able to make any sense at all of the claim that liberalism is a tragic doctrine.

1

~

Liberalism and Moral Pluralism

Both in theoretical debates and in practical politics, it has often been claimed that liberalism has become the dominant political ideology of the Western world. This seems to be true, especially since the term *liberalism* refers to a general political outlook that is shared by most citizens and political parties—whether they call themselves liberal or not. The main characteristics of this general outlook consist of a constitutionally warranted sense of respect for the life and liberty of each individual, a concentration on equal rights, an affirmation of the value of democratic government and moral pluralism, and the advancement of a market economy. As Richard Bellamy puts it: "From New Right conservatives to democratic socialists, it seems that we are all liberals now."[1] To the extent that liberalism can be understood as a general political outlook, it provides a relatively solid modus vivendi on the basis of which often fierce battles of interpretation take place over the question of what a just and good society should look like.[2] However, this characterization of liberalism is so general that it calls for further specification.

Liberalism

It is important to stress the fact that I will focus on normative liberal political theories. These are philosophical theories that discuss the normative grounds on which liberalism should be defended and how this relates to more specific questions of, for instance, social justice, institutional design, and civic virtue. Such theories start from basic

intuitions and empirical knowledge as to the autonomy and vulnerability of human beings, their capacity to act reasonably and
morally, the sense of justice and good that comes with this capacity,
and the purposes a just society serves—most notably the protection
of personal and political freedom.[3] In this section, I will briefly discuss concepts of freedom, equality, state neutrality, and the good life
that should not be understood as describing empirical realities of existing liberal societies. Rather, they should be understood as core
concepts of theories that aim to articulate pictures of how humans,
understood as members of political communities, could and should
live together. In this sense, they are ideal notions; however, they are
not as abstract as they often seem to be. A convincing ideal notion
stays in close contact with empirical reality.[4] For example, the notions of freedom and equality are so influential in contemporary normative theory because they seem to articulate the normative
expectations of many citizens of existing liberal societies. They do
not want their fellow citizens, the government, social organizations,
the business sector, religious authorities, and so on, to control their
lives. Furthermore, they expect to be protected by the institutions of
constitutional freedom.[5] The aim of normative political theory is to
articulate the normative expectations implicit in these claims, to tie
them to general conceptions of justice, reasonableness, freedom,
equality, and so on, and to mold them into a coherent conceptual
framework that is suited to help people reflect on questions of social,
legal, and political order and legitimacy. The hope of normative political theorists is that, by doing so, they will provide society with
well-articulated insights.

Let me begin my discussion with the concept of freedom. Most
contemporary liberal thinkers agree that citizens of liberal-democratic societies should be considered free in two different, yet closely related, respects. First, they should be able to form, revise, and
rationally pursue their own conception of a good life.[6] It is not always
clear why people choose to walk different paths in life, but it is clear
that they do. One person may pursue a career as a gardener and be a
convinced atheist, while another may pursue an academic career and
be a devoted Catholic. Of course, factors such as their intellectual and
physical abilities and their social and cultural backgrounds are likely
to introduce their choices. But this does not necessarily mean that
personal choices cannot be made. Freedom is a lived experience. Generally put, it is the experience of successfully deciding for oneself how
one wants to lead one's life and being respected as a person who does
so. Liberalism embraces this general notion of freedom.

The first type of freedom is often labeled "personal freedom." But as I just noted, the experience of deciding for oneself how one wants to lead one's life presupposes that others respect one's ability to do so. Humans are social beings, and their aims and choices affect the lives of others. In order to deal with the conflicts that often arise from this inescapable fact, every society needs a stable regime of social integration that defines the limits of personal freedom. Within liberal societies, and certainly within liberal theory, such a regime is usually conceived of in terms of social, moral, and legal norms; principles; and procedures that set standards for interaction within society. Furthermore, this is meant to reflect—in some way or other—the democratic will of the people to whom they apply. Behind this expectation lies the second idea of freedom constitutive of liberalism. This is the idea of the public autonomy of the citizen, understood as her capacity to reflect on the adequateness and legitimacy of the norms, principles, and procedures that set limits to her own personal freedom and to the personal freedom of her fellow citizens, and to her capacity and fundamental right to play a role in their generation. Of course, this notion can be justified in many different ways.

These two ideas of freedom—which at first sight seem to logically presuppose and complement each other perfectly—are crucial to most accounts of the normative core of pluralist and liberal societies.[7] The first is often thought to reflect typically modern ideas of personal autonomy and authenticity. In fact, these are separate ideas. One can act autonomously without being authentic and vice versa. But both involve the notion that the good life for human beings consists of the active participation "in the determination of their lives,"[8] that being true to one's own "originality," that "doing your own thing," and that "finding your own fulfillment," are valid ideals.[9] Both notions imply that one should be respected not only as a reasonable agent in some general sense, but also as one who has a unique self-determining authority in the formation, revision, and pursuance of a conception of the good life. The uniqueness of this authority is important because it has a bearing on what, in modern pluralist societies, can count as a good life. The ideals of personal autonomy and authenticity do not prescribe the content of conceptions of the good life, but they do set limits to their structure, that is, to the way in which individuals are expected to form such conceptions and to identify with them. Autonomous and authentic persons lead their lives "from the inside." In light of these ideals, the question of the good life is primarily a question for self-determining individuals, not for collectives.[10]

These brief remarks concerning personal autonomy and authenticity are certainly not as uncontroversial as they may seem to be at first sight. Leading "politically liberal" theorists such as John Rawls and Bruce Ackerman will find the ideals of personal autonomy and authenticity too "perfectionist" to allow them to play a fundamental role in liberalism as a political tradition.[11] In Rawls's words, political liberals will claim that personal autonomy and authenticity present ideals of human excellence that the government "can no more act to maximize . . . than it can advance Catholicism or Protestantism, or any other religion."[12] Although I suspect that these authors would be willing to acknowledge that these ideals primarily affect the structure and not the content of personal conceptions of the good, they would certainly reject any suggestion that the liberal state should deliberately foster them. For this would undermine another important liberal idea, that of the liberal state's aim for neutrality among competing conceptions of the good life. So, political liberals and many other liberals would not accept the ideals of personal autonomy and authenticity as uncontroversial facts of social life that liberalism can unproblematically embrace. Rather, they welcome them as possible ways of thinking about the good life that exist among other ways, for example, the idea that there is no real value in examining one's "authentic" identity, or that the unautonomous imitation of someone else's life is not necessarily a bad thing.[13]

An important question in the present study will be whether liberalism, understood as a political doctrine, presupposes the ideals of personal autonomy and authenticity. I will argue that it does, especially so with respect to personal autonomy, but that this does not mean that it should not respect persons who do not adhere to these ideals. However, until I will have shown this we should be reluctant to be too perfectionist about the liberal notion of personal freedom. Let us for now characterize this notion minimalistically as the freedom to live one's life according to one's given conception of the good life, and not say anything more about the exact quality of such conceptions.[14]

I mentioned that, for political liberals, the neutrality of the liberal state with respect to different conceptions of the good life is important. In fact, state neutrality is important for most liberals.[15] The liberal state does not only aim for neutrality among competing reasonable conceptions of human excellence within a liberal order; it also respects all citizens as being equally entitled to having their voice heard in the generation of the norms, principles, and procedures that govern life in liberal society. Again, there are many different ways in which the liberal principle of neutrality can be accounted for. Some

authors primarily concentrate on the "hypothetical" consent of all citizens to general principles of liberal justice; others concentrate on the
normative core of "actual" empirical processes of democratic opinion
formation and parliamentary decision-making.[16] In both accounts,
the idea of equality plays an important role.

The idea of equality lies behind the liberal idea that all citizens
have the fundamental right to be respected as free and reasonable
persons. This assumption is based on a post-Enlightenment belief in
the reasonableness of human beings, which is based on their capacity to act autonomously in the "public" sense that was just described,
and also, in a more general sense, on their capacity to acquire knowledge of the natural and the social world by following the logic of their
own thought and perception (as opposed to following the logic of systems of thought offered to them by, e.g., tradition or political and religious authorities). One of the basic ideas of the Enlightenment era
was that if genuine knowledge of the world could be attained by all
reasonable beings, then all reasonable beings should have an equal
say in a society's attempts to shape and control the world.[17] This idea
motivated political thinkers such as John Locke and Immanuel
Kant—who we now think of as "early liberals"—to question tradition, convention, and forms of heteronomous political authority as
the basis of social order and political legitimacy, which concern all
members of society. And since they should in principle be seen as
reasonable beings, there is no reason why they should not have a
voice in the generation of the norms and principles and procedures
that govern their lives. The idea is that as long as these are generated and controlled in ways that all reasonable individuals can
(could) agree to, they may be said to be legitimate.[18]

So liberal theories are egalitarian when it comes to the question
of their legitimation. The theories I will focus on are egalitarian in
other respects too, most importantly with respect to the notion of
equality of opportunity. When thinking about equality, we can distinguish between formal equality and substantive or effective equality.[19]
Formal equality is legal equality per se. The formal egalitarian argues
that a just society is one in which all citizens have equal rights. But
are "equality of libertarian rights" (Robert Nozick) or "equal legal and
political treatment" (James Buchanan) enough to effectively treat
human beings as equals?[20] The liberals I will concentrate on in this
study answer this last question in a negative manner. They believe
that formal equality is not enough. Their well-known argument is that
in order to really count as equals, some citizens may require special
attention. They are not exclusively preoccupied with the vague notion

that, on a very fundamental level (e.g., the level of their ability to act reasonably), everyone is equal and should, therefore, be treated equally, but with the substantive moral position that everyone, whatever their resemblances and differences may be, should have equal opportunities in life. The idea that people should not always be treated equally, but should be treated as equals, is the idea that the conditions for the full development of person A may require different measures than the conditions for the full development of person B, and that the liberal state has the responsibility for providing everyone with basic conditions of well-being. In a society in which everyone has the same rights, but in which some of them cannot make effective use of these rights because they lack the minimum conditions that will enable them to flourish in that society (e.g., a minimum income, basic education, and basic health care), the liberal state has the responsibility to support these citizens—particularly if their position is not one of choice but of chance. In a world characterized by huge, nonvoluntary inequalities in economic and cultural capital and opportunities, this substantive notion of equality or distributive justice is a minimum requirement for a liberal theory that poses the fundamental question of how the liberal state could treat its citizens as equals.[21] The liberal theories I focus on are usually understood as interpretations of what, in practical political terms, is known as welfare liberalism or social-democratic liberalism.[22]

Finally, the idea of equality plays a role in liberal thought in what one could call a presumption of equal value regarding different conceptions of a good life.[23] Liberalism and ethical pluralism go hand in hand. Therefore, liberal citizens as well as liberal governments will at least have to presume that the often quite different conceptions of the good life of different persons are, in some way or other, of equal value. This means that they will have to acknowledge the fact that value schemes that are not their own may well contain valuable ethical orientations, both for those who adhere to these value schemes and even for those who do not. Of course, there are limits to the presumption of equal value. The liberal state cannot tolerate blatantly unreasonable conceptions of the good life. This can only be pursued at the cost of the freedom and equality of others. But so long as individuals respect the limits set by legitimate general norms, principles, and procedures for peaceful interaction, they must be equally entitled to pursue their own conceptions of the good life.

Again, not all theorists account for this presumption of equal value in similar terms. All agree that tolerable conceptions of the good should at least promote in those who adhere to them toleration for other conceptions of the good. But liberal authors disagree about whether more substantive judgments as to the validity of conceptions of the good can be made. Some defend noncognitivist views that border on moral skepticism, the idea that the value of conceptions of the good cannot be rationally assessed. They regard conceptions of the good as subjective preferences, the value of which the liberal state cannot (and should not try to) assess. From this perspective, all that matters is that citizens understand that their personal conceptions of the good are theirs, not everybody else's, and that claims to the validity of such conceptions of the good should not be brought into deliberations concerning matters of public and political concern.[24] Other theorists, however, maintain that the value of conceptions of the good can in principle be rationally assessed through reasonable dialogue,[25] or by looking at received standards of what must be considered valid conceptions of the good within a liberal society.[26] In later chapters, I will argue for a combination of the second and third accounts and show why the first approach should be rejected. My argument will have considerable consequences for the question as to whether liberalism presupposes a substantive conception of the good life. I will argue that it does. For now, however, it suffices that we understand that the liberal state aims to respect its citizens both as "publicly" autonomous reasonable subjects and—within certain minimalist limits—as individuals who must be presumed to have valid reasons to orient themselves to their particular conception of a good and valuable life.

To conclude, I am primarily interested in liberal theories that allow all citizens to enjoy personal freedom and public autonomy equally.[27] These are prerequisites for leading a good life within a liberal society. Therefore, it is in order to claim that the central question of this study is *how a liberal society could let the interests of all citizens in leading a good life matter equally.*

Pluralism and how (not) to defend liberalism

As I said earlier, I want to defend the thesis that liberalism is a tragic doctrine; that it is characterized by conceptual tensions and practical conflicts that are inescapable, to a considerable extent irreconcilable, and that involve the experience of loss. In the general characterization of liberalism I just presented, I did not stress any of those aspects of my tragic view because the main defenders of

liberalism I will focus on concentrate on the decidedly untragic notion of reconciliation. As thoroughly modern theorists, they look for
ways in which human beings could think of social, legal, and political order that do away with the agonizing experience of irreconcilable tension, conflict, and loss, and that unite them in a just and
reasonable society that benefits them all. The basic premise is that
reasonable persons, capable of acting freely, should in principle be
able to live together in ways in which conflicts can adequately be
transcended and, possibly, even reconciled.

I do not want to deny that this is a highly valuable way of viewing reality. Both for questions of social order and for questions of individual well-being, the importance of the ideal of reconciliation can
hardly be overestimated. One of the great achievements of modern
liberalism is that, from the days of the religious wars of the six-
teenth and seventeenth centuries onward, it has pacified social strife
by fostering modes of toleration that enable people to live peacefully
together despite their moral and cultural differences. The reconciliation that liberalism aims at is not achieved through homogeniza-
tion. It is rather based on trust in the power of public reason; the
reason of a community of citizens who shape their pluralist social
world in a collective effort to attain justice and personal freedom for
all. As John Rawls puts it, within the liberal tradition "pluralism is
not seen as disaster but rather as the natural outcome of the activities of human reason under enduring free institutions."[28]

But how should this "natural outcome" be conceived? Should it
be accounted for in terms of humanity gradually coming to live up
to its quasi-innate moral core? Or should it be conceived of in terms
of a more contingent pragmatic achievement that has gradually
been morally embraced by a great many people who flourish as a result? This is an important and difficult question, which goes straight
to the heart of contemporary philosophical debates over liberalism.
On the one hand, we see authors such as Rawls and Jürgen Habermas, who use notions such as autonomy, reasonableness, and justice
in what I would call an a prioristic mode.[29] To put it simply, here the
basic idea is that if all human beings were true to their essential capacities for autonomy, reasonableness, and justice, social and political reconciliation could be attained. Because these authors tend to
view these capacities as essential human capacities, they can rather
unproblematically assume that it would be good for all citizens of liberal societies to embrace and act upon them. On the other hand, we
see what we could call historicist authors such as Joseph Raz,
Richard Rorty, and William A. Galston, who stress the fact that lib-

eralism is a lived tradition whose historically contingent central notions developed within, and have proven to be of great value for, individualist and pluralist cultures.[30] These authors believe that so-called essential capacities for autonomous and reasonable action are not so much capacities of all human beings, but rather culturally situated capacities that are conducive to particular—liberal—forms of social cooperation. They emphasize that, although these capacities are highly valuable characteristics of virtuous members of liberal societies, one cannot simply assume that they are essential characteristics of human beings per se. In this study, I will opt for a variant of this second approach. I will not so much show that humanity has no essential moral core, but rather that it is wise to accept that we cannot decide that question and that we, therefore, should look at liberalism and at its central notions in the second way. For we do know from experience that, despite its historical successes, liberalism has always been, and still is, a contested tradition. It seems wise to take that experience seriously.

Of course, the choice for the second approach has significant implications for anyone who wants to defend liberalism. Typically, those who choose the first approach have a standard answer to those who contest liberalism. They argue that these contestants are wrong, or unreasonable, because they simply do not understand what it means to live up to the real meaning of—the postmetaphysical philosophical truth about—autonomy, reasonableness, and justice. In a way, this is a comfortable position. It provides the theorist with an Archimedean point from which many, if not all, conceptual tensions and practical conflicts that may spring from liberalism can be assessed and—at least theoretically—resolved. It assures the Archimedean liberal that she is right about her fundamental theoretical beliefs, although she will admit that she may not yet have fully grasped all of liberalism's practical and theoretical implications. Theorists who opt for the second approach, however, cannot be so sure about their basic beliefs and assumptions. They have no Archimedean point to argue from. Rather, they are faced with a world full of different and often conflicting values, orientations, and principles that at first sight cannot be fitted easily into a coherent scheme. They believe that liberalism is one among many possible ideologies that aim to organize society, and that there simply are no knock-down arguments that could ultimately show that, among these, liberalism is the only viable option. Still, from their historical and political perspective, they choose to defend liberalism rather than any other doctrine. They account for the capacities for autonomy, reasonableness, and justice in terms that are not a prioristic. They understand them as critical values and virtues characteristic of a particular political tradition that is well worth arguing for, simply because it is conducive to forms of social interaction, pluralism, and personal freedom that represent good answers to questions that modern societies pose—not necessarily because liberalism's basic assumptions are thought to be more "true" or "less controversial" than those of other doctrines.

In contemporary liberal theory, the battlefield on which discussions over how to defend liberalism take place is very often that of moral pluralism. Moral pluralism exists if people, who in some way or other (are forced to) live together, hold different moral views, that is, views that are critical to their identity and that give meaning to their being in the world. The clause "who in some way or other (are forced to) live together" is important here. The term *moral pluralism* makes sense only if people with different moral views interact and consequently run the risk of getting into normative conflict over questions that call for morally motivated answers. If a group of three isolated islands in the Pacific Ocean were inhabited by three peoples with different moral views and if each people were to stick to an island of its own and live a self-contained life there, we would not say that moral pluralism was a feature of social life on the archipelago. If, however, they were to take up economic and cultural relations, visit each other's islands, and become political allies (or enemies), they would soon find out what moral pluralism consists of. They would experience what has been called difference: through interactions with strangers from other islands they would realize that these strangers attach significance to persons, values, and objects in ways formerly unknown to them. And they would find that severe normative conflicts can spring from the collision of different worldviews.

Of course, difference and moral pluralism are not necessarily the same. There are many sorts of differences that can be experienced as morally neutral: bodily differences, differences of accents within one language, and differences of taste are good examples.[30] But it is true that difference is often indicative of moral pluralism. As J. Donald Moon puts it: "Ties to family, love, friendship, and attachments to land and home can give rise to moral pluralism when they lead to distinct group identities and significant differences within a society."[32] And we might add that ties to religion, ethnicity, culture, gender, and ideals of personal excellence may give rise to the same phenomenon. Particularly so if they inspire social and political action that aims to gain influence over important institutions associated with education, culture, politics, law, and so forth.[33] It seems, then, that moral pluralism exists if distinct group identities and significant and morally relevant differences occur within one social setting. This kind of pluralism is labeled moral, because the difference between groups originates from the existence of two or more conflicting moral frameworks—which will in most cases encompass both conceptions of general social norms, principles, and procedures and ideals of personal excellence—within one society or community.

Now, an important question for the assessment of moral pluralism is how "real" the differences between moral frameworks are. In liberal theory, many attempts have been undertaken to show that what we, following Habermas, might call ethical pluralism—the kind of pluralism that springs from the incompatibility of nongeneralizable substantive ideals of personal excellence[34]—need not really bother the liberal theorist. Such personal or "private" ideals, many liberals claim, are best understood as subjective preferences that cannot be argued for in a generalizing mode. From the perspective of normative political theory, these theorists claim, such personal preferences should not be understood as the locus of the moral capacities for autonomy and reasonableness that are so important for the sustenance of a just society. These latter capacities, they maintain, are primarily capacities of persons qua human beings, not capacities of members of groups who happen to value these capacities. In moral and political theory, they conclude, generalizable principles that are deduced from essential capacities should always override claims that are born of subjective preferences. And this not just because only the former make it possible for human beings to successfully control and, if necessary, counteract the severe normative conflicts that may spring from the clash of irreconcilable subjective preferences, but rather because the dignity of human subjects is defined by their ability to act according to the essential capacity for autonomous moral action.[35] Moral pluralism cannot be a genuine problem for theorists who start from these assumptions. For them, the moral is one, while the ethical is many.[36] And, at least for normative political theory, the moral must be more real than the ethical, because—or so the assumption goes—we all share the same capacities for moral deliberation, while we are deeply divided over questions of personal excellence.

As has been often noted, the main problem with this line of thought is that it—perhaps unwillingly—presupposes a conception of individuality that borders on the schizophrenic.[37] It expects citizens to be able to largely abstract from personal interests, attachments, and purposes in public life (the life of autonomous, reasonable, and generalizable reasons and actions), while it encourages these same citizens to find their personal fulfillment in substantive and possibly controversial notions of the good in their private lives. And it suggests that a liberal society is neutral among ethical notions of the good because its thin, capacity-focused notion of the autonomous and reasonable citizen does not favor any particular ethical conception of the good. Which personal ideals of excellence should be of value to individuals is left to these individuals to decide. This kind of liberalism genuinely aims to combine the best of both worlds—the world of autonomy and reasonableness and that of nongeneralizable ideas of human excellence—without compromising either of them. Its intentions are very sympathetic, its moral promise alluring. But somehow, it all seems too good to be true.

To get to the heart of this approach, let's pose some straightforward and commonsensical questions.[38]

> 1. Is it not true that we know from experience that a successful, well-educated citizen of a liberal society stands a better chance of being recognized as an autonomous and reasonable person than most poorly educated citizens?
>
> 2. Is it, therefore, not true that liberalism is no more than a cleverly disguised ideology that will primarily benefit successful members of society?
>
> 3. Is it not true that we cannot act autonomously and reasonably without being motivated by personal (ethical) convictions?
>
> 4. Is it not true that there are many people who would rather be damned than let public morality be ruled by the individualist-secular idea of autonomous reasoning alone?

Of course, "Archimedean" liberals have standard answers to these questions—with which their critics confront them all the time. Let me try to answer these questions on their behalf.

1. Yes, that is entirely true. And that is exactly why we stress the fact that people should have equal opportunities in life. Our belief in the political priority of autonomy and reasonableness should not be mistaken for the naive idea that every human being, in every situation, will automatically be capable of acting autonomously and reasonably in our sense. It is just the belief that, in principle, every human being should be respected. This implies that she should be

granted full citizenship status and that she may be entitled to extra measures by the state, which will enable her to successfully live up to these capacities and, therefore, flourish in both her public and her private life.

2. No, liberalism is not a disguised ideology that primarily favors the already well-off. On the contrary, it stands for equal liberties and opportunities for all, guaranteed and protected by a state that aims for neutrality among competing conceptions of the good life. Of course, liberalism leaves a lot of room for personal choice. So some citizens may concentrate on economic success, while others may devote their lives to personal purposes that will not be as lucrative. Liberalism is neutral on such issues. It does not prescribe how people should lead their lives. Because of the far-reaching freedom of choice it grants to citizens, liberalism cannot be held responsible for inequalities that result from free choices made by individuals. As long as the principles of the liberal state can be freely accepted by all citizens, liberalism neither favors nor disfavors the interests of any particular group of citizens.

3. That is an important question. And yes, it is true that we often cannot act autonomously and reasonably without being motivated by our deepest personal convictions. However, our capacities for autonomy and reasonableness set limits to what we may legitimately expect of the outcome of public deliberation. Respect for these essential capacities and their role in democratic deliberation entails that citizens should be willing to let their personal convictions and aims be trumped by legal and political forms of consensus and compromise. Note, however, that consensus and compromise should not be understood as expressing a mere modus vivendi of competing groups and individuals. The idea is that citizens will understand that consensus and compromise are genuine goods, that is, that they will respect them as legitimate and highly valuable aspects of a well-ordered pluralist society.

4. That is a tricky question. Classic examples of the problem can be found in discussions concerning the right to abortion or to euthanasia and the right to self-government of religious groups such as the Amish or native people such as Native Americans and Australian aboriginals. The problem is that some people indeed believe that they have valid moral reasons—reasons that they think everybody should accept—not to accept the liberal principle of autonomous and reasonable self-determination of citizens as the highest standard for a just ordering of society as a whole. Archimedean liberals offer two possible answers to this dilemma.

The first is simply to point out to these people that they are not being reasonable, that they are unwilling to recognize that we need to transcend ethical pluralism, and that we can do so only by giving priority to capacities we all share. This may seem to come down to begging the question but the idea is that, in deliberating with us about these issues, our opponents cannot but presuppose the validity of public autonomy and reasonable consensus-seeking as guiding ideals for conflict resolution. By denying this, they would engage in a performative contradiction, for they would reject the very kind of reasonable consensus-seeking that they engage in. The idea is that the contestants of our strategy do not understand the normative presuppositions of their own (communicative) actions. If we succeed in pointing this out to them, they might eventually come to accept the impartiality and acceptability of at least the basic terms of the strategy we propose.[39]

The second strategy is more modest. Here, the idea is that even if we accept the fact that public autonomy and reasonableness cannot be understood as an Archimedean point by all individuals and groups within liberal societies, we may find an alternative—although slightly weaker—Archimedean point in the "public culture" of liberal societies. We then are able to state that, when public issues are at stake, public autonomy and reasonableness override private conceptions of the good life because, in our liberal society, we have found that this is the best—or if you want, the least controversial—way of dealing with pluralism. It is a consequence of this approach that, as John Rawls has recently pointed out, we may reach a point at which we cannot do anything other than override the claims of our opponents without their consent.[40] Although this approach offers a very realistic and pragmatic solution to problems of pluralism, it is true that it also has an illiberal ring to it.

I think that these answers to our commonsensical questions, which I have tried to present as fair-mindedly as possible, are only partly convincing. More precisely: the first is convincing, the second is slightly less convincing, the third is problematic, while the fourth shows that there is something seriously wrong about the self-understanding of Archimedean liberals.

1. The liberal Archimedean is right in pointing out to us that our first question is based on a misunderstanding of the aims of normative political theory. The empirical fact that some groups benefit more from existing liberal societies than others does not show that normative liberal theories merely try to sustain that unjust status quo. After all, such theories often explicitly try to point out to

what extent these existing societies do not succeed in living up to the normative core of their constitutive documents and legal and political institutions. However controversial the idea of the priority of autonomy and reasonableness may seem to be to some, there seems to be nothing wrong with the attempts of many theorists to show that if we want to stick to this priority in our public language, we had better look for ways in which all citizens could fully live up to it.

2. It follows from this, that liberalism is not a conservative doctrine. It genuinely tries to stand for the interests of all citizens. However, the stress on freedom of choice and autonomous self-determination may be more controversial than it seems to be at first sight. Liberalism allows some citizens to devote themselves to making a fortune on Wall Street, while others choose to work for Amnesty International or Greenpeace (trying to counteract, among other things, some of the less favorable consequences of the financial speculations of many of their fellow citizens). In this sense, it is a tolerant doctrine, which aims to let citizens decide for themselves how they want to lead their lives and how, if at all, they want to contribute to the common good. But the liberal framework that allows for freedom of choice and for autonomous self-determination, and that finds its principle of legitimacy in the hypothetical agreement of all citizens to its basic terms, will have to presuppose that these values (will eventually) be wholeheartedly embraced by all citizens. This highly demanding criterion of legitimacy, it seems to me, is the Achilles heel of Archimedean liberalism.

3. The demanding character of this criterion becomes clearer once we accept the fact that people cannot but act from personal convictions about what is right and what is good. This means that, whatever the precise Archimedean qualities of public autonomy and reasonableness are thought to consist of, liberalism can only be considered a legitimate doctrine if the "moral character" of all citizens of a liberal society is structured in such a way that they can wholeheartedly accept the priority of public autonomy and reasonableness in the public life of that liberal society. Archimedean liberals cannot simply reply to this that their normative theories reflect on the principles of legitimacy of an ideal liberal society, that is, a society in which all citizens would be able to accept this priority. A convincing ideal notion stays in close contact with empirical reality. And the empirical reality in which liberal theorists stand clearly shows that not all citizens of liberal societies show the personality traits of the ideal liberal citizen. The conceptions of personal and collective freedom of

some not necessarily unreasonable groups and individuals—orthodox Christians, Muslims, Jews, Native Americans, Australian aboriginals, and so on—are sometimes clearly at odds with liberal principles of moral, legal, and political order and legitimacy. This raises the question as to how Archimedean liberals could ever be true to their aim to allow all citizens to lead a good life.

4. The two answers to this problem we just saw indicate the seriousness of this problem. The first answer states that we should always be willing to deliberate with nonliberal citizens, but only on the premise that they are willing to accept that—by engaging in deliberative attempts at conflict resolution—they are using a formal vocabulary that is biased toward (liberal understandings of) public autonomy and reasonableness. The second answer basically states the same, although it understands the moral grammar of liberal deliberation as a culturally situated good. These answers are certainly not to be condemned. Both are given with understandable reluctance and come with the explicit guarantee that liberalism will always treat "dissidents" with the utmost respect. However, what worries me about these answers is that they seem to beg the question. The unquestionable belief in the correctness of our way of consensus-seeking, of the values central to our public culture, has a very dogmatic ring to it. It seems to say something like: "We propose a way of including you in our just order; we know that, as a human being, you are capable of acting autonomously and reasonably, of distinguishing public aims and purposes from private ones, so please feel free to join us." In many ways, this is a very humane and tolerant strategy. But it overlooks the very real possibility that those who do not fit easily into the liberal framework might have important and valid reasons not to accept that liberal framework. Such reasons are deliberately ignored by Archimedean liberalism.

We may conclude that Archimedean liberalism tries to take pluralism seriously by sidestepping its most inflammatory building blocks. In practice, this strategy has some major advantages. Most importantly, it gives liberalism the opportunity to grant citizenship rights universally, without having to scrutinize the ethical beliefs of all citizens. This is a highly valuable aim of liberalism that should not be abandoned. Yet, from a philosophical perspective, with a view toward finding out what liberalism's relation to pluralism consists of, the Archimedean approach appears to be deeply problematic. Most importantly, because of its basic terms and assumptions, Archimedean liberalism seems to make it impossible for itself to look at pluralism in an open-minded and self-critical way.

In the course of this study we will find that there is a more viable way to think about the relationship between liberalism and pluralism. It starts by genuinely accepting the fact that liberalism has a problem with pluralism. And this not just in the sense of acknowledging that there indeed are empirical cases in which the limits of liberal tolerance seem to have been reached, but rather in the sense of acknowledging that—as a matter of the ethical orientations of members of liberal societies—the tension between, on the one hand, general liberal principles of public autonomy, reasonableness, and state neutrality and, on the other hand, nonpublic ideals of individual and collective self-realization is at the heart of liberalism. If we accept the fact that liberalism can only be a viable doctrine so long as there are individuals who are willing to let their ethical beliefs be trumped by liberal standards of public reason and public autonomy, then we also have to accept the fact that liberalism is not the ethically neutral and undemanding doctrine it is often purported to be. For the willingness to let one's most deeply felt beliefs be trumped by the overriding values of public autonomy and reasonableness will have huge consequences for the hierarchical ordering of one's ethical orientations.

For any self-critical brand of liberalism, this must mean that it should understand conflicts that spring from pluralism not primarily as problems caused by individuals or groups who refuse to be fitted into the allegedly ethically neutral liberal framework. It should rather look at such conflicts as conflicts that liberalism cannot help but generate itself. Indeed, I hope to show that the liberal aim to grant all citizens the equal right to lead a good life is—paradoxically—both rather unrealistic and highly valuable. It is unrealistic because it seems that there are not always decisive reasons that can show why everybody should affirm those ideas of a good and valuable life that liberalism cannot help but presuppose and foster. But it is highly valuable because for us—liberals, that is—there is no better way to think about public issues than the one articulated in the highest liberal aim. It is necessary to abide by the liberal aim, because it is the aim that underlies our deepest personal and political self-understandings. Yet, if my articulation of this problem is more or less correct, it seems that we will have to seriously ask ourselves whether we understand the negative and even exclusionary consequences of our allegedly ethically neutral doctrine well enough to be true to liberal ideals.

I will defend the thesis that it is best to admit straightforwardly that liberalism is—both in its moral foundations and in its effects on the lives of individuals—not an ethically neutral doctrine. Only if we admit this, will we be able to gain valuable knowledge concerning the limits and scope of this political doctrine. I will argue that liberalism should not so much be embarrassed by the tensions and conflicts it simply cannot transcend and reconcile, but that it should rather take them seriously as essential characteristics of its own normative framework that have a tremendous heuristic value. The idea is that by acknowledging the inescapability of these conflicts and tensions, liberalism will be able to both generate a more adequate self-understanding and come up with more promising ways to deal with them. In my account, the idea that liberalism is a tragic doctrine will play an important role. I will now turn to this idea.

2

~

The Tragedy of Liberalism

Let me start with a stipulative definition. It is characteristic of a tragedy—either as a play, as a single event, or as a persistent situation—that human beings who, as free and responsible individuals, try to control the world in order to be true to values that are of great importance to them, find that they ultimately fail in their attempts because of certain inescapable or even necessary traits of their fate, of the world, or of the frameworks of value from which they draw their motivations. This is why a tragic experience necessarily results in the loss of high hopes and the loss of the possibility to act according to one's deeply held beliefs.[1]

Perhaps this definition is most famously illustrated by Sophocles' *Oedipus Rex*. In this play a human being perishes precisely because of the actions he deliberately undertakes to avoid his own downfall. Oedipus flees from Corinth in order to escape the oracle's prediction that he will kill his father, who, Oedipus believes, is Polybos, king of Corinth. How could he possibly have known that this action, born of the best of intentions, would result in his meeting and killing his real father, Laios, on the way to Thebes, the place where he thought he would be safe? In trying to flee from his horrible fate, killing his father and sleeping with his mother, Oedipus ends up doing both. It is this predicament (and the predicament of many other tragic figures in world literature) that makes the German critic Peter Szondi state that "the unity of liberation and destruction" ("*die Einheit von Rettung und Vernichtung*") is one of the fundamental characteristics of the tragic.[2]

27

Two views of tragic liberalism

There is, of course, an influential tradition in modern thought that tries to do away with the tragic experience. This is the tradition, going back to Plato and Aristotle, and with modern roots in both Kant and Hegel, which primarily focuses on the reconciliation of conflicts and inconsistencies in the social, moral, and political fabric of society through the use of reason. As Bernard Williams has shown in a perceptive discussion of the relationship of this tradition to tragic accounts of the irreconcilableness of many conflicts of value, representatives believe "in one way or another that the universe or history or the structure of human reason can, when properly understood, yield a pattern that makes sense of human life and human aspirations."[3] What they seek, Williams maintains, is an understanding of human reason, of the world, or of history that will make us understand that, ultimately, a harmony of ethical motivations and conflicting interests with the refractory world we act in is possible because this world is shaped to the "ethical interests" of human beings.[4] Williams seriously doubts that the world is structured in such a way. Therefore, he comes up with the idea that the tragic representation of humans dealing "with a world that is only partially intelligible to human agency and in itself is not necessarily well adjusted to ethical aspirations," as it is found in Greek tragedy, may be surprisingly well suited to fit the experience of many late twentieth-century members of Western societies.[5]

It is tempting to a see a parallel between the pre-Socratic view of irreconcilable value pluralism, sustained by a quasi-polytheist—nonmonolithic—understanding of the supernatural, and contemporary "postideological" or "postmodern" thought. Of course, most of us do without a clearly defined view of the supernatural, and many think that they can do without such a view altogether. From a liberal point of view, the widespread agnosticism concerning these matters is one of the main reasons why one should presume that the orientations of others may well be as valuable as our own. Moreover, there is a widely shared experience that it is not at all easy to make sense of our existence in a world in which we are confronted with so many different and seemingly incommensurable, yet valuable ideas of personal excellence, cultural belonging, religious worship, and so forth. Our intellectual debates are certainly dominated by the experience of a sort of value pluralism which, in many cases, cannot easily be overcome by reference to some kind of overarching and uncontroversial view of politics, reason, or world history. So whatever may be true of the speculative ontological point Williams tries to make—the point that the world may not be shaped to ethical reconciliation—we certainly have the fundamental epistemological experience that the plurality of human values set free in late modernity cannot easily be overcome by reference to values that all individuals could (quasi-monotheistically) understand and embrace.

In a way, all tragic views of politics rest on—and in their turn reinforce—accounts of value pluralism and moral pluralism.[6] However, it is important to understand that not all tragic views of politics—or of liberalism for that matter—are the same. Restricting myself to contemporary views, two views stand out. The first view is grounded in what we might call an ontological account of value pluralism, the second in an account characteristic of what we might call a method of normative political theory. The two views cannot always be clearly distinguished from each other, for they share many assumptions. But I think that it is fair to say that both the famous tragic liberalism of Isaiah Berlin and Bernard Williams's ontological view fall within the first category. On the other hand, recent accounts by authors such as J. Donald Moon, Christoph Menke, and Susan Mendus fall within the second.[7]

It is characteristic of the ontological approach that it starts from an account of irreconcilable value pluralism and goes on to defend liberalism as a viable answer to social and political questions that arise from conflicts of pluralism. To quote a famous passage from Berlin's celebrated "Two Concepts of Liberty": "If, as I believe, the ends of men are many, and not all of them are in principle compatible with each other, then the possibility of conflict—and of tragedy—can never wholly be eliminated from human life, either personal or social."[8] The possibility of conflict and tragedy Berlin is talking about emanates from human life, not from the normative framework that a specific political doctrine such as liberalism brings to human life. Berlin's argument that liberalism—here of course understood as the antiperfectionist defense of negative liberty over positive liberty—is the best answer we have in face of irreconcilable conflicts of pluralism, rests on an analysis of the sometimes tragic nature of value pluralism as such, which is conceptually independent of his affirmation of liberalism. To be sure, Berlin has repeatedly stressed the fact that the conceptual structure of liberalism is not free from serious and irreconcilable tensions such as the one between the ideal of freedom and equality. But his central argument remains that conflicts of pluralism lead us to accept liberalism because it is simply the best—that is, the least oppressive—political system we can think of. Liberalism is presented as the best (although not perfect) solution to pluralism, but not as an important source of persisting conflicts of pluralism.[9]

The other approach I mentioned—the one emanating from a method of normative political theory—is not primarily interested in the tragedy of human life, but in the tragedy of liberalism. With this I mean to say that it focuses on exactly those practical conflicts and conceptual tensions that spring from liberal attempts to structure the social world. This approach investigates to what extent the epistemological experience of the irreconcilability of many conflicts of pluralism might be conceptually dependent not on value pluralism as such, but on the liberal framework that purports to give an answer to conflicts of pluralism. Moreover, this approach investigates the sacrifices liberalism demands of citizens in return for its promise of liberty, equality, and toleration. It represents a highly self-critical recent development in liberal political theory, which seems to have been strongly influenced by the recent communitarian and feminist critiques of Rawlsian liberalism in particular.[10] I label this approach one of normative political theory, because it starts from an analysis of the moral promise of a specific normative political theory and from the social, legal, and political practices it inspires, not from a prepolitical ontological account of value pluralism.

Where in Berlin's day and age liberal ideas represented an oasis of reasonableness and toleration in the face of—at the level of social patterns of expectation—narrow-minded intolerance and inegalitarian beliefs and—at the level of government—state paternalism and cold-war threats, liberal ideas nowadays often structure much of both the government and citizens' intuitions regarding questions of conflict, toleration, and social justice. Against this background, it comes as no surprise that recent tragic accounts of politics have started to make liberalism itself, not its external enemies or the nature of value pluralism, responsible for some of the seemingly irreconcilable conflicts of pluralism within liberal-democratic societies. In this spirit, J. Donald Moon defends an alternative understanding of political liberalism that "recognizes that *even within its own sphere* there will be oppositions that it cannot overcome. [Political liberalism] offers, then, a tragic view of political life and its possibilities, resting on the recognition of the inevitability of conflict and the experience of imposition on the part of those whose ideals are denied."[11] Conflicts that arise from clashes of orthodox-religious and liberal-secular frameworks of value and clashes of traditional community-based and liberal rights-based conceptions of justice and politics play an important role in Moon's book. He does not try to make such conflicts look harmless by linking liberal secularism and rights-based doctrines to the ideas of negative liberty, state neutrality, or strong consensuality on constitutional essentials. On the contrary, Moon vehemently stresses the fact that liberalism often cannot avoid being understood as a substantive moral and political doctrine which, just as any other doctrine, promotes controversial ideas as to the value of possible conceptions of the good. For this very reason, he maintains, liberalism will not always be able to transcend conflicts of pluralism. In such cases, it will sometimes tragically override the interests of at least some citizens.[12] Moreover, and this is a claim that can be found in all recent tragic accounts of liberalism, Moon maintains that the conceptual framework of neutralist liberalism often makes it difficult both for itself and for nonliberal members of liberal societies to perceive the potentially oppressive nature of its liberating exercise of power. One might ask, how could a deeply egalitarian political doctrine that genuinely aims for justice by way of neutrality among citizens' conceptions of the good life ever seriously harm some citizens' interests in leading a good life? Perhaps the answer to this question is best phrased by Susan Mendus, who claims that the tragedy that is characteristic of liberal thought "arises not from the operation of a cruel and arbitrary fate; it arises from the belief that we can escape fate by extending the power and scope of justice."[13]

From an ontological point of view, we may lament our "cruel and arbitrary fate" of having to live in a pluralist world in which all true values do not always combine. And I do not doubt that liberalism is the best answer presently available to the question of how—when it comes to social and political cooperation—we might learn to live with this fate. This is Berlin's famous argument. But today, this way of looking at the tragic character of pluralist politics is not the most promising one. Especially in light of the vehement communitarian and feminist critiques of liberalism of the last two decades, which have continually stressed the fact that liberalism is a far less neutral and far more substantive political doctrine than it purports to be, the second approach should be preferred. I will argue throughout this book that an open eye for the tragic conflicts that liberalism itself generates opens up the possibility of formulating an internal critique of liberalism. Such a critique remains sensitive to the possibility that a tragic "unity of liberation and destruction" may hide behind liberalism's aim to let the interest of all citizens in leading a good life matter equally. The ultimate aim of such an internal critique is to overcome this tragic unity—although that may prove to be an unreachable aim. But its first goal must be to present a diagnosis of the seemingly inescapable fundamental tensions within the liberal normative framework that constitute tragic conflicts of pluralism in the first place.

A working hypothesis

Let me start by looking at the crucial concepts of tragic "inescapability" and "necessity." What is it that is inescapable or even necessary about tragic conflicts? We tend to look to ancient Greek tragedies in search for an answer to that question. According to Bernard Williams, in Greek tragedy there is first "the necessity encountered when an agent concludes that he must act in a certain way."[14] This we may call performative necessity, the necessity to act. For a thinking and acting being it is not only inescapable or unavoidable to act, but it is also necessary in a stronger sense, for thinking and acting are fundamental human capacities. Without referring to or making use of these capacities, human agency cannot be explained and understood. Second, there is the kind of "necessity consisting of the application of power by a person to another, a necessity imposed on some human beings by others."[15] This we may call the necessity of consequences of our actions. Here Williams uses the term *necessity* in the loose sense of "inescapability." I will later argue that, in order to make sense of tragic conflicts characteristic of liberalism, the necessity of consequences of our actions should be understood in a stronger sense than that of causal inescapability alone. I will argue that these consequences must follow from the very ethical self-understandings of the parties to the conflict within a liberal society. For now, however, it suffices to follow Williams's view.

The first two issues that Williams sketches are fully intelligible. They are facts of everyday life, springing from our beliefs, from our actions, and from their consequences in the world. The third issue, however, is far less intelligible. This refers to "supernatural necessity," involving "an idea that the structure of things is purposive: that it is, so to speak, playing against you. Things are arranged in such a way that what you do will make no difference to the eventual outcome, or will even help to bring about what you try to prevent."[16] It is characteristic of modern and liberal worldviews that we do not fear such a purposive structure of reality that will frustrate our aims and actions. The natural world is a "fact," and often also a value, but in our demystified age it is usually not understood as having a purposive structure or will of its own. This raises the question as to whether it makes any sense at all to talk about tragic conflicts in a demystified universe. In order to answer this question, we have to ask whether the first two kinds of necessity could—upon their collision—generate tragic conflicts.

If we take moral pluralism seriously, I think that it is clear that this possibility should not be ruled out in advance. As I have said earlier, taking moral pluralism seriously means that, in assessing a normative conflict, we should try not to reason this conflict away by immediately referring to "higher" human capacities or principles which, from a liberal perspective at least, could help resolve or transcend the conflict. We should first look at the conflicting values at hand, and presume that they have genuine value. In order to do so, we have to presume that, at least for the people who hold these values, these values are real, that is, that they are not merely subjective preferences, but rather constitutive parts of their identities that cannot be sidestepped in moral reasoning. The meaning and existential significance of orthodox religious beliefs and strong ties to an individual's cultural community may not always be intelligible to the secular and cosmopolitan liberal. But this does not necessarily mean that the beliefs and practices associated with such outlooks are not of genuine value for those who abide by them, and possibly even for the wider pluralist societal culture that liberals share with these people. At any rate, in this study I follow those liberals who in recent years have begun to take cultural and communal belonging as well as religious belief seriously as conditions of individual and collective well-being which, when public-political questions are at stake, cannot be restricted to the private domain.[17] If we look at conflicts of pluralism in this way, tragic collisions of values render themselves intelligible.

Of course, in liberal societies, social and political conflicts that are deemed tragic do not develop in a social or political vacuum. On the contrary, they develop within a well-defined normative framework, the framework of liberalism. Before their collision, the irreconcilable views that eventually collided already existed; they were part of what we could call the ethical life—the complete structure of accepted norms, laws, rights, practices, and personal convictions—of liberal society. It is important to remember this. For if we want to maintain that liberalism is a tragic doctrine, then the colliding views have to exist and even have a certain validity within the liberal framework. Only if it is characteristic of the liberal framework that its aim to protect citizens' interest in leading a good life sometimes necessarily results in the destruction of the not unreasonable conceptions of the good of at least some citizens, can we truly maintain that liberalism is a tragic doctrine.

In an extremely interesting study on Hegel's understanding of the tragic, Christoph Menke makes a similar point.[18] According to Menke, a tragic conflict is made up of two moments. First, the colliding views have to have a certain validity within the social setting in which they eventually collide. They have to be valuable aspects of both the individual self-understandings of their bearers and of the ethical life of society at large, at least in the minimal sense that society recognizes an obligation to tolerate them. So what has to be at stake in the conflict is the ethical validity of values that are genuinely thought to be valid in the social setting in which the conflict occurs. Second, Menke maintains, it is important that the collision can be understood as a necessary consequence of the ethical self-understandings of the parties to the conflict. For what seems to be the question in tragic conflicts thus construed is to what extent persons can act upon personal beliefs that liberalism in principle allows as soon as these collide with the beliefs of others.

To get a grip on this rather abstract understanding of the tragic, it seems wise to apply it to an ethical-political controversy we all know. Let us look at the much debated topic of abortion. For the sake of clarity, we will assume that there are only two clearly identifiable parties to the conflict: a prochoice and a prolife party. The debate—and the conflict that underlies it—is inescapable because (a) for both parties life is an ultimate value and both parties want society to protect this value;[19] (b) many people feel that for social, medical, and psychological reasons, undesired pregnancies exist; (c) there are medically safe techniques for terminating pregnancies; and (d) people are deeply divided over the question as to whether or not abortion is morally defensible. We assume here that both parties to the conflict are willing to give reasons for their views and to seriously consider the reasons given by others. So we rule out terrorist extremists. We do so because we assume that the debate takes place within a liberal framework of public deliberation. Within such a framework—as in every defensible framework of social and political cooperation and deliberation—reasonableness starts where people are willing to respect, or to learn to respect, the needs and beliefs of others and to manage their common concerns and conflicts through dialogue, not through physical or mental violence.

The prochoice party states that the question of abortion should be left to individuals to decide. This idea of free choice—of individual self-determination—implies that women have the right to abortion.

The liberal framework supports the idea of individual self-determination. Therefore, abortion should be legalized. The prolife party, on the other hand, states that, in this debate, individual self-determination is not the highest value at issue. According to them, the value of unconditional respect for life, even for unborn life, trumps the value of self-determination. Because the right to abortion harms their highest value in this debate, they claim that abortion should not be legalized, because this would mean that liberal society admits a practice that deeply offends some of its members' most fundamental ideas about human dignity. And they are right in stressing the fact that a liberal society—which, after all, aims for neutrality—should always try to avoid that.

Both kinds of necessity we accepted earlier as constitutive moments of tragic constellations are involved in this debate. In the first place, both parties feel that it is necessary for them to voice their beliefs because some of their most deeply held values (and the interests that spring from them) are at stake. Both parties live by values that the liberal framework tolerates and even, through the rights it upholds, protects. In this minimal but important sense, these values can be said to be valid. Second, it is a necessary trait of the debate over abortion that the views of both parties collide. For what is at stake is an inflammatory issue of public concern that is understood differently by various groups of citizens who, on the one hand, hold ethical views that the liberal framework allows and protects and, on the other hand, that all have the right to let their voice be heard in debates concerning the issue. The situation is so grave that settling the issue according to the beliefs of just one of these groups will deeply offend the worldview of the other party. So both parties have good and indeed inescapable reasons to engage in public debate over this issue. By engaging in the conflict, the parties test the boundaries and possibilities of the very normative framework that both guarantees them important conditions of their individual and social freedom and sets possibly tragic limits to the extent to which their personal needs and deeply held beliefs are reflected in public policy and law. Moreover, by engaging in the conflict citizens gain the possibility of influencing and changing the terms that both guarantee and set limits to their freedom.

In most liberal societies, abortion has been legalized; however, there is by no means a moral consensus concerning the legitimacy of the right to abortion and the beliefs and practices associated with it.[20] From time to time, the conflict returns to the public agenda. Prolife pressure groups come up with horrifying stories of abuse in abortion clinics; politicians bring up the issue for electoral reasons; judges, doctors, and psychiatrists discuss the conditions that should be met before an abortion may be carried out, and so forth.

Behind the conflict lies the problem of the irreconcilableness of the worldviews that underlie the conflicting positions. As writers on the issue have demonstrated, Self-determination and Respect for Life are competing slogans behind which very rich and comprehensive, and often not coherently articulated frameworks of value are hidden.[21] The prolife view is sustained by a worldview that values narrowly circumscribed, traditional social roles for men and women. It is of great importance to this worldview that the emotional, caring, life-giving qualities it ascribes to women are not undermined by the practice of abortion. Prolife activists understand very well that abortion, like birth control, can and will be used as a social and political tool to liberate women from traditional roles. They detest not only the practice of abortion, but also important aspects of the worldview that admits it, based on the value of freedom of choice, which is deeply egalitarian in its understanding of male and female roles.

Now, how would Archimedean liberalism have the parties discuss the issue of abortion? It would stress the fact that it is important that the parties engage in a reasonable public deliberation and find a solution to which all can agree. But because of the irreconcilableness of the worldviews involved, they will not find such a solution. In order to find a way of dealing with this problem, liberal authors such as John Rawls and Bruce Ackerman have suggested that controversial "private" beliefs—such as religious beliefs—should not play a role in public deliberation, or only a minimal one.[22] This would certainly rule out those prolife arguments that are sustained by theological arguments. But it would not bring us any closer to a morally legitimate solution to the conflict. For this strategy would most likely result in the solution that has been institutionalized in most liberal societies, and that is the very subject of practically all conflicts in liberal societies over abortion; women are given the right to abortion, and because this right does not oblige people to make use of it, both the prochoice and the prolife parties can remain true to their own private beliefs. As a liberal, I do not doubt that this is the best pragmatic solution to the problem currently available. But for most prolifers, finding a pragmatic solution to the problem is not what the debate is about. They feel that the value of individual self-determination that underlies both the prochoice view and the "neutral" liberal framework is fundamentally biased against one of their most deeply held beliefs which, ironically, liberal society genuinely aims to tolerate. But it tolerates this belief as a "private" view only, not as a view that may be called upon in deliberations about the legitimacy of the liberal strategy of the radical "secularization" of the public domain.[25]

What the case of abortion suggests, then, is that the prochoice view and the public liberal framework are much more closely intertwined than neutralist Archimedeans are willing to admit. Indeed, it seems that the liberal framework does not really transcend parties to conflicts within liberal society; it rather—however unwillingly—structures the possibilities for conflict resolution in ways that will always be biased toward substantive values such as individual self-determination, public autonomy within a secularized framework of reasoning, and equality of opportunity among the sexes. Furthermore, the issue of abortion suggests that these values promote or are founded in more comprehensive "private" conceptions of the good that are conducive to personal life-styles guided by substantive liberal ideals. Here, we must seriously consider the possibility that, contrary to what it often claims, liberalism is not just a political doctrine but rather a cleverly disguised comprehensive moral doctrine with a purposive structure that both builds upon and fosters "private" conceptions of the good with its ideals of personal autonomy and moral pluralism. We have seen earlier that influential liberals such as Rawls vehemently deny the fact that political liberalism presupposes comprehensive conceptions of the good. Still, if in hard-to-decide ethical-political cases the liberal framework is consequently biased toward the value of individual self-determination, then it is hard to see why it would not presuppose the ideal of personal autonomy as a necessary component of a truly valuable conception of the good life. In later chapters we will see that such a conception also presupposes an affirmation of the worth of pluralism, because personal autonomy presupposes the ability to choose, and the ability to choose presupposes the existence of a wide range of valuable options to choose from.[24] Admittedly, I have not shown that this is in fact the case. For now, the reader has to content herself with the idea that it is not at all strange to suspect that liberalism builds upon values that are not just public.

We may (albeit for now only in a hypothetical mode) conclude that what liberalism has to offer for conflict resolution in a pluralist world—public deliberation among publicly autonomous and reasonable citizens—generates serious ethical tensions that may be labeled tragic, and this is very discomforting. Because most influential liberals are "Archimedeans" when it comes to the defense of the public liberal framework, it is very hard for them to recognize that this framework has a definitely nonneutral, purposive structure that promotes controversial ideals of personal excellence such as personal autonomy, individual self-realization, and the affirmation of ethical pluralism. And although most liberals will recognize that, to stick to our example, the prolife party will experience moral loss in the face of a liberal abortion politics, they usually do not recognize that within a liberal framework, loss is inescapable. This is the loss of the liberal hope that it should be possible to decide hard ethical-political cases in such a manner that the interests of each and every citizen in leading a good life could be taken into account on an equal basis. Therefore, there is something to be said for the suggestion that in modern societies the political domain, which has such a huge bearing on the lives of individuals, has some characteristics that resemble those of supernatural necessity.[25]

In this study, I will mostly be concerned with the critical analysis of normative political theories that present a picture of politics according to which social and political structures are nothing more and nothing less than controllable, man-made institutions which, on principle, could serve the legitimate interests of all citizens. Still, there is something strangely alluring in the idea that even the most sophisticated normative theories could generate consequences which, in some cases at least, necessarily run counter to the very ideals they are meant to defend. At any rate, I believe it is valuable to test some of the most humane and tolerant normative theories we know of with this possibility in mind. Before I set myself to that task, however, let me list some of my hypotheses that will be tested in this book.

1. Because liberalism has a purposive structure—that is, it is not an ethically neutral doctrine—there are normative conflicts in which its aim to let the interests of *all* citizens in leading a good life matter equally cannot but generate tragic conflicts.

2. In generating tragic conflicts, liberalism sometimes undermines conceptions of the good life that it aims to tolerate; and (thereby) its own aim to let the interests of all citizens in leading a good life matter equally.

3. This tragic predicament of liberalism seems to be related to its explicit aim to promote moral unity when it comes to the use of public reason and public deliberation; and its implicit aim to promote key components for "private" conceptions of the good life such as the ideal of personal autonomy and the affirmation of ethical pluralism.

~

PART II

Political Liberalism versus Liberal Perfectionism

Introduction

One of the most controversial questions for liberal political philosophy is how liberalism is best defended under conditions of pluralism. We already touched upon that question in the preceding chapters. In this part, I will try to critically analyze the differences between the most influential answers. These differences can best be understood by asking liberal theorists: Are liberal institutions justified because they have instrumental value in the promotion of a specific view of human well-being and personal excellence, or are they justified simply because they treat humans as equals while trying to say nothing at all about the value of "private" conceptions of the good life? Among those who believe the first view to be correct, an important role is played by "liberal perfectionists." Among those who opt for the second view, "political liberals" are at the front of the debate.[1]

In chapter 3, I will discuss politically liberal ideas concerning the justification of liberal institutions. Political liberalism respects all citizens equally—irrespective of their private orientations. This doctrine sidesteps controversial comprehensive ideals of well-being and personal excellence. As John Rawls puts it, it tries to make sense of the legitimacy of the basic structure of society in terms "of certain fundamental ideas seen as implicit in the public political culture of a democratic society."[2] The doctrine presupposes that citizens with all kinds of comprehensive ideals of well-being and personal excellence participate in this public political culture and are able to affirm its fundamental ideas. Political liberalism stresses the fact that citizens of a just order should act from their capacities to act autonomously and reasonably as this is expected of them by the public political culture. But it also stresses the fact that this cannot mean that "the ideal of autonomy has a regulative role for all of life."[3] The idea is that if liberalism were to demand such a role for autonomy, it would cease to be a tolerant liberal doctrine. However, it turns out that political liberalism implicitly presupposes the affirmation of some values that cannot but demand specific comprehensive orientations of citizens. This cannot easily be reconciled with the politically liberal interpretation of the aim to let the interests of all citizens in leading a good life matter equally. For the doctrine presupposes the value of specific conceptions of the good life—conceptions central to which are ideals of personal autonomy and the affirmation of ethical and moral pluralism—which necessarily discredit conceptions of the good that do not fit well in the liberal normative framework.

Liberal perfectionism holds that political liberalism should straightforwardly admit that this is the case and reframe its affirmation of public autonomy, reasonableness, and toleration in these terms. Perfectionists maintain that liberalism is a comprehensive moral doctrine that is ultimately grounded in specific conceptions of the good life. They see liberalism as a political instrument to not only protect and promote public or political principles, values, and virtues, but also to protect and foster at least those that they believe to be valid for all members of modern democratic societies. Among the many values that can be found in modern societies, for liberal perfectionists the values of personal autonomy and an affirmation of pluralism stand out as values that each liberal society should actively promote.[4] Conceptually, this turns out to be a sound proposal. This conclusion, however, should not be understood as a reason for the unqualified acceptance of liberal perfectionism. Rather, in combination with the critique of political liberalism, it helps unveil an inescapable dilemma within liberal thought. As seen from the conceptual level, liberalism can only be defended as a moderately perfectionist doctrine. But as seen from the normative level, perfectionism sometimes appears as an intolerant doctrine which, therefore, should—if at all—be only very reluctantly accepted by liberals. This dilemma will eventually help me to come back to the hypothesis that liberalism is a tragic doctrine. In the final section of chapter 4, I will ask to what extent this hypothesis can be said to be valid for political liberalism and for liberal perfectionism.

3

~

Political Liberalism:
Justification through Public Reason

Liberalism is characterized by a specific notion of the justification of our social and political world. This notion is born of a deep suspicion of any form of arbitrary government. In the words of Stephen Macedo, liberals hold that "the application of power should be accompanied with reasons that all reasonable people should be able to accept."[1]

As I have noted before, it is not hard to see the influences of Enlightenment thought in this idea. The idea that of the many characteristics of man, reason stands out as a first among equals or—far more likely for thoughts born in the age of the Enlightenment—even as his very essence, has had huge implications for the concepts of social and political order and political authority. The early modern (re)discovery that humans can gain valid knowledge of the natural world by following the logic of their own thought and perception changed their relation to the social and political world as well. The idea was that if it is possible to understand the laws of the natural world by careful perception and reflection, then rational knowledge, and hence control, of the social and political world should be possible as well. Tradition, convention, and forms of heteronomous political authority were no longer accepted, at least not by liberals, as legitimate bases of social and political order. The liberal idea that government should always be able to convince the citizenry that it is entitled to respect, was born.

In contemporary liberalism, the demand for transparency and hence public control of the main institutions of society is universal.

The idea is that a social order is legitimate if and only if reasonable citizens of this order can be expected to acknowledge the reasonableness of the principles and norms on which it is built. But when can citizens, principles, and norms be said to be reasonable? Political liberals and liberal perfectionists give different answers to that question.

John Rawls: Political liberalism

Let me begin my discussion of the politically liberal view by quoting John Rawls's influential liberal principle of legitimacy: "[O]ur exercise of political power is proper and hence justifiable only when it is exercised in accordance with a constitution the essentials of which all citizens may reasonably be expected to endorse in the light of principles and ideals acceptable to them as reasonable and rational."[2] Given the pluralism and sometimes even incommensurability of worldviews in contemporary societies, political liberals hold that citizens should, when questions of public justification are at issue, abstract from their individual economic interests and from their possibly controversial private worldviews, and concentrate instead on what would be good for all. The main political, social, and economic institutions of liberal society are said to be reasonable and therefore legitimate if all citizens can freely accept the reasonableness of the basic principles that underlie them. The stress is on the consent of individuals to such basic principles. The motivation to accept these premises, however, is not solely grounded in their being reasonable. From the point of view of the citizen, understood as a single agent, it is also important that they be rational, that is, that they be instrumental to "ends and interests" peculiar to the agent in question (50). Political liberalism allows individuals to pursue their own ends in society, both concerning their material and their immaterial well-being, but it also stresses the fact that the limits of this individual pursuit of rational goals are established by general moral principles that all can and should accept.

This raises the question as to why citizens of liberal societies should be considered able and willing to accept such general principles. Rawls wrote two influential books on this question. In the first, *A Theory of Justice* (1971), he argued that the idea of a just liberal order can be achieved by theoretically articulating a comprehensive philosophical doctrine the basic premises of which are acceptable to all citizens of a liberal society, because they mirror ideas of autonomy, reasonableness, and rationality that, understood as rational subjects in an almost Kantian manner, they simply have an essential capacity for. These capacities were seen as central to all defensible moral doctrines. And because they were seen as such, Rawls could assume that the account of justice and social stability he presented was acceptable to all citizens of liberal-democratic societies.[3]

This is a highly Archimedean way of viewing things. It starts from premises that Rawls thought to be both inescapable and uncontroversial and which, therefore, seemed to be a rather ideal starting point for a liberal theory. However, many critics pointed out that these premises were nowhere near as inescapable and uncontroversial as Rawls assumed. Most importantly, communitarian authors stressed the fact that Rawls's liberalism presupposed an unconvincing atomist metaphysics of the person, and was far too rationalistic and voluntaristic to present a convincing picture of justice and social stability understood as social practices.[4] They argued that Rawls had perhaps succeeded in developing an ideal theory of justice and social stability for Kantian subjects, who in their moral reasoning are not bothered by ties to family, community, culture, and so forth, but had failed to develop such a theory for real people, whose capacities for autonomy, reasonableness, and rationality differ greatly because, as an inescapable trait of the human condition, these capacities are always embedded in, and substantially shaped by, particular frameworks of value. These frameworks, they maintained, are constitutive of moral character, of a character capable of understanding claims to justice. Therefore, abstracting from them in a theory of justice would necessarily result in a theory that evades the real problems that face any genuine attempt to reflect on how to conceive of justice in pluralist societies.[5] For this reason, Rawls's crucial assumption in *A Theory of Justice* that all reasonable and rational human beings will eventually choose the same principles of justice and live up to them turned out to be rather problematic.

Rawls denies that the communitarian critique of his theory seriously influenced its further development since the publication of *A Theory of Justice*.[6] Be that as it may, it is at least remarkable that his recent work is dedicated to showing how liberalism should deal with pluralism and the tension between cultural, communal, and ethical belonging on the one hand, and the unifying claims of public justice and democracy on the other. In another book, *Political Liberalism* (1993), he claims that his liberal theory should not be understood as a comprehensive philosophical or moral doctrine, but rather as a moral doctrine that is, both in its application and in its claim to validity, restricted to the public-political domain. I will concentrate on this recent theory, because it is the theory Rawls now espouses. In the remainder of this section, I will reconstruct his argument. In the next section, I will ask to what extent he is successful.

As I have said earlier, Rawls presents a "freestanding" moral doctrine for social and political cooperation; a doctrine that people with different comprehensive ideas of the good life could all voluntarily accept. The reason for this is simple. In *A Theory of Justice*, he now says, he did not really take "the fact of pluralism" seriously. In pluralist societies, comprehensive moral, religious, and philosophical frameworks will always be controversial because the beliefs central to them are accompanied by claims to moral truth that will often be incompatible with beliefs central to other comprehensive frameworks. Because it will just be too controversial, a theory that presents an ideal picture of social and political cooperation in a pluralist society should not start from a comprehensive philosophical framework. Therefore, Rawls now chooses another strategy. In *Political Liberalism*, he does not start from controversial metaphysical speculations concerning essential human capacities (or, as he himself would put it, from ideas that could easily be mistaken for comprehensive metaphysical speculations), but from certain fundamental and uncontroversial ideas implicit in "the public culture of a democratic society" (15). The most important of these is the idea of society as a fair system of cooperation. Such a system, Rawls says, is fair when it is guided by "publicly recognized rules and procedures," and when all participants in the cooperation may expect to gain "rational advantage" from it (15f.). Of course, this presupposes that these participants be understood as free and equal citizens. Rawls explains the freedom of citizens in terms of two moral powers: a capacity for "a sense of justice" and a capacity for "a conception of the good." A sense of justice is "the capacity to understand, to apply, and to act from the public conception of justice which characterizes the fair terms of cooperation." It expresses a willingness "to act in relation to others on terms that they can also publicly endorse." And the capacity for a conception of the good is "the capacity to form, to revise, and rationally pursue a conception of one's rational advantage or good" (19). Persons who have these capacities, Rawls maintains, should be considered free and equal citizens. These capacities should be seen as minimum requirements for successful participation in a fair system of social cooperation.[7]

Rawls explains the fairness of his freestanding view of social cooperation in terms of reasonableness. A well-ordered society, he claims, is one sustained by "a diversity of reasonable comprehensive doctrines" (36). These are doctrines that recognize that there are other beliefs than just their own comprehensive beliefs, and that various comprehensive doctrines will have to cooperate within a framework of "reasonable pluralism." Such doctrines accept "the very same principles of justice," and recognize and obey the "main political and social institutions" of society, insofar as these comply with the principles of justice (35). Rawls, of course, gives a fairly precise definition of the main principles of justice for a just liberal society.[8] But he stresses the fact that acceptance of these principles is not the primary focus of his account of reasonableness. Rather, doctrines within the broad liberal tradition "may differ about these principles and still agree in accepting a [political] conception's more general features. We agree that citizens share in political power as free and equal, and that as reasonable and rational they have a duty of civility to appeal to public reason" (226). In a sense then, the affirmation by all citizens of a shared notion of public reason is more important for liberal society than their acceptance of the very same principles of justice. Rawls ultimately aims to give reasons for the adequacy and legitimacy of his principles, but the acceptance of a shared notion of public reason from which these as well as other principles can be argued for is more important to him. Therefore, I will concentrate on the notion of public reason.

What is public reason? Rawls distinguishes two basic aspects of reasonableness. First, reasonable persons are willing to deliberate on fair terms of cooperation and "to abide by them provided others do." Second, reasonable persons are willing to recognize "the burdens of judgment" that accompany the willingness to act reasonably (54). I already discussed the first aspect. With the second aspect Rawls stresses the fact that the goal of liberal reasonableness cannot always be to reach total agreement on all politically relevant issues that might come up in a pluralist society. Often, the aim should rather be to reach an agreement to disagree. But in order for such an agreement to be reasonable, it must involve "an account of the sources, or causes, of disagreement between reasonable persons" (55). These sources, or causes, Rawls labels the burdens of judgment (ibid.). They spring from the fact that in many deliberations the evidence for a certain view may be conflicting and complex; that reasons that are considered relevant may still be ascribed different degrees of importance by them in their overall arguments; that the concepts they use are "essentially contested"; that they speak from different social and ethical backgrounds; that their normative considerations are sometimes so different that it becomes hard to make an overall assessment; and that a structured social space simply cannot give equal concern to every cherished value (56–57). These burdens of judgment add up to the conclusion that, in many cases, "it is not to be expected that conscientious persons with full powers of reason, even after free discussion, will all arrive at the same conclusion" (58). But the idea is that as long as reasonable persons understand this, disagreement over many issues, particularly those concerning the incommensurability of many comprehensive doctrines, need not necessarily threaten the stability of a just framework for social cooperation.

Together, the two aspects of reasonableness point to the idea of public justification and to a form of toleration. Public justification is a practice between representatives of reasonable comprehensive doctrines. These are doctrines that accept the fact that the two aspects of reasonableness define limits that all members of pluralist societies should recognize. The pluralism of a liberal order must be a reasonable pluralism. Within the boundaries of such a reasonable pluralism, people accept the fact that their reasonable comprehensive doctrine exists alongside others that may well be equally reasonable. This does not mean that adherents of a particular doctrine should not believe that their doctrine is correct or true. It just means—in the sense of what I earlier called a presumption of equal value—that citizens should accept the fact that others may have equally good reasons to believe that their comprehensive doctrines are true, and that disagreement over the truth of comprehensive doctrines is not a sufficient reason to risk civil strife. From this it follows that adherents of reasonable doctrines are tolerant and believe in liberty of conscience and freedom of thought (61). They accept the fact that their belief in the correctness or truth of their own beliefs is not a sufficient reason to repress other doctrines by the use of political power.

For questions of the public justification of a system of fair cooperation, Rawls argues, this means that claims concerning the truth of a particular comprehensive doctrine should never decide them—not even when almost all citizens believe that doctrine to be true. Questions of public justification should be answered through the use of public reason since it is "the reason of the public," "its subject is the good of the public and matters of fundamental justice," and its "nature and content is public, being given by the ideals and principles expressed by society's conception of political justice" (213). The reasonable and pluralist public agrees that fighting over the truth of comprehensive doctrines is not a matter of public concern and that, therefore, claims to the ethical truth of public reasons should not be their concern. Such claims should, in general, not "be introduced into political discussion of constitutional essentials and basic questions of justice" (16).[9]

It is important to recognize that Rawls's political doctrine for a reasonable and pluralist society should not be understood as a mere modus vivendi view. Although his account of political community is not a comprehensive but a freestanding doctrine, Rawls stresses the fact that it still is a moral doctrine. It is sustained by an "overlapping consensus" of reasonable comprehensive doctrines that affirm it for their own religious, philosophical, or moral reasons. They all agree that a freestanding political doctrine should be a moral and reasonable doctrine, not just "some kind of balance of forces" that coexist in society (39). For such a balance would lack the stability that is needed to sustain a just society. It would shift as soon as some of the forces in society became stronger. Political liberalism aims for more than that, and that aim is guaranteed by the moral threshold presented by the notion of the reasonable. Reasonable citizens respect each other's liberties—irrespective of the question whether their comprehensive views are or are not overwhelmingly prevalent in society. From a moral point of view, this is not important. What is important, however, is whether the comprehensive doctrine in question sustains the overlapping consensus. Insofar as it does, it has the moral right to fully participate in liberal society.

Rawls, like many other liberals, claims that the normative force of his political conception is ultimately rooted in the idea of the priority of right over the good. By this Rawls means that within a liberal society, political and judicial solutions to normative conflicts must ultimately be supported in terms of what, for the issue at stake, is the right or just decision as seen from the public conception of justice. The solution should be argued for in terms of public reason, not in terms of comprehensive conceptions of the good. The reason for this is, again, that in a pluralist society only the former way of arguing for a decision can claim to be uncontroversial. Yet, Rawls acknowledges that no decision can be accepted in terms that wholly evade reference to ideas of the good. He says that, in itself, this need not be a problem for liberalism so long as these ideas of the good are "shared by citizens regarded as free and equal" and "they do not presuppose any particular fully (or partly) comprehensive doctrine." The priority of right means that "admissible ideas of the good must respect the limits of, and serve a role within, the political conception of justice" (176).

Several ideas of the good may be referred to in public deliberation. First, there is the idea of the goodness of rationality (the goodness of valuing human life and the desire to fulfill one's basic human
needs) (179). Second, the political doctrine aims to guarantee and
protect several "primary goods," goods that are taken to be of the utmost importance for all citizens of the liberal order. These include
basic rights and liberties, freedom of movement and free choice of occupation, equal political and economic opportunities for all, income
and wealth, and the social bases of self-respect (181). I think that
these primary goods—which are central to the constitutions of most
liberal-democratic societies—speak for themselves,[10] although it is
important to emphasize that Rawls takes citizens' self-respect to be
primarily generated by the experience that their society is made up
of just institutions and that the public political culture of this society
recognizes them as free and equal persons in the political sense.
These goods may be referred to in public deliberations, because the
question of their distribution is the stuff of most fundamental public debates. Third, citizens may explain their public claims by pointing out that the state should guarantee them equal opportunity to
affirm a permissible (reasonable) comprehensive conception of the
good (194). Fourth, citizens may refer to strictly political ideas of the
good citizen, that is, to virtues such as fair social cooperation, reasonableness, civility, tolerance, and a sense of justice (195). And fifth,
citizens may claim that a solution to a particular political question is
preferred because it enhances the good of a well-ordered society; a
society that enables citizens to exercise the two moral powers we discussed earlier and that provides them with firm institutional bases
for self-respect (201). In public deliberation, Rawls says, these goods
must play an essential role. Only by referring to them will citizens
be able to make firm, yet more or less acceptable moral claims. But
although the needs of citizens can be explained only in terms of
these substantive goods, public deliberation is limited by the notions
of the reasonable and the right. Therefore, in processes of public deliberation and justification, the perspective of what is right can, in
this normative sense, be said to be prior to the good.

Finally, because, in this sense, the right is prior to the good, political liberalism can be said to be a neutral political doctrine—but
neutral only in a restricted way. Rawls corrects several misunder-
standings of his notion of neutrality. I think that he is right in emphasizing that political liberalism is not procedurally neutral.
Procedural neutrality is either legitimized by reference to no moral
value at all, or by reference to values such as impartiality and equal

opportunity, which are neutral in themselves (191). The substantive ideas of reasonableness, overlapping consensus, and fair cooperation that political liberalism builds upon are not neutral in this way. Rather, political liberalism seeks "neutral ground" given the fact of pluralism (192). And its neutrality starts where society accepts that pluralism should be reasonable. Political liberalism aims for neutrality in a reasonable pluralist society. The liberal state, it says, is neutral in the sense that it aims to "secure equal opportunity to advance any permissible conception [of the good]" (193).[11] And permissible conceptions are reasonable conceptions. Furthermore, from the idea of the priority of right it follows that the state should not deliberately foster certain comprehensive doctrines, while frustrating others. In these two senses, the politically liberal state aims to be neutral among conceptions of the good. But political liberalism acknowledges that the state cannot be neutral in effect. Political liberalism shapes the social world, and therefore it will always affect the conditions under which comprehensive doctrines flourish. Some such doctrines may gradually lose their attractiveness to people, and die out. Rawls maintains that political liberalism cannot be held responsible for this. For it cannot be said that political liberalism is arbitrarily biased against any particular life form. This it would be only if it promoted individualism or the value of personal autonomy as ideals that should govern all of life (199). Here, Rawls points to the restricted political nature of his doctrine, and claims that political liberalism does not do this.

The two-stage path to an overlapping consensus: A critique

One cannot but admire the systematic coherence and balance of Rawls's theory. It provides us with a precise and careful reflection on the bounds of pluralism in a just society, and the bounds of justice and morality given the fact of pluralism. It does not defend some far-fetched notion of liberal neutrality that is primarily based on wishful thinking, while it emphasizes that its ideals are far from realized in existing liberal-democratic societies, and may very well never be. Why then did I suggest in the first chapters of this study that there is something seriously wrong with this theory? My argument will be that while the notions of the reasonable, of pluralism, of the overlapping consensus, and even the account of neutrality are in many ways well suited to defend liberalism, Rawls hesitates to take one crucial step, admitting that political liberalism does build upon nonpublic, comprehensive conceptions of the good life that should, at a minimum, include an affirmation of the ideal of personal autonomy. Furthermore, this step implies that political liberalism must accept that it does not succeed in finding "neutral ground" given the fact of pluralism. Rather, political liberalism is a doctrine that affirms pluralism, because it recognizes value in a pluralist social world.

We have seen that Rawls claims that his political conception does not presuppose acceptance of any particular comprehensive doctrine, and that it is not formulated in terms of a comprehensive doctrine, but in terms of fundamental ideas implicit in the public culture of a liberal-democratic society. These ideas, he states, can be accepted from any reasonable comprehensive view and may therefore be expected to be sustained by an overlapping consensus of reasonable doctrines. In order to get to the heart of his approach, I will critically discuss his ideas concerning how such an overlapping consensus might come about.

Rawls introduces two stages. The first he calls a constitutional consensus, the second an overlapping consensus (158ff.). He presents a constitutional consensus as a compromise: a modus vivendi based on a balance of forces arrived at by competing individuals and groups. Here, there is agreement on some basic rights, liberties, and principles of justice, while there is disagreement regarding the precise content of many other principles and rights. Most importantly, there is disagreement on the definition of primary goods and the question as to whether or not the principles for their distribution should apply to the basic structure of society. So while there is agreement on the need for a minimal modus vivendi guaranteed and protected by a democratic government, there is no agreement on a substantive notion of justice applying to the basic structure of society. Just as in the historical modus vivendi accepted after the Reformation, Rawls maintains, a principle of toleration would be crucial to this modus vivendi.

Now, what does such a modus vivendi presuppose? According to Rawls, it presupposes "a certain looseness in our comprehensive views" (159). This enables citizens to see that the modus vivendi, in combination with the principle of toleration on which it is based, results in favorable circumstances for all groups and individuals in society. And their acknowledging this, Rawls claims, would enable citizens to affirm the modus vivendi. Without really arguing for it, Rawls conjectures that "[s]hould an incompatibility later be recognized between the principles of justice and [citizens' wider comprehensive] doctrines, then they might very well adjust or revise these doctrines rather than reject those principles" (160). He suggests that citizens will in most cases be willing to let their personal beliefs be trumped by their, indeed overwhelming, need for political rights and liberties. Gradually, they will come to accept these rights and liberties for their own sake. Reasonable pluralism will be reached, for citizens will—partly out of self-interest, partly because they understand the political principles to be valuable in themselves—be willing to deliberate with each other on terms of public reason. Gradually they will even come to embrace cooperative political virtues, such as a sense of fairness and a willingness to compromise (163).

Although Rawls acknowledges that his sketch of the development of a constitutional consensus is speculative, he stresses the fact that, as a matter of moral psychology, it is not unlikely to happen.[12] I think he is right about this. Once citizens discover that certain principles enhance social stability, reduce social conflict, and generate a cooperative spirit, they are likely to accept these principles as valid, and recognize the boundaries of a reasonable pluralism. Rawls seems to be right, then, when he concludes that "at the first stage of constitutional consensus the liberal principles of justice, initially accepted reluctantly as a modus vivendi and adopted into a constitution, tend to shift citizens' comprehensive doctrines so that they at least accept the principles of a liberal constitution" (163). When this has been achieved, the main obstructions to a broader consensus (an overlapping consensus that extends the political conception to include agreement on a full set of basic rights and liberties that applies to the basic structure of society) can be removed. Independent political allegiance to this consensus by reasonable citizens then becomes a possibility.

Rawls's argument, which in the context of his book is meant to show that the idea of an overlapping consensus need not be utopian, is sound; particularly so, because Rawls does not deny the fact that an overlapping consensus can only come about if citizens are willing to reconsider not only their political beliefs, but also the comprehensive doctrines that guide them through their nonpolitical lives. As we have seen, Rawls states this explicitly. And there is another passage in which Rawls makes a similar claim:

> [I]n affirming a political conception of justice we may eventually have to assert at least certain aspects of our own comprehensive religious or philosophical doctrine (by no means necessarily fully comprehensive). This will happen whenever

someone insists, for example, that certain questions are so fundamental that to insure their being rightly settled justifies civil strife. The religious salvation of those holding a particular religion, or indeed the salvation of a whole people, may be said to depend on it. At this point we may have no alternative but to deny this, or to imply its denial and hence to maintain the kind of thing we had hoped to avoid. (152)

It turns out then, that Rawls's insistence that his political doctrine must be affirmed for reasons given by this doctrine itself does not mean that, in the end, the doctrine is not rooted in comprehensive doctrines. He himself clearly admits that it is. But this is paradoxical, for in other parts of the book he vehemently denies this. However, a clear distinction between the closely intertwined yet separate stages of consensus-seeking Rawls comes up with can make sense of this paradox. The first explains that, and how, an overlapping consensus could come about. The second reflects on the independence of the political doctrine sustained by this consensus once it has been reached. At the first stage, Rawls has to account for tensions that spring from the fact that some citizens will be willing to act according to public reason as he conceives of it, while others will not. At this stage, Rawls cannot but make clear that a true overlapping consensus is only possible if the ethical orientations of all members of society have such a structure and content that they can wholeheartedly affirm this consensus. In this sense then, political liberalism cannot be defended independently of comprehensive doctrines—reasonable comprehensive doctrines that is, which recognize the priority of the right over the good. But at the second stage it can, at least to a certain extent. Once all citizens accept that pluralism can only be defended as a reasonable pluralism, and agree that in public deliberation they should only refer to reasons that may be expected to be acceptable to all, the liberal political doctrine will indeed be accepted for its own sake. Only at this stage will it appear as a doctrine that not only aims for but that actually achieves some sort of neutrality among competing comprehensive notions of the good. However, this will be no more than neutrality within a nonneutral political order that presupposes the acceptance of certain comprehensive ethical orientations.[13]

This distinction, then, makes sense of the paradox just identified. But making sense of this paradox was not our main goal. Rather, our goal was to investigate whether Rawls's theory presupposes a nonpolitical, comprehensive notion of the good. The conclusion must be that it does because, logically, the first stage is a necessary step in the emergence of the second. Admittedly, the comprehensive notion of the good presupposed by political liberalism is rather thin. It does not define the good life. In Rawls's own words, we could best describe it as a "partly comprehensive notion" that "comprises a number of, but by no means all, nonpolitical values and virtues and is rather loosely articulated" (13). This partly comprehensive notion must include a general willingness to tolerate the beliefs of others, an undogmatic presumption of "equal value" of different reasonable purposes and aims in life and, perhaps most importantly, an affirmation of reasonable pluralism as a precondition for people's ability to decide autonomously for themselves how they want to shape their lives. Indeed, Rawls's assumption that, as free persons, people have the capacity to "form, revise, and rationally to pursue a conception of [their] rational advantage or good" rather straightforwardly presupposes the validity of a notion of personal freedom understood as personal autonomy. At a minimum, the political doctrine guarantees that free persons can anchor this capacity in their moral character in a special way. They should be willing to decide for themselves what the good life consists of, and let others decide nonpolitical questions in a similar fashion. But this is not an ethically neutral demand. Rather, the demand presupposes the validity of at least one controversial character ideal: that of personal autonomy, understood as the ideal of people determining their own lives in light of their own choices for certain social and moral options (and against others) that their reasonable, pluralist environment offers them.[14]

It is true that Rawls's theory does not in any way claim that the aim of democratic politics or the basic structure of society must be to impose this "thin" but substantive conception of the good on people's personal lives. But although it does not deliberately aim to do this, it presupposes the validity of personal autonomy. We cannot make sense of the meaning of "substantive rights such as liberty of conscience and freedom of thought, as well as fair equal opportunity," or Rawls's primary good for that matter, in any other way (164). For they cannot be supported in any other way than in terms of the protection and sustenance of the free choice and the personal autonomy of individual citizens—if only the freedom to decide for oneself whether one wants to appeal to these rights or not. Political liberalism does not only foster personal autonomy, value pluralism, reasonable deliberation, and ethical toleration (understood as the effects of its framing of the social world); it can only justify its normative outlook by assuming that these values and practices should not only be protected in a just liberal society, but should ideally have their proper place among the "habits of the heart" of citizens of a just liberal society.

This conclusion has far-reaching consequences for political liberalism. Most importantly, it will have to admit that the nonneutrality of the effects it has on comprehensive beliefs of citizens does not only spring from the inescapable fact that every political doctrine sets limits. Contrary to what Rawls claims in his discussion of neutrality, political liberalism does favor autonomy-enhancing comprehensive doctrines. In search of "neutral ground" given the fact of pluralism, it embraces the partly comprehensive ideal of personal autonomy, understood as an answer to not just the fact but the value of pluralism. Admittedly, it does not do this in an arbitrary way. It draws a limit that says what, on moral grounds, should be understood as permissible in a just social order. But it cannot deny that this limit is inspired by what I would call a moderate form of perfectionism; political liberalism does presuppose—already at the level of justification—a thin but nonetheless substantive conception of the good life, which it cannot but foster once it has the power to structure social and political space. This may seem to be a highly alarming conclusion. But there is no real reason for alarm. For even if it acknowledges my point, liberalism can still remain a doctrine that is primarily political. I will come back to this part in later chapters. For now, let me just briefly point to a problem that political liberalism will have to overcome in order to achieve a new, and in my view better, understanding of its political aims.

We can identify this problem by asking from which of the two stages just identified political liberalism should argue when it tries to make sense of normative conflicts that arise in existing liberal-democratic societies. Since Rawls himself makes it quite clear that until now no society complies with his politically liberal doctrine, it seems that the first stage would be most appropriate for this. This is the stage at which political liberalism has not been accepted by all citizens, but at which something like a constitutional consensus has been achieved. It is a stage at which we are somewhere between a mere modus vivendi among citizens and a minimal overlapping consensus in which citizens begin to see political principles and virtues as achievements that can be valued for their own sake. We saw that at this stage, political liberalism cannot but admit that it is rooted in a partly comprehensive notion of the good life that is conducive to toleration, personal autonomy, moral pluralism, and public reason.

Because at this stage the fundamental ideas that political liberalism takes from the public political culture of society are not accepted by all citizens who are at least willing to search for a political modus vivendi, it can—for reasons of toleration and reasonableness—not simply assume that all citizens will accept the basic terms it proposes for public deliberation. It will rather have to articulate and argue for the partly comprehensive notion of the good that citizens will have to accept before they can successfully engage in liberal public deliberation.

In discussing normative conflicts in liberal-democratic societies, political liberals usually argue from the second stage. By doing so, however, they evade the very core of these conflicts, which in the context of our discussion must be understood as springing from the fact that, in such societies, an overlapping consensus has often not been reached. Rawls allows for public discussions concerning the question as to how different comprehensive views relate to the politically liberal idea of public reason, but—strangely enough—only insofar as these discussions "strengthen the ideal of public reason itself" (242). This begs the question, because in hard ethical-political cases such as those of abortion, euthanasia, and cultural belonging the issue is not how nonliberal views could strengthen the politically liberal idea of public reason, but rather, given the inescapable bias of liberal public reason toward liberal views, what valid reasons nonliberal views could have not to accept the liberal framework of public deliberation.[15]

We can better understand this point if we approach the question from the first stage, at which allegiance to a liberal overlapping consensus is not self-evident. Let us, again, take conflicts over the right to abortion as an example. At the first modus vivendi stage the prochoice view will, provided it generates enough support within society, get its way (because the interest-based balance of forces in society will support the view). The right to abortion will be incorporated in the constitution. Provided the constitutional consensus develops according to the expectations implicit in Rawls's moral psychology, most citizens will shift their comprehensive doctrines so that they can accept ever more aspects of the developing consensus. Let us say that at a certain point, most citizens do indeed accept an overlapping consensus in Rawls's sense. Others, however, will still have great difficulty accepting this consensus, because they still feel it frustrates some of their most fundamental comprehensive beliefs. Even if they accept many of the liberal framework's aspects (its promotion of freedom of conscience and of thought, political rights, many social arrangements, etc.), they seem to be right in saying: "Wait for us, we believe that we have valid ethical reasons not to accept at least some of the basic terms by means of which you—the liberal majority—want to frame the discussion." But political liberalism does not allow for the articulation of these ethical (presumably theological) reasons, which are comprehensive reasons, because it will look at the conflict from the second stage, at which it is presupposed that, in public debate, comprehensive reasons are not valid reasons. Even Rawls's entirely correct recent claim that in hard cases "unanimity of views is not to be expected," cannot take away my concerns regarding this exclusionary trait of political liberalism.[16] For the exclusion, at the second stage, of comprehensive reasons from public deliberation is the point at which political liberalism starts treating personal beliefs as mere preferences that are best sidestepped in public debate. Political liberalism forgets that its second stage is no more than a substantive guiding ideal. And it subsequently reifies this ideal into an Archimedean starting point for public deliberation.

This blindness of political liberalism to dissidents' attempts to look for reasons for their views is perhaps best illustrated by Bruce Ackerman's work on these questions. Ackerman holds that, for members of liberal-democratic societies it is a moral duty not to persuade their fellow citizens to accept that their controversial comprehensive beliefs might be relevant to issues of public concern. He proposes a method of "conversational restraint" that is supposed to help citizens achieve this goal: "When you and I learn that we disagree about one or another dimension of the moral truth, we should not search for some common value that will trump this disagreement; nor should we seek to translate it into some putatively neutral framework; nor should we seek to transcend it by talking about how some unearthly creature might resolve it. We should simply say *nothing at all* about this disagreement and put the moral ideals that divide us off the conversational agenda of the liberal state."[17] Ackerman envisages a liberal state in which the public sphere is cleansed of controversial moral beliefs so that social conflict is minimized. This does not mean, however, that he holds that there is no need for public deliberation whatsoever; he just holds that for liberal society to flourish, it is necessary that citizens can engage in dialogue in "an appropriately neutral way," which does not call into question their personal beliefs.[18]

Ackerman's variant of political liberalism is a mere modus vivendi view that remains at the stage of constitutional consensus. But at that stage, he wrongly assumes that his method of "conversational restraint" is uncontroversial. Rawls's account of the "stages" of consensus-building makes it possible to see why this assumption is wrong. Usually, Rawls argues from the second stage. But at least he is able to acknowledge the existence of problems that spring from the first stage. To a certain extent, he has to argue from the second stage, because political liberalism stands for an ideal moral doctrine that can only be articulated in substantive terms at that later stage. But at the same time, this ideal doctrine will have to acknowledge, as it can at the first stage, that it is in many ways not ethically neutral. It seems, then, that in discussing severe normative conflicts, political liberalism will have to go back and forth between the two stages; making clear which ideal normative conception it ultimately stands for at the second stage, while acknowledging the ethical roots of this conception, and trying to understand the ethical roots of other conceptions, in unconstrained debates, at the first.[19] For what we seem to need is an understanding of how public deliberation could not just stabilize but rather narrow the ethical differences that divide members of liberal-democratic societies in which a stable overlapping consensus has not been reached. There is a practical necessity here, for if we cannot resolve severe normative conflicts that divide us on the basis of wholeheartedly shared moral principles, it may become necessary to settle them by force. And that seems to make a mockery of the liberal principle of public consent.[20]

Given this unattractive alternative to public deliberation, it seems that the liberal notion of public reason will have to be supplemented with a notion of convincing others by means of a less constrained or even unconstrained understanding of public deliberation. Only if it is legitimate for citizens to raise questions concerning the truth or validity of different comprehensive views in public debate is it possible for them to create, strengthen, and problematize shared understandings in an open-ended practice. Furthermore, we need such a concept to account for all those emancipatory processes in liberal-democratic societies in which matters that had long been considered controversial private matters burst on to the scene of public deliberation, and radically changed the public's understanding of justice, toleration and individual liberty. Examples are the socioeconomic and cultural perception of women, blacks, gays, and issues such as abortion, pornography, and euthanasia. In these cases, many citizens were gradually convinced that the highly controversial questions related to the perception of excluded groups and silenced themes are genuine matters of public significance.[21] Such changes in perception—which seem to be important for a flourishing liberal society—could not legitimately take place if the boundaries between private and public morality were to be as rigid as Ackerman and Rawls—at the second stage of his argument—think they should be.

To be fair, there is at least one politically liberal author who would wholeheartedly agree with this conclusion. In light of my argument, J. Donald Moon's version of political liberalism is interesting because it is in part based on a criticism of Rawls and Ackerman that is quite similar to mine. Furthermore, Moon recognizes a tragic aspect in the tension between, on the one hand, political liberalism's aim to treat all morally motivated people as equals and, on the other hand, the undeniable partiality of its own conception of political justice and public reason. He concentrates on "situations in which the principles and institutions that appear to be necessary for the liberal strategy, and that are intended to be inclusive, function in such a way as to burden or even exclude some citizens, based on their possession of property or skills, their gender or their cultural identities."[22]

Moon's answer to political liberalism's tragic predicament has two main components. First, a specific conception of public discourse and, second, a specific notion of agency rights. His notion of public discourse is meant to constitute a type of ethical-political dialogue that makes it possible for all citizens to effectively thematize instances in which reigning substantive understandings of public reason—and the political and legal actions they make possible—are considered impositions by at least some reasonable citizens. Here, Moon tries to sail between the Scylla of all-too-constrained liberal notions of public dialogue and the Charybdis of all-too-unconstrained deliberative democratic such notions (74–97). Against Rawls and Ackerman, he argues that dialogue that is constrained along the rigid lines of the public-private distinction cannot be neutral, because it will inescapably be based on contestable choices regarding the very definition of what should be considered private and public issues. Rawls and Ackerman construct what I have earlier called Archimedean interpretations of liberalism that cannot "recognize . . . their own limitations" (72).

One way of overcoming the exclusionary consequences of constrained dialogue would be to adopt a less constrained or, if possible, even unconstrained understanding of public deliberation. However, Moon is as wary of the idea of unconstrained dialogue as he is of that of constrained dialogue. He discusses Seyla Benhabib's notion of unconstrained dialogue, and rejects it.[23] What he is most afraid of is that antiliberal consequences may flow from the "moral-transformative" dynamics between private and public needs and interests that such a notion allows and—in Benhabib's case—even fosters: "The problem, in [Benhabib's] analysis, is that needs and interests should not be taken as given but must be seen (at least in large part) as a result of processes of socialization and the life experiences of individuals in particular social formations" (88). Contrary to the constrained politically liberal strategy, the unconstrained strategy does not confine itself to "finding rules that bridge the differences among given constellations of interests and identities." Rather, in a critical theoretical fashion, it calls "into question the conflicting interests, needs, and aspirations that lead to conflict" in the first place (88–89). Here, Moon opts for a "generalized" notion of discourse that limits itself to matters of public concern and does not try to increase social order and moral consensus by means of an unconstrained search for our "true" interests, needs, and aspirations. For that would demand an amount of ethical self-disclosure that liberalism has always been most wary of.

As we will see in chapters 5 and 6, there are less dramatic accounts of unconstrained dialogue than Moon's somewhat one-dimensional reconstruction suggests. Still the dilemma he describes is real enough: "[W]e appear to require unconstrained discourse in order to settle what the boundaries of the private should be, but such discourse itself violates any such boundaries because it rests upon a demand for unlimited self-disclosure" (93). Confronted with this dilemma, Moon aims to develop a notion of public discourse which (1) contrary to unconstrained conceptions, "protects the integrity of the participants in discourse"; (2) contrary to constrained conceptions, "opens itself to criticism of its own presuppositions and assumptions"; and (3) acknowledges "the possibility of its own silences and evasions" (97).

In order to arrive at such a notion, Moon introduces the concept of "agency rights." His choice for this concept is inspired by, first, the intuition that, as seen from the perspective of comprehensive doctrines, a liberal theory should be as ethically uncontroversial as possible and, second, the observation that "the sense of oneself as an agent" is "significant to (virtually) everyone" (109). I agree with the second point, but disagree with the first. And given Moon's rejection of the aim for neutrality, it is not quite clear why he keeps defending this first intuition. Sure enough, "rights to bodily integrity," "freedom from physical coercion," "the right to control the use and powers of one's body," political rights, "rights of privacy," and rights to basic goods will be accepted by all reasonable citizens, whether they call themselves liberals or not (111). But before reaching his own systematic proposal, Moon has several times convincingly argued that the meaning of most moral and political concepts is essentially contested, and that liberalism cannot avoid being a substantive and contested doctrine (75ff.). Now why would formal agency rights, and the possibilities and limits they confront citizens with, not be controversial? Why would—when "Aristotelean," "contractarian," "perfectionist," and "thin-self" groundings of liberalism all turn out to be ethically controversial[24]—the agency-rights approach be more acceptable? Moon's answer is that the agency-rights approach is the only one that leaves liberalism's fundamental principles and assumptions open to criticism and revision. And he is right about that. Still, he does not offer an account of public deliberation that solves the problems of the models of constrained and unconstrained dialogue. The general thrust of his argument is that the extent to which dialogue should be constrained must be decided in individual cases and contexts, in light of the agency-undermining characteristics of the concrete situation. And, quite rightly, he adopts a "two-stage" approach to questions of public discourse (100). But his account remains too unspecific to satisfy the expectations as to the merits of the discursive model he initially set out to develop. For it entirely leaves open the question which exact conceptions of agency are conducive to a practice founded on liberal agency rights.

In the end, Moon's account of political liberalism leaves me puzzled. Most importantly, his position on the character ideal of personal autonomy remains unclear. He rejects the liberal-perfectionist suggestion that liberalism should be understood as a comprehensive doctrine that promotes the ideal of personal autonomy. Again, the moral-transformative demands of a perfectionist approach seem to worry him. But as seen from his own account of liberalism's tragic situation, the reason he gives for the rejection of liberal perfectionism—that personal autonomy cannot be accepted as a valid ideal by all citizens of pluralist societies (33)—is not convincing. For the whole point of his (and of any) account of liberalism's tragic situation is that it cannot avoid being a substantive and therefore controversial moral doctrine: "The decision to use the liberal strategy is itself a moral choice, one that may exclude certain perspectives, certain experiences, certain ends, and moral ideas" (10).

So, after convincingly having identified liberalism's tragic situation, Moon opts for a strategy that seems to rest on the type of strategy he has earlier rejected—that of trying to ban all controversial moral substance from the best account of liberalism's normative foundations. And although he elegantly shows how even agency rights can come into tragic conflict with various needs, interests, and conceptions of the good, I think that the real problem is not that of the contestedness of the liberal account of agency rights, but rather that of the contestedness of the substantive (partly) comprehensive conception of the good life that the agency-rights approach presupposes: "Respecting persons' capacity for agency requires, in the most general terms, responding to them in terms of their abilities of rational self-direction, by giving them reasons for acting and not attempting to control their behavior through force and manipulation" (111). Agency is not the foundational value here. What is foundational is a partly comprehensive view of agency that comes close to the ideal of personal autonomy as rational self-determination. We cannot abandon that partly comprehensive view without abandoning the dynamics of a conflictuous "two-stage" account of deliberation and the idea that even the most reasonable account of liberalism's normative foundations will always run the risk of being confronted with tragic conflicts.

We may conclude that even a highly self-critical politically liberal theory such as Moon's does not succeed in founding liberalism on purely political values. We seriously have to consider the possibility that the fact that personal autonomy is a controversial value does not by definition discredit attempts to ground liberal theories on this value. Indeed, if we take seriously our earlier idea that liberalism has to go "back and forth" between, on the one hand, the explication of its ideal conception of social cooperation and of the good life and, on the other hand, the acknowledgment of the controversial comprehensive roots of these conceptions, then it does not seem all that threatening to admit that the ideal of personal autonomy may play a foundational role at the "second stage" of liberal thought. Furthermore, this way of looking at the problem makes us understand to what extent liberalism might be considered a doctrine that need not be overly afraid of the "moral-transformative" dynamics of less constrained public debate. After all, if liberals were to agree that personal autonomy is of foundational importance for them, then would this not mean that a perfectionist liberal politics will not simply override people's capacity for autonomous action, but rather appeal to it in order to convince people that they might benefit from making a "moral transformation" from their given beliefs and interests to more autonomy-based ideas of the good life? And would this not imply that the most worrisome consequence of perfectionist doctrines—that they tend to override the given beliefs and interests of individuals—would on principle not be open to liberal perfectionists?

4

~

Liberal Perfectionism:
Autonomy and Pluralism

So what if liberals simply were to admit that liberalism promotes a nonpolitical substantive idea of the good life for all citizens based on an affirmation of personal autonomy? Would it fare any better? There are liberals who believe that it would. Joseph Raz, for instance, holds that the liberal state is "duty-bound to promote the good life."[1] And there are others who defend similar views.[2] For our discussion, however, Raz's account of liberalism is the most interesting. For he explicitly claims that the liberal state should promote the value of personal autonomy and backs this claim with an ingenious account of pluralism. Since autonomy and pluralism are critical to my interpretation of liberalism and have also played an important role in my discussion of political liberalism, it is in order to turn our attention to Raz's theory.

Joseph Raz: Liberal Perfectionism

We can immediately gain an understanding of some of the central features of Raz's perfectionism by looking at his comments on the widespread idea that political authority rests on consent. We have seen that this plays an important role in political liberalism. That doctrine, it may be said, is a reflection on the conditions under which the public's consent to basic social, political, and economic institutions may be said to justify these institutions. The idea is that these institutions—and the restrictions and obligations they impose on people—are legitimate only if these people have voluntarily consented to them. Political liberalism holds that its directives are valid because all reasonable people would consent to them. Raz, however, comes up with a different view. It is different because it says that not consent as such, but rather the content of the directives to which people consent, make directives legitimate: "Authoritative directives ought to be such that their subjects will be acting as they should act in virtue of reasons that apply to them independently of the authority's action, and an authority is legitimate and its directives are binding only if, by and large, they meet this condition to such a high degree that its subjects will better conform to reason if they try to follow the authority's directives than if they do not."[3] In other words, one can only wholeheartedly consent to directives which, as expressing right reason, apply to one anyway. However, this is not the whole story. Raz claims that members of liberal-democratic societies have an essential interest in autonomy. His use of the notion of autonomy does not rest on the assumption that autonomy is intrinsically valuable, that is, that the value of autonomy is independent of the quality of the choice one makes. Rather, he claims that the autonomy of a person is only valuable insofar as this person chooses valuable options. These are options that can be reconciled with what he calls right reason. Yet, he concedes that, particularly when the question of the government's authority over people's lives is at stake, there are matters on which right (governmental or political) reason should be silent. For "sometimes it is more important that we should decide for ourselves than that we should decide correctly." Therefore, the "first condition of legitimacy has to be supplemented with a second, to the effect that governments can have legitimate authority only over matters regarding which acting according to right reason is more important than deciding for oneself how to act."[4] This second condition of legitimacy does not concern the content but rather the limits of right (governmental or political) reason.

Raz's argument concerning the issue of consent is complex. I presented it briefly since this is a characteristic of Raz's thought that runs throughout all his arguments. He is a master at articulating values and presuppositions—in our case: right reason and the interest in autonomy—which still underlie political theoretical concepts that are generally taken to be independent values in themselves. He does this not only regarding the notion of consent, but also, as we will see, regarding the concepts of autonomy, individual rights, and toleration. And if we recall the conclusions we reached in our discussion of political liberalism, we immediately see how beneficial this strategy can be. There, we concluded that the political doctrine that John Rawls, J. Donald Moon, and others defend cannot be valued for independent, strictly political reasons. With Raz, the real criterion of the legitimacy of political liberalism should not be looked for in the consent of citizens to independent substantive principles of justice and social stability, but rather in the value of the ethical orientations and the social practices that these principles are bound to promote. In the case of Rawls, we saw that this value can be tracked down by closely studying the substantive characteristics of the conditions of liberal consensus-seeking he advocates. It turned out that these conditions—which are conceptualized as reasonable conditions—do in fact express a nonpolitical notion of the good.

So let us turn to Raz's account of personal autonomy, which is the central feature of his perfectionism. In his book *The Morality of Freedom* (1986), he claims that citizens of liberal-democratic societies have an essential interest in autonomy, in a sense that might seem to be illiberal to some: "The value of personal autonomy is a fact of life. Since we live in a society whose social forms are to a considerable extent based on individual choice, and since our options are limited by what is available in our society, we can prosper in it only if we can be successfully autonomous" (394). Personal autonomy is instrumentally valuable in an autonomy-enhancing culture; a culture that sustains social forms (practices) that are conducive to autonomous life-styles (372). An autonomous life is a life of independence, free from coercion and manipulation by others and characterized by the pursuit of projects a person wholeheartedly identifies with. It is a life of self-control and self-creation in a pluralist society characterized by a range of options from which individuals choose forms of work, leisure, love relationships, ethical orientations, political affiliations, and so forth (391).

Of course, many liberals maintain that within a society in which individuals are free to choose among many life-styles, an autonomous personal life-style should be seen as just one of the many options from which individuals can choose. Raz, however, maintains that an autonomous life-style is not just an "option," but rather a necessary feature of what, in modern pluralist societies, can be called a good life. Many of the most valuable options for leading a good life such that societies present their members with presuppose that they be chosen for and pursued in an autonomous fashion. The meaning of these options, one could say, is such that expectations as to the autonomy of those who choose them are already implied in them. The practice of marriage as we know it in contemporary liberal-democratic societies is a good example. Raz holds that we cannot adequately account for it by saying that a marriage is a legal (and sometimes religious) bond between a man and a woman which, in our society, is further characterized by the idea that the man and woman have voluntarily chosen each other. Rather, he says, this latter characterization defines the very nature of the bond as we value it. Therefore, the idea of free choice is not external to, but rather implied in the very meaning of this practice (392–95). (Consider the way in which liberal governments and courts nowadays think about invasions of the private sphere of marriage or the family in cases of marital abuse. It is praiseworthy that the "sanctity" of family life is understood as insufficient reason not to invade this sphere when the physical and mental integrity of one of the spouses or children is threatened by this very institution.) Since the ideal of personal autonomy or free choice is internal to the meaning of many highly valued practices in liberal societies—education, entrepreneurial activity, working ethos, political activity, art, academic activity, parenthood, and so on—Raz seems to have a strong case when he says that an autonomous personal lifestyle is not just another option. Rather, it is a prerequisite for leading a good life.

Now what does this mean for liberal politics? Raz holds that "[t]he government has an obligation to create an environment providing individuals with an adequate range of options and the opportunities to use them. The duty arises out of people's interest in leading a valuable autonomous life" (417–18). The state as well as individual citizens are obligated to help all members of society lead autonomous lives by first, the classic liberal duty not to coerce or manipulate others; second, the duty to "help in creating the inner capacities required for the conduct of an autonomous life," and, finally, the duty to provide people with an adequate range of valuable options from which to choose (407–8).

Here, it is in order to go further into the assumptions of Raz's theory.[5] As I already noted, his use of the term *autonomy* is somewhat different from that of many other liberals, political liberals in particular. Raz writes: "Autonomy is valuable only if exercised in pursuit of the good. The ideal of autonomy requires only the availability of morally acceptable options. This may sound a very rigoristic moral view, which it is not. A moral theory which recognizes the value of autonomy inevitably upholds a pluralist view. It admits the value of a large number of greatly differing pursuits among which individuals are free to choose" (381). From the point of view of political liberalism, Raz's conception of autonomy may seem to be overly narrow and normative. Political liberals will say that living an autonomous life has to do with deciding for oneself, without being coerced or manipulated by others, what options—either good or bad—one wants to choose. Of course, one might be punished for choosing bad options, such as stealing or dealing in drugs, but according to the political liberal this does not necessarily mean (although it might) that the choice one made was not autonomous. According to Raz, however, autonomy is only valuable if exercised in pursuit of the good. The free choice to bully others, or to embark on a criminal career, is not a valuable choice. For personal autonomy as it is valued in liberal societies is not an aspect of the social meaning of these practices. These practices are not good in themselves. An autonomous life is not simply a life one has voluntarily chosen. Rather, it is a life of self-determination led in pursuit of the good as defined by social practices that are, within a liberal culture, considered valuable. That is why Raz maintains that autonomy only requires a plurality of valuable options. For only if such a plurality is guaranteed will the agent be able to lead a valuable life.

Raz is committed to a view of the well-being of persons that is, again, somewhat atypical of liberalism understood as a theoretical tradition with rather individualistic premises. He holds that a "person's well-being depends to a large extent on success in socially defined and determined pursuits and activities" (309) In these pursuits and activities—and this is important with respect to Rawls's view— comprehensive goals play an important role. According to Raz, these are goals that permeate important aspects of one's life—such as the goal to become a violinist, a gardener, a politician, a Roman Catholic priest, a good Muslim, a writer, a parent, and so forth. Raz stresses the fact that "a person can have a comprehensive goal only if it is based on existing social forms, i.e. on forms of behavior which are in fact widely practised in his society" (308). Comprehensive goals can only be as pervasive as they are because they are embedded in social forms, which "consist of shared beliefs, folklore, high culture, collectively shared metaphors, imagination, and so on," which support them, that is, which render them socially recognized activities. And it is through participation in, and observation of, existing social forms that people come to accept particular comprehensive goals as their own (408).

Now, the central argument of Raz's perfectionism is that both the state and individual citizens have an obligation to provide members of society with a pluralist social environment that is conducive to the autonomous pursuit of valuable options, that is, comprehensive goals. We have seen that this is the third, most demanding autonomy-based duty of the state and its citizens. The first two duties (not to coerce or manipulate others and to help create the inner capacities required for the conduct of an autonomous life), so it seems, can also be supported from a nonperfectionist perspective. For these only concern strategies needed to guarantee the conditions of autonomy or, put more moderately, free choice, which do not presuppose a judgment concerning the value of the options people might choose. In order to prevent people from coercing and manipulating each other, and to provide them with the mental and physical capacities required for the conduct of a life led in liberty, one need not say anything about the ethical quality of their lives. One need not even claim that only an autonomous life is of value. But as soon as the state goes one step further and starts defining and providing "valuable options," it can no longer claim to be neutral on questions concerning the good life. It then creates a social and political world in which a life led in pursuit of options that are generally regarded as valuable is the only valuable life imaginable.

Against this background, Raz has interesting things to say about the meaning of individual rights. He vehemently argues against the widespread liberal view that individual rights "represent the individual's perspective or interest against the general or public good or against the claims, demands, needs, or requirements of others generally."[6] What he thinks is distorted about this view is not that it sees a close link between people's interests and their rights. Although he concedes that people's interests do not tell the whole story about rights—for example, the intensity of a person's interest is no valid reason for her fundamental rights trumping the rights of others—Raz does see a close link between rights and interests. This link becomes intelligible once we understand that fundamental civil rights such as the freedom of thought, of religion, of speech, of association, of occupation, and so forth, "are all important not because it is important that people should speak, should engage in religious worship, . . . etc., but because it is important that they should decide for themselves whether to do so or not." Again, Raz points to the value of personal autonomy as the chief justificatory force in legal and political thought. People have an essential interest in leading an autonomous life, because in a pluralist liberal culture autonomy is a basic condition of individual well-being. Individual rights protect and foster this interest. So Raz holds that rights and, more generally, liberal institutions are indeed interest-based. But he denies that the interest in personal autonomy should primarily be defended in terms of the interest of individuals to be protected against the common good and against the demands of others. Rather "[t]he protection of many of the most cherished civil and political rights in liberal democracies is justified by the fact that they serve the common or general good." Although it very often seems that protecting the rights of individuals is the highest aim of law in liberal societies, Raz maintains that the (autonomy-based) circumstance that the most fundamental rights are individual rights does not mean that these rights prevail "over the interest of the collectivity or the majority." By protecting the rights of individuals, liberal society eventually protects the common good, that is, a culture in which individual well-being remains an attainable good for all. Individual rights protect and promote an environment in which autonomy-enhancing social forms flourish. Because of the values they are based on, they contribute to a flourishing liberal culture.[7]

Finally, attention should be paid to Raz's views concerning the liberal aim for state neutrality. Raz does not think highly of, for instance, Rawls's notion of neutrality (117ff.) For reasons that resemble my argument against Rawls's unwillingness to reflect on the value of personal autonomy, Raz cannot accept Rawls's restricted use of the idea of the autonomy of citizens—understood as public autonomy alone—and concludes that Rawls does in fact presuppose the validity of personal autonomy as a basis of his theory. Political liberalism, he claims, is a comprehensive doctrine.[8] This motivates him to understand Rawls's aim for liberal neutrality as an aim for "neutrality between those conceptions of the good that greatly value an autonomous development" of citizen's lives (133). But this, he states, means that liberalism should no longer be understood as a doctrine of neutrality but rather as a perfectionist doctrine of moral pluralism, that is, a form of liberal "pluralism which allows that certain conceptions of the good are worthless and demeaning, and that political action may and should be taken to eradicate or at least curtail them" (133).

The limits of perfectionism

It is time to evaluate Raz's perfectionist account of liberalism. Of course, the differences between his theory and political liberal theories are striking. Raz's most important conclusion is that our most cherished social forms and the ideals implicit in them presuppose an affirmation of personal autonomy and value pluralism. In line with my critique of political liberalism, I believe that we have to concede that, in the end, Raz does straightforwardly say what is not just true of his account of liberalism, but also of more neutralist approaches such as the one professed by political liberals. Liberalism is at least a partly comprehensive political doctrine, based on an affirmation of personal autonomy and pluralism, and it would be wise to acknowledge this. But what to do once this fact has been acknowledged? Should liberalism still try to be as neutral as possible, or should it rather defend its own comprehensive view as acceptable to all? Raz does not hesitate to claim that the liberal state should protect and foster the conditions for leading autonomous personal lives. It is mainly because of this last step that his theory has a conservative or illiberal ring to it.

What is most problematic about Raz's theory is his trust in the value of given liberal social forms and in his readiness to accept, as a fact of life, that these social forms sometimes exclude the social and legal recognition of other social forms that might well be equally valuable. The problem springs from a dilemma that is at the heart of the theory itself. Remember that Raz distinguishes between three autonomy-based duties of the state and of individual citizens: first, the duty not to coerce or manipulate others; second, the duty to help create in people capacities for autonomous action; and third, the duty to provide people with an adequate range of valuable options from which to choose. Taken together, these duties confront us with a dilemma. For how could liberal societies define and support a limited (although pluralist) range of valuable options without running the risk of coercing or manipulating some of their members?

Raz would say that this dilemma is no more than a paradox; a contradiction which, upon reflection, turns out to be no contradiction at all. Since he assumes that a given, always limited, range of options in a particular society will provide most citizens with options that they believe to be genuinely valuable—options that are in line with the right reason of both the state and its citizens—the fostering of these options does not appear as coercion or manipulation to him. Even though his argument of valuable social forms conducive to personal autonomy is sound in theory, Raz overlooks some problems when he applies it to normative questions. To illustrate this point, let me return to the example of marriage. As we have seen, Raz makes the convincing point that the legal bond between spouses is defined by much more than its formal definition. In liberal cultures, this bond is characterized by the autonomous choice of a man and a woman. This characteristic is implied in the social meaning of the bond. And the same goes, according to most people, for the idea that a marriage is a bond between a man and a woman. In valuing social forms, Raz gives priority to the widely shared social meanings they actually have. When discussing the possibility of gay marriages, he observes that it is not at all impossible to recognize marriages of people of the same gender, and that it "merely requires the passing away of the current type of marriage, which is exclusive to people of differing genders."[9] It seems that he is saying that the traditional meaning of the good of marriage has to change or wither away before liberal societies can decide to recognize, or even consider recognizing, marital bonds with other social meanings. But Raz does not go into the important question at what point this meaning will have shifted enough to make institutional changes both possible and legitimate. In other words, the theory does not provide us with the conceptual means to understand how struggles over the social and/or legal recognition of not (yet) accepted social forms could have cultural and political significance. I fear that it relies too much on the value of existing social forms, and on the government's wisdom in assessing right reason, to be wholly convincing as a normative theory for an autonomy-enhancing liberal society.

Raz acknowledges that his theory has conservative traits. His concern is with liberal societies in which certain social practices are valued highly. These social practices should be protected and promoted as valuable options for their members. And he emphasizes that "[t]he fact that any one society makes realization of only a small fraction of them [i.e., routes to the good life] possible is inevitable." The only thing that matters, he says, "is that everyone will have an adequate range of options realistically available to them."[10] But that statement is more problematic than it might seem at first sight. Although Raz is surely right in claiming that his theory is not conservative but radical in showing why people should have full and equal access to available state-supported options, the question as to who decides which possible range of options would be "adequate" remains largely unanswered. Surely, it is not enough to say that these options offer many different possibilities for leading an autonomous life. For wholeheartedness is a condition of autonomy (382).[11] When some members of society cannot wholeheartedly lead the life they aspire to lead because it is not socially and legally recognized, the conservative "adequate range of options" of Raz's liberal society will not be of much use to them. They will feel that it manipulates their sense of freedom. Raz is aware of this problem. He states that the

"need to secure adequate access, like the need to provide basic capacities, overrides any fondness for existing forms of activity and relationship. If access to some requires a change in options to all, so be
it."[12] This is a reassuring remark, which suggests that Raz's radicalism is meant to go further than a radicalism within a conservative
framework. Still, the question remains as to how the conservative
and the radical perspectives could be reconciled.

On the last pages of *The Morality of Freedom*, Raz identifies
some serious problems that every perfectionist politics will be confronted with. First, at the level of government, he concedes that there
are "dangers inherent in the concentration of power in few hands, the
dangers of corruption, of bureaucratic distortions and insensitivities,
of fallibility of judgement, and uncertainty of purpose, and . . . the in-
sufficiency and the distortion of the information reaching the central
organs of government" (427). He acknowledges that, out of concern
for personal freedom and autonomy, "the limitations of governments
force one to compromise the purity of the ideal [perfectionist] doctrine
of freedom" (428). A considered view of the defects of government, he
says, will lead to much greater freedom from governmental action
than a firm commitment to autonomy ideally requires. This, he says,
is both a good thing and a bad thing. If the perfectionist powers of
government are limited, citizens will not necessarily lose the opportunity to lead autonomous lives. And this is good. But—and this is
the bad consequence of the fallibility of government—because the
freedom from governmental interference will be much greater than
the commitment to autonomy ideally requires, citizens who do not
manage to lead autonomous lives because they lack the support of a
perfectionist liberal state will not be able to lead good lives in the
modern, liberal sense. And so the liberal perfectionist ends up acknowledging what more neutralist theorists have always taken as
one of the most important starting points of liberal political thought:
that, in the imperfect social world we inhabit, the dangers of perfectionist politics are so widespread that liberalism should try to resist
the conceptual and political attractiveness of perfectionism as much
as possible. This means that liberalism will have to be permissive of
personal life-styles and social practices that it thinks do not fit well
with its cherished social forms. This, liberal neutralists will wholeheartedly say and perfectionists will reluctantly admit, is the price
liberalism has to pay for its attempt to construct a morally defensible
political theory for an imperfect world, inhabited by imperfect people.

Raz concedes that there is still a second source of discontent
with perfectionist projects that should be taken seriously: "The pur-

suit of full-blooded perfectionist policies, even of those which are entirely sound and justified, is likely . . . to backfire by arousing popular resistance leading to civil strife" (429). In such cases, the only viable way to protect the social and political order in society is to look for compromise or a modus vivendi—the least perfectionist political strategy imaginable. Apparently, perfectionist measures require a large measure of social consensus. In all other cases, the civil strife that such measures generate can be understood as a call for freedom from government, so that the freedom of individuals will not be restricted.

What is striking about Raz's insights concerning the fallibility of perfectionist governments is that he does not really reflect on the ways in which the government's idea of what right reason consists of could be controlled and strengthened by social and political participation of the citizenry. His basic outlook seems to be that the government should just know what right governmental reason is and that, if it does, it will govern in just ways. But this is a strange assumption. I think that Raz should focus more on the meaning of the highly valued and autonomy-enhancing practice of democracy. In trying to deal with the paradoxes of liberalism, he could—just like political liberals—benefit from the idea of public deliberation. Raz is correct in claiming that it is not consent to a just government but rather the right reason implicit in a government's actions that makes a government legitimate. Right reason stands for substantive ideas that benefit the good of a just society. And it is the substance that matters most: it provides citizens with the reasons for consent. So here, the good is prior to the procedural notion of consent. But this does not at all mean that public deliberation over issues of public concern such as the legitimacy of the government's actions and the validity of existing social forms could not be of prime importance in assessing right reason. Although Raz does not explicitly deny this, he does overlook the importance of public debate understood as a crucial link between the needs and aims of "private" citizens and the right reason that liberal government and institutions represent. As Raz himself makes clear, the right reason of liberal government and institutions has to be responsive to valuable social forms. But if that is true, then how else could we think of right reason other than as a reason that draws its content from public deliberation? In public deliberation within institutions of civil society such as the media, interest-based pressure groups, religious institutions, universities, and so on, a continuous debate is taking place over the question as to how valuable practices characteristic of our liberal-democratic societies really are. This is the place where the radical perspective that Raz needs to counterbalance the conservatism of his perfectionism will be articulated most vehemently. And a good government, just like a good parliament, will take notice of this perspective because it articulates points of view that are essential to a successful assessment of the question as to what extent governmental, parliamentary, and legal reason are really responsive to valuable social forms. It is only through public debates, or through other public forms of symbolic representation, that an issue such as that of gay marriages reaches the political agenda. For a convincing political theory, it is not enough to just state that the issue will be taken seriously once it turns out that existing social forms cannot answer to authentic needs and purposes of some members of society. The theory has to have some understanding of where in society shifts in social practices can best be identified, and how its normative claims relate to the conception of right reason of liberal governments and institutions.

Implicitly, Raz's theory provides us with insight that could be supplemented with a notion of public deliberation. In his discussion of the virtue of toleration, he stresses the fact that an autonomy-enhancing culture will always generate serious normative conflicts. The pluralism of such a culture, he says, will inescapably be competitive. "[C]ompetitive pluralism admits the value of virtues possession of which normally leads to a tendency not to suffer certain limitations in other people which are themselves inevitable if those people possess other, equally valid, virtues" (404). Because a pluralist culture will only flourish if it provides individuals with often incompatible options, many seemingly irreconcilable conflicts may be expected to spring from it. Individuals who have wholeheartedly chosen particular options will believe that their deepest convictions are valid. This will sometimes prompt them to react intolerantly to people who are motivated by other beliefs and projects. Yet, out of respect for the autonomy of those with whom they disagree, liberal citizens will often have to curb the very intolerant reactions that they believe to be valid. This, Raz maintains, is the stuff toleration is made of.

This is a convincing account of toleration. It explains why the reasonableness and the personal autonomy of liberal citizens do not rule out the possibility of normative conflict. An autonomy-enhancing culture is not a homogenous culture. Even if all citizens were to be reasonable and autonomous, serious normative conflicts over moral and ethical questions would still arise. Yet, Raz does not sufficiently address the question as to what role the practice of toleration, understood as the curbing of intolerant reactions, could play with respect to the reproduction of the symbolic order, including the framing of right reason, within liberal society. He does not make clear to what extent liberal citizens are or are not allowed to articulate the deeper grounds of their intolerant feelings toward others. Should they always re-strain themselves? I believe that this would be an invalid perspective, for it would sustain the status quo of accepted social forms and life-styles within society. It seems to be far more promising to ask to what extent the virtue of toleration could enable citizens of liberal societies to engage in "transformative" debates over questions of what is right and what is wrong, what is good and what is bad. Toleration should not only be understood as self-restraint. As a virtue that draws its value from the curbing of sometimes intolerant yet deeply cherished beliefs, it should also be understood as an important source for the ar-ticulation of critical and radical perspectives on existing social forms. After all, in an autonomy-enhancing culture, intolerance of nonvalu-able or outdated social forms is often a virtue. In trying to supple-ment liberal perfectionism with a notion of public deliberation, this insight could be highly valuable.

My critique of Raz's perfectionism resembles my earlier critique of political liberalism. Both liberal theories seem to be in need of an understanding of how its basic assumptions could be assessed through public debate. One might say that they suffer from a demo-cratic or deliberative deficit. In the case of political liberalism, the critique was that its substantive notion of public reason unknow-ingly and unwillingly tends to frustrate potentially valuable notions of the good because it overlooks its own bias toward personal auton-omy. In the case of liberal perfectionism, this point could not be made. Still, because of its conservative affirmation of existing op-tions for leading a good life in liberal society, which also runs the risk of frustrating certain valuable ideas of the good, it is in need of a critical self-reflexivity to prevent it from merely sustaining the sta-tus quo. If it does not, this status quo will take on the status of a du-bious, highly substantive and, despite its pluralist sympathies, culturalist Archimedean starting point—"our way of doing things"— for the assessment of right reason.

Rephrasing some key concepts of liberal thought

We have come a long way in discussing the justification of liberal in-stitutions and, indeed, of liberalism itself. We began these chapters on political liberalism and liberal perfectionism with a simple question: Are liberal institutions justified because they have instrumental value for the promotion of a certain view of well-being, or are they justified simply because they treat human beings as equals while trying to say nothing at all about the value of particular "private" ideals of well-being? We found that only the first view is correct. Liberalism is a moderately perfectionist doctrine that cannot but promote, through its major institutions, a view of well-being based on the ideal of personal autonomy and on an affirmation of moral pluralism. However, we also found that Raz's liberal perfectionism, which explicitly defends this view, is not by far an unproblematic doctrine. Because of its conservative implications, its explicit aim to defend primarily autonomy-enhancing social forms that are widely valued in liberal society backfires. These implications are all the more worrying because Raz seems to suggest that the government is the main authority in deciding which options within society are valuable. Because of this, one would almost long for the aim for the neutrality of the politically liberal view, even if one knows that it cannot be defended as the freestanding doctrine that at first sight makes it so attractive. This leads to the unsatisfactory conclusion that while liberal perfectionism is, at the conceptual level at least, the more convincing theory, from a normative perspective political liberalism still appears to be a more desirable doctrine. We have to conclude that the liberal aim for impartiality or neutrality and the ideal of personal autonomy cannot be reconciled by the variants of liberalism we have studied. In the following chapters, we will have to ask to what extent it is possible to combine the strengths of both doctrines while leaving their weaknesses behind.

Yet, much has been established. Not only has a serious dilemma that runs through liberalism been traced. We have also gained deeper insight into the meaning of such concepts of liberal thought as autonomy, reasonableness, pluralism, toleration, the good life, and neutrality. Let me, for reasons of clarity, recapitulate the meaning of these concepts.

Autonomy—Autonomy is both a capacity of liberal citizens who engage in public deliberations concerning the validity of the general rules that govern social cooperation, and an ideal central to permissible comprehensive social practices and conceptions of the good. The first meaning of the term we label public autonomy, the second personal autonomy. Liberalism presupposes the validity of personal autonomy in the sense that it is—both in its strategies of justification and in its practical effects—biased toward a society in which persons aim to lead autonomous lives. Liberalism will be most readily accepted by persons who are, or aim to be, autonomous in this sense. Note, however, that this does not necessarily imply that liberalism has no reason to tolerate conceptions of the good that do not embrace the ideal of personal autonomy. For it seems that respect for each and every person's capacity for personal autonomy implies that seemingly nonautonomous persons cannot simply be forced into accepting this ideal.

Reasonableness—Reasonableness is a virtue of liberal citizens. It acknowledges that people may have different yet valuable reasons to choose options that society has to offer. They understand and accept the fact that their reasonableness imposes burdens of judgment. Put generally, they understand that the intensity of their most deeply held beliefs, and the interests that spring from them, does not provide them with a valid reason to disrespect the beliefs and rights of others. They understand that the comprehensive ideas of others may well be as valuable as their own. In their public lives they are willing to reach an "agreement to disagree" with others over questions both of the good life and of public issues. And they accept the fact that others may have different reasons for accepting a common doctrine of "public reason." Yet, their respect for the beliefs of others does not prompt them to say nothing at all about controversial issues. On the contrary, they acknowledge that, in order to understand the nature of certain controversies, they will often have to engage in unconstrained public dialogue. The exact characteristics of this notion of public dialogue have not yet been properly discussed. But we have found that reasonableness cannot consist in simply drawing a sharp line between a "public domain" of constrained dialogue and a "private domain" of given interests, needs, and conceptions of the good. There is no reason to assume that the "moral-transformative" quality of reasonable deliberation should be dogmatically rejected by liberalism.

Pluralism—For liberal citizens, pluralism is not just a fact but a value. Liberal citizens understand that it is precisely the pluralism of the social world that enables them to lead an autonomous life. The pluralism they value is a reasonable pluralism, a pluralism sustained by autonomous and reasonable persons who seek to sustain and foster valuable conditions for their individual and collective well-being. Therefore, reasonable pluralism can be said to be a common practice sustained by liberal persons and institutions. But it is important to recognize that the liberal affirmation of the value of pluralism is not the only option open to those who recognize—as all members of modern societies must—the fact of pluralism. There is no prima facie reason to believe that the rejection of the liberal understanding of pluralism and personal autonomy must necessarily be an unreasonable act.

Toleration—Toleration is a virtue of liberal citizens and of liberal institutions. It does not mandate that conflict and competition be totally curbed. On the contrary, toleration is necessary because, in truly liberal societies, conflict and competition will never be totally curbed. Out of respect for the capacity for personal autonomy of others, tolerant individuals curb their own inclinations to be intolerant. Yet, toleration should not lead to a social status quo or to the toleration of all beliefs and practices. Again, toleration of all "given" interests, needs, and conceptions of the good in liberal societies does not seem to be a promising option. We will have to examine how controlled intolerance (toleration) could benefit liberal societies that aim to learn from normative conflict.

Conceptions of the good—Liberalism is biased toward conceptions of the good where the ideals of personal autonomy and an affirmation of moral pluralism are critical. But the conclusion that liberalism should simply limit its normative appeal to those citizens who embrace autonomy-based conceptions of the good seems to be unsatisfactory. All liberals agree that an "objective" and fully comprehensive definition of the good life cannot be given. But we also found that a simple toleration of given "subjective" conceptions of the good would not benefit liberal purposes. So it seems that we have to go beyond objectivism and subjectivism and opt for a more intersubjectivist approach. Such an approach would be a deliberative one, which starts from the intuition that the question as to what the good life consists of for members of liberal societies can only be answered in open deliberations among those members in which the defensibility of their given beliefs is tested in light of their own interests and those of their fellow citizens. On the "second stage" of liberal reasoning—the stage at which liberal ideal conceptions are being articulated—"thick" autonomy-based conceptions will be defended. But on the first stage—that of a modus vivendi of liberal and other ideals—other conceptions may be tolerated as well, if only for reasons of respect for the capacity for autonomy. As Raz's argument concerning the importance of social practices made clear, an assessment of the importance of flourishing social forms for individual well-being will be important here. Against this background, the free choice of members of traditionalist cultures to protect their social practices against undesired consequences of liberal individualism need not necessarily be disqualified from a liberal point of view. Indeed, Raz's perfectionism helps us understand how important cultural situatedness is for the well-being of liberals as well as for members of nonliberal, but not necessarily unreasonable cultures.

Neutrality—Liberalism is not a neutral political doctrine. It demands that citizens affirm the values of autonomy, reasonableness, pluralism, the good life, and toleration. This being said, a liberalism that is true to its own ideals will still have to aim at several forms of neutrality. First, it is neutral among comprehensive notions of the good life that affirm the values or character-orientations discussed herein. And second, it defends a notion of public deliberation that is not only acceptable to liberal individuals but that also provides nonliberal members of liberal societies with opportunities to have their voices heard. It is true that liberalism affirms a pluralist yet substantive idea of a good life. But liberalism should not be too dogmatic about this ideal. For if it were, it would rob itself of the opportunity to learn how exactly this idea relates to those conceptions of the good that conflict with it, but that may well be of constitutive importance to those who adhere to them.

Conclusions to Part 2

It is time to ask to what extent, on the basis of the shortcomings of political liberalism and liberal perfectionism identified in chapters 3 and 4, it is legitimate to state that liberalism is a tragic doctrine. The simplest way to answer this question is to confront my findings with the hypothesis I presented in chapter 2. I will begin by discussing the first two parts of the hypothesis.

> 1. Because liberalism has a purposive structure—that is, it is not an ethically neutral doctrine—there are normative conflicts in which its aim to let the interests of *all* citizens in leading a good life matter equally cannot but generate tragic conflicts.

> 2. In generating tragic conflicts, liberalism sometimes undermines conceptions of the good life that it aims to tolerate; and (thereby) its own aim to let the interests of all citizens in leading a good life matter equally.

Tragic conflicts, we said, are conflicts that are both necessary and, to a considerable extent, irreconcilable. And we conjectured that the tragedy of liberalism might be related to the purposive structure of the conceptual framework by means of which liberalism makes sense of the social world. One important conclusion is that the liberal framework does have a purposive structure. It necessarily sustains and promotes autonomy-enhancing comprehensive conceptions of the good and a plurality of autonomy-enhancing social practices, because it is founded on a firm belief in the value of personal autonomy. Yet, liberalism is confronted with a social world that is recalcitrant in two ways.

First, not all notions of the good and not all social forms are autonomy enhancing. The liberal notion of respect for autonomy must play an important role in liberalism's dealings with such social forms. Liberal societies cannot simply force "dissident" groups to affirm liberal notions of autonomy and reasonableness. Such a move cannot be justified by the liberal notion of personal autonomy. In a nutshell, this is the dilemma that both variants of liberalism are confronted with. The conceptual frameworks that these variants of liberalism present us with are, in a sense, a prioristic. When it comes to discussing the value of the ethical and moral demands that liberalism makes on citizens, liberalism's purposive conceptual framework leads to what we might call an intercultural stalemate. As seen from this framework, this stalemate appears to be both necessary and irreconcilable. It's necessary because liberalism cannot jump over its own shadow (its a prioristic normative assumptions) and irreconcilable because liberalism offers no clear notion of practical reason or public deliberation that could help it take seriously claims of individuals and groups that do not embrace liberal values and principles. The conflict between the variants of liberalism we have studied and such nonliberal individuals and groups is a tragic conflict because, as a general rule, true liberals will want to respect and tolerate the genuine beliefs of individuals they firmly disagree with. Adhering to a "presumption of equal value," they would like to find ways to let these beliefs matter equally, but the conceptual frameworks of political liberalism and liberal perfectionism do not tell them how they could live up to this moral aspiration.

Second, with the pluralism of autonomy-enhancing notions of the good and social practices severe normative conflicts among people who all affirm the value of personal autonomy are by no means impossible. But are such conflicts tragic? I think they can be. Personal autonomy is not a substantively defined life-style but a condition for leading a good life in a liberal society. People who affirm the value of personal autonomy can still lead different lives. Remember our prolife party? Its adherents may well recognize values such as personal autonomy, reasonableness, and toleration. This is a central theological trait of (moderate interpretations of) monotheistic religions such as Islam, Christianity, and Judaism. The very fact that prolifers recognize these values implies that they have no valid general reason to condemn dogmatically liberal-democratic modes of consensus-seeking and lawmaking. Indeed, the strength of the politically liberal notion of an overlapping consensus is that it shows how people could have different reasons to accept the fundamental characteristics of a liberal public culture. Yet, the fact that the members of our prolife group do in fact hold that a liberal public culture is valuable does not oblige them to identify wholeheartedly with some of the practices that this public culture allows. The practice of abortion, which is validated by the liberal framework they accept, harms some of their most deeply held beliefs.

So these citizens of liberal societies find themselves in a tragic predicament. In affirming the value of personal as well as public autonomy, they morally approve of a practice of lawmaking that sometimes generates effects they morally condemn. Again, in liberal societies, the conflict is both necessary and irreconcilable. It is necessary (inescapable) because these people cannot abandon or disregard their personal beliefs without abandoning the very framework of value that inspires both their ethical beliefs and actions and their recognition of the public liberal framework. And it is irreconcilable because the purposive structure of the liberal public culture they recognize promotes a freedom of choice that is not bound by the substantive characteristics of their own comprehensive doctrines. The conflict is tragic for wholehearted liberals as well. For the liberal framework as we have come to know it thus far does not allow the full articulation of the comprehensive beliefs that inspire the view that freedom of choice should never—not even within a liberal framework—be extended to a choice against (in this case fetal) life. Since the true liberal, just as liberal institutions, aims to respect and take seriously the notions of the good of all citizens, this is clearly unacceptable.

What the tragic conflicts at issue present us with is an insight into the problematic nature of the liberal aim to let the interests of all citizens in leading a good life matter equally. What is problematic about this aim is, of course, not the general thrust of the aim itself. It articulates a deep respect for human life and individual flourishing that must be valued for its own sake. Because of this, liberalism grants civil, political, and social rights to all citizens, not just to those who wholeheartedly affirm the value of personal autonomy and the practices it justifies. In granting citizens such rights, liberalism recognizes the fact that citizens are to a large extent free to choose their own values and life-styles. However, it thereby allows a form of pluralism which, in practice, it cannot adequately deal with. For its purposive structure cannot avoid frustrating the free articulation of those ethical views that liberalism tolerates but that do not fit in easily with the notion of the good liberalism ultimately stands for.

> 3. The tragic predicament of liberalism seems to be related to its explicit aim to promote moral unity when it comes to the use of public reason and public deliberation; and its implicit aim to promote key components for "private" conceptions of the good life such as the ideal of personal autonomy and the affirmation of ethical pluralism.

The main problem with both political liberalism and liberal perfectionism is that they define moral unity in too rigid terms. Personal and public autonomy, reasonableness, and state neutrality are ideals that are critical to liberal normative theories. They are not simply traits of the social world everyone can accept. Of course, liberalism cannot be blamed for claiming that they should be accepted as valid ideals. However, the variants of liberalism we discussed can be blamed for not providing us with sufficient understanding of how substantive liberal ideals relate to struggles over the legitimacy of the main institutions of society. The conceptual makeup of the theories we studied tends to exclude perspectives on society that seem to be at odds with liberal ideals—either by a method of conversational restraint or by an appeal to existing social forms. In order to live up to their highest aim, liberals should at least be capable of open-mindedly assessing the (consequences of) assumptions that underlie their own ideals and those of others. As we concluded in our discussion of political liberalism, liberalism should at least be able to go back and forth between a mere modus vivendi to which it is just one of the parties and the full articulation of the assumptions underlying its own ideals of a good and just society and the burdens of judgment it lays on individuals.

Maybe liberalism could gain a more open-minded understanding of pluralism. Maybe the idea of public deliberation could help us develop an idea of toleration that does not just passively tolerate social forms that cannot easily be fitted into practices that liberalism wholeheartedly approves of, but that enables those who cherish them to engage in forms of cooperation that are less frustrated by the high threshold of substantive a prioristic starting points. Although it is likely that such forms of cooperation would often not bring the parties to a consensus, they could generate shared understandings. If the parties to public deliberation would only learn that some of them are genuinely interested in the points of view of others, much would be won. Provided that liberal ideals are widely shared within society, it is of course true that the public culture of society will still frustrate the aims of nonliberal groups. But their awareness that liberal society genuinely aims to take their beliefs and ideals seriously could well have a positive influence on their self-respect and on their willingness to compromise or even transform some of their more controversial beliefs.

What we are looking for, then, is an idea of public reason through which the validity of ideals of personal excellence as well as ideals of justice could be assessed. It should not be based on dogmatic assumptions that suggest an Archimedean point. Yet, it should incorporate enough right reason to be acceptable to morally motivated members of liberal societies. While, out of respect for personal autonomy, it should not promote wholly comprehensive ideas of the good life, it should at least make it possible to assess open-mindedly the validity of such ideas. Our hope is that it will help us come to terms with the tragedy of liberalism. If it cannot overcome the tragic predicament of liberalism, it may at least point to ways in which we could come to accept and learn to live with it.

PART **III**

~

Deliberative Democracy
as a Way Out?

Introduction

Now that it has been shown that a good case can be made for maintaining that liberalism is in fact a tragic doctrine, it remains to be seen whether it could be defended in alternative ways that evade the tragic predicament. First, is it possible to develop a way of thinking about public deliberation that would not oblige citizens to refrain from appeals to "comprehensive" reasons in public debate? Second, can such a notion of public deliberation be defended in a non-perfectionist mode? If the first question can be answered affirmatively, then the exclusionary effects of the use of public reason for those citizens whose values and interests do not combine easily with the demands of public reason could perhaps be mitigated. And if, in addition, the second question can also be answered affirmatively, then a strong notion of the liberal principle of neutrality might be developed after all. For in that case, liberalism would not have to be defended as a perfectionist doctrine, nor would its notion of public deliberation have morally unjustifiable exclusionary effects.

In this section, I will study the theory of "deliberative democracy." More precisely, I will study Jürgen Habermas's account of deliberative democracy. His account is undoubtedly one of the most influential to date.[1] Furthermore, it builds upon an impressive notion of practical reason that makes it fairly easy to compare it with politically liberal and liberal-perfectionist accounts—which also build upon notions of practical reason. Moreover, Habermas's theory is a thoroughly liberal one.[2] Finally, the theory rests on a specific account of public deliberation. Deliberative democracy, unlike political liberalism, does not from the outset accept a substantive notion of justice and public reason (or the sharp distinction between "private" and "public" interests inspired by it). And neither does it, or so Habermas claims, presuppose a comprehensive and perfectionist idea of positive freedom understood as personal autonomy that would be characteristic of "our" liberal culture.

I will begin with a short exposition of the general idea of deliberative democracy. After that I will compare Habermas's notion of public deliberation with the politically liberal account. At first sight, it appears to be a much less constrained notion of public deliberation than the politically liberal one. Yet, it is not until after Habermas's discourse ethics and the substantive assumptions toward moral character that this moral theory presupposes have been examined that we can really begin to answer these two questions. The deliberatively democratic notion of public deliberation is indeed less constrained than its politically liberal counterpart. But I will argue that deliberative democracy should still be defended as a moderately perfectionist interpretation of liberalism, based on a firm affirmation of pluralism, the value of personal autonomy, and, generally, the value of posttraditional worldviews.

In chapter 6, I will discuss the deliberatively democratic understanding of law and democracy. Subsequently, it will be asked in what way the theory of deliberative democracy makes it necessary to revise the notions of autonomy, reasonableness, pluralism, toleration, the good life, and neutrality that were discussed in part 2. At the end of chapter 6, I will ask to what extent deliberative democracy can be understood as a way out of liberalism's tragic predicament. The conclusion will be that it can somewhat mitigate, but not overcome the tragedy of liberalism.

5

~

Discourse Theory
and Moral Character

It is often said that the idea of deliberative democracy is obsolete in pluralist and institutionally highly complex societies. One is tempted to agree with this view as long as one associates the idea of active democratic participation with images of the Greek agora or early-modern republican city-states, where, so tradition tells us, men endowed with the status of full citizenship gathered to discuss issues of public interest and to decide on strategies of collective action. Seen from this perspective, contemporary mass societies, which are divided into many semiautonomous spheres of action and in which full citizenship is an almost universal status of the adult members, do not seem to be suited for a participatory democratic regime in the strong sense. We simply cannot imagine how the ancient idea of citizens "gathering" to discuss issues of public concern could be conceptualized today. Furthermore, in contemporary liberal-democratic societies private projects are much dearer to citizens than their political engagements. Most of them simply see politics as a means to create private opportunities, not as the highest and most fulfilling form of human action.[1] Therefore, according to many critics of deliberative democracy, it seems necessary to take the idea of representative rather than direct democracy as a starting point, and to introduce "the voice of the people" as an instance of control (through voting and lobbying) only, not so much as a fundamental defining force in democratic processes of decision-making. As Mark E. Warren aptly summarizes this line of thought: "The best possible democracy is one in which groups and coalitions can check (but not guide) experts and political elites through the formal powers of voting and lobbying."[2]

Preliminary remarks on deliberative democracy

There is, however, a way of thinking about democracy that is conducive to the idea of participatory democracy while avoiding essentialist images of the citizen as a political being. The theory of deliberative democracy starts from the simple intuition that respecting people, recognizing them as social beings with a responsibility for their own actions, consists of taking them seriously as actors who can and should have a voice in the generation of the norms and laws they are subject to. It is a radicalization of the liberal idea we encountered in the previous chapters that the government should always be able to convince the citizenry that it is entitled to respect; a radicalization, because it does not content itself with the idea that a liberal government should try to be true to a hypothetical consensus concerning fundamental questions of justice, democracy, and solidarity. Rather, deliberative democrats avoid talk of a substantive hypothetical consensus and look for ways to locate the touchstone of legitimacy of the public order in public debates within diverse social spheres in society. However, this does not mean that deliberative democrats use the notion of actual consent as the ultimate touchstone of legitimacy. Although the idea of actual consent plays an important role in their theories, they maintain that actual consensus in itself is no guarantee of legitimacy; in order to answer questions of political legitimacy, deliberative democrats turn to a normative notion of public deliberation that sketches the conditions under which legitimate forms of consent could be reached.

Before I turn to this notion of deliberation, let me first say a few more words on some general characteristics and assumptions of deliberative democracy. Deliberative democracy is not primarily a theory about the purposes, principles, and rationality of the state or right governmental reason, and the ways in which it could serve the basic interests of members of civil society.[3] Liberal political theorists in particular still use these two notions to point to a supposedly clear distinction between the political sphere of government and political control on the one hand (state), and prepolitical social and economic spheres on the other (civil society).[4] Yet, in contemporary liberal societies, it is almost impossible to make a clear distinction between political and prepolitical spheres. Corporatism in questions of social and labor politics; economic, fiscal, and monetary control of private capital; questions concerning environmental issues and the development of modern science and industry; and the politics of education; emancipatory measures such as affirmative action imposed on the "free" market by the state—they all blur the supposedly clear distinction between civil society and the state. Private, economic, and cultural interests and conflicts have become strongly politicized, and so has civil society. Therefore, deliberative democrats maintain, questions of political democracy have become relevant to its institutions—from the economic sphere to science, education, culture, and the family.[5] The increased politicization of civil society, which has its main roots in the struggle for, and the subsequent granting of, full civil, political, and social rights to ever more citizens by the state, and the subsequent claiming of these rights in diverse institutions of civil society,[6] undercut many conventional means of social coordination within civil society—such as tradition, markets, and coercion. Once citizens have been recognized as equals under the law, social coordination increasingly becomes a collective task for them. According to deliberative democrats, the egalitarian politics of equal citizenship rights makes democratic discourse the most likely means for social coordination, particularly because it is the only means of coordination which, by definition, has to view all parties to social and political questions as equals—that is, as defined by their formal status of equal participants in democratic discourses, not by their status as determined by the market, tradition or other power-based relations.

So deliberative democracy breaks with the liberal idea that democracy is primarily concerned with decision-making at the level of the state. It aims to decentralize the idea of democracy. Although deliberative democrats by no means deny that a centralized state and a democratically elected government are necessary conditions for the enactment of law, a well-functioning bureaucratic system, and the protection of civil order, they do maintain that the politicization and democratization of civil society is an equally necessary condition for a free society. The idea is that the egalitarian ideology of liberal-democratic societies can only be realized if its members are able to play a guiding, not just a controlling, role in the political processes of decision-making that affect their lives.

Jürgen Habermas: Theoretical foundations of public deliberation

There is a twofold question that structures this discussion of deliberative democracy: the question whether, in terms of access to public deliberation, Habermas's account has less exclusionary effects than the one defended by politically liberal authors and whether it is really free of perfectionist substantive assumptions that would affect its neutrality.[7] In order to answer this double question, it seems to be a good idea to first look at Habermas's comments on political liberalism.

Habermas is sympathetic to the normative aims of political liberalism, particularly to this doctrine's universalistic aim to defend a notion of public reason that is "common to all humans."[8] He admires political liberalism's aim for neutrality toward conflicting worldviews but fears that, in the end, it rests on a justificatory strategy that cannot sufficiently guarantee this neutrality. In short, Habermas argues that the basic normative concepts from which political liberalism starts—most importantly the concepts of the politically autonomous citizen, of fair cooperation, and of a well-ordered society—are too substantive and (therefore) too controversial to function, as I would put it, as Archimedean points on which a liberal theory may rest. He holds that this theory of justice should not try to "bracket the pluralism of convictions and world view from the outset." For if a theory starts from controversial substantive normative assumptions and does not include a notion of practical reason (public deliberation) by means of which these assumptions can be questioned from various comprehensive perspectives, it will inescapably generate exclusionary effects that cannot be morally justified. As a way out of these shortcomings of political liberalism, Habermas concentrates on "the open procedure of an argumentative practice that proceeds under the demanding presuppositions of the 'public use of reason'" that would make such a bracketing of comprehensive ideas unnecessary.[9]

According to Habermas, it is possible to understand the relation between political and comprehensive doctrines in cognitive or epistemic terms that are genuinely ethically neutral. In order to arrive at these terms, which he says are essential to understanding the moral point of view, he proposes that we look at "the socio-ontological constitution of the public practice of argumentation, comprising the complex relations of mutual recognition that participants in rational discourse 'must' accept (in the sense of weak transcendental necessity)."[10] According to Habermas, this is genetically prior to the substantive concepts of the moral person and of social cooperation in political liberalism. In other words, it is not the substantive liberal concepts of the moral person and of legitimate forms of social cooperation that motivate us to value the practice of public deliberation, but rather the weakly transcendental presuppositions of rational deliberation. Here, it is in order to look at the theoretical core of Habermas's theory of practical reason.

In his *Theory of Communicative Action*, Habermas uses rational-reconstructive—"weakly transcendental"—arguments in order to state that language use "always already" builds upon certain normatively rich yet nonsubstantive conceptual presuppositions. As Seyla Benhabib puts it, the aim of rational reconstruction is to gain an understanding of the *"deep structures* of cognition and action which are operative in the activities of individuals" through an understanding of the often implicit "rule competencies" they follow.[11] These competencies, Habermas maintains, can only be adequately reconstructed if their analysis is tied to an understanding of the cultural-political development of a certain society over time. This development will show a certain logic that can subsequently be reconstructed in terms of implicit rules for rational action coordination that govern the actions of those who participate in this cultural-political development.

Habermas focuses on the modernization (the Enlightenment) of Western societies over the last few centuries. In the process of modernization, he discerns a development that he, following Piaget, refers to as a "decentration of world views."[12] The idea is that, quite analogous to the moral development of maturing individuals, in the course of the process of modernization of different forms of cognitive access to the world—objectifying thought (the natural sciences, economy, technical knowledge, and administrative reason), moral-practical insight (morality, law, and politics), and aesthetic-practical experience and expression (individuality, authenticity, and art)—have gradually been "set free" to become cognitive-practical powers in their own right.[13] He reconstructs the normative core of modernization as a learning process through which the adequacy and legitimacy of quasi-uncriticizable substantive worldviews are gradually being called into question.[14] In short, the idea is that individuals and social groups gain, through learning processes, the ability to be more rational and critical of the substantive worldviews—the social patterns of expectation—which underlie both their own beliefs and the beliefs of those they interact with. A life form can be said to be rational if it admits of social forms that allow of, and possibly even foster, critical questions as to the truth of factual beliefs, the rightness of social norms, and the authenticity of personal dispositions and expressions.[15] Therefore in modern societies, communicative action—a form of rational action by which people deliberate on the right reasons to accept or reject prevailing beliefs and norms—carries the burden of cultural reproduction. By acting communicatively, and by instating institutions that make communicative, deliberative action coordination possible, modern individuals free themselves of the reign of uncriticizable worldviews, and take responsibility for both their personal and their collective beliefs and actions.

Habermas's theory of modernization and rationalization is highly complex. It suffices if we know that this theory supports a notion of rationality that finds its foundation in a formal and procedural understanding of the weakly transcendental presuppositions of language use in terms of validity claims. When we reject a statement made by someone we talk with, we reject the validity of (aspects of) her claim.[16] Parallel to the three different forms of cognitive access to the world he distinguishes, Habermas discerns three kinds of linguistic validity claims. The first concerns the truth of a statement (its correctness as a statement concerning an identifiable state of affairs in the world); the second concerns its truth-analogous correctness (the extent to which it can be morally reconciled with norms and rules all reasonable persons could voluntarily accept and the extent to which the speaker is willing to defend the appropriateness of her view in moral argumentation); and the third concerns its authenticity (the extent to which it can be regarded as a statement that the speaker really believes to be true or correct). The fundamental presupposition behind this way of looking at the use of language consists in the idea that, in order to act rationally, people must always—although often counterfactually—assume that they themselves and their fellow men aim to speak the truth, live by rules and norms they voluntarily agree to, and are willing to defend and act in an authentic way. The most well-known and, to my mind, most convincing way of showing that this presumption is correct consists in the simple argument that even the liar and the cheat have to presume that those they are lying to and cheating, respectively, do in fact believe that they are speaking the truth and are acting authentically. They strategically manipulate others who trust in their adherence to the normative presuppositions implicit in everyday language use.

Against this background, we can now better understand Habermas's critique of political liberalism. His argument is that the epistemic relation between the legitimacy and the ethical neutrality of political liberalism should be understood in terms of the rationality of the form of public deliberation it makes possible. Since political liberalism is a moral doctrine, it is the truth-analogous correctness of its claim that it is a valid political doctrine that is at stake. Here, the procedural requirements of testing the moral legitimacy of this doctrine trump the boundaries set by its substantive presuppositions. For, or so Habermas argues, it is characteristic of the modern notion of rationality that such substantive presuppositions may always be questioned: "Precisely those [substantive] principles are valid which meet with uncoerced intersubjective recognition under [procedural] conditions of rational discourse."[17]

We can now also understand why Habermas claims that a theory of justice and democracy should not bracket the pluralism of comprehensive worldviews from the outset. For it follows from his notion of public deliberation that respecting a person's capacity to act morally consists of respecting her ability to freely articulate her views on the substantive principles and concepts that structure the public-political domain of society. In order for her to make use of this capacity, she may want to defend comprehensive or otherwise controversial moral convictions that she believes should be universally accepted. At the same time, however, she has to accept the fact that these convictions will in turn be scrutinized in the light of the procedural norm that only those substantive principles are morally valid which could be accepted in rational discourse.

So on the one hand, Habermas's notion of public deliberation has less exclusionary effects than its politically liberal counterpart. In the previous chapter we saw that one of the major limitations of the politically liberal notion of public deliberation is that it does not include perspectives that question its substantive normative assumptions. Provided that it is true that Habermas's notion of deliberation can be grounded without having any recourse to substantive assumptions (I will go into that claim in a little while), we may conclude that it should be welcomed by liberal thought. Liberalism will greatly be served by this rather unconstrained understanding of public deliberation. In principle, it enables all citizens to engage in political debates over the legitimacy of the rules and principles that govern the understanding of justice, rights, and democracy and, therefore, the institutional arrangements that set limits to their personal freedom.

On the other hand, however, many liberals will say that this perspective is not so tolerant when it comes to respecting "private moral

truths." As we have seen, it is one of the chief aims of political liberalism to keep religious and metaphysical questions of moral truth off
the political agenda. Yet, if we replace the politically liberal notion of
public deliberation with the deliberatively democratic one, this is no
longer possible. We then have to accept that all kinds of "private" beliefs that people appeal to in public deliberation will become vulnerable to a kind of moral scrutiny founded on the procedural logic of
communicative deliberation that may undermine (or, put in more positive terms, morally transform) these comprehensive beliefs.[18] So
while, as far as questions of access to public deliberation are concerned, deliberative democracy is more tolerant than political liberalism, it seems that there is reason to fear that the actual outcomes of
such deliberations are less tolerant than political liberals would wish.

    However, this point should not be exaggerated. First of all, it
does not follow from the fact that a controversial "private" belief may
not be accepted as a valid reason in public deliberation that the comprehensive worldview underlying it should not be tolerated at all. It
only follows that this worldview should not dominate the public life
of society. Deliberative democrats are as hospitable to the freedom of
conscience as political liberals. Second, it is somewhat misleading
and perhaps even false to state that the outcomes of public deliberation in terms of deliberative democracy will be less tolerant than the
outcomes of politically liberal deliberations. It only appears as less
tolerant as long as it's directed at the protection of given comprehensive worldviews. Here, the emphasis is on noninterference. By
contrast, deliberative democrats stand for a notion of toleration that
is "active" or "militant"; the greatest good is not noninterference, but
"a form of mutual respect" or "militant toleration" in which difference is not only tolerated, but, as Kenneth Baynes puts it, "in which
individuals seek to understand one another in their differences and
arrive at a morally-reasoned solution to the controversy in question."[19] Although this notion is more demanding than the one professed by political liberals, it is a necessary complement to the notion
of public deliberation that has been sketched here. If we want to adhere to a procedural notion of deliberation by means of which we can
test the acceptability of principles and substantive assumptions that
govern our public life, then we have to make the private and the
comprehensive political. And this indeed means that we will have to
be willing to understand each other despite our differences. We may
even hope that such an attitude will benefit social integration and
social stability, for we may conjecture that where there is mutual respect, understanding, and appreciation, there is social stability.[20]

Discourse ethics and the limits of formalism and proceduralism

We have now reached a rudimentary understanding of the similarities and differences between the theory of deliberative democracy and political liberalism. Still, in light of the findings of part 2, the claim that this theory does not presuppose substantive values derived from reasonable worldviews cannot be easily accepted. For this reason, we have to study Habermas's moral theory, which provides the theoretical basis for his deliberatively democratic perspective.

Habermas has taken up the critical and emancipatory potential inherent in rational language use to develop a "Diskursethik," a discourse ethics. Its main goal is to settle the dilemma as to how moral norms and principles could be grounded, that is, how their content could be understood as not just offering contingent guidelines for action, but rather as presenting moral imperatives with an epistemic status analogous to truth claims. Habermas starts from the formalistic Kantian conviction that only those moral beliefs are just that all rational beings could will. It is understandable that he should do so. After all, his aim is to develop a universalistic moral theory, a theory which, at least in principle, could be accepted by all beings who act morally. Whereas Kant lays the burden of moral judgment on isolated autonomous subjects, Habermas lays it on intersubjective procedures of moral deliberation. He translates Kant's categorical imperative—"Act only according to that maxim by which you can at the same time will that it should become a universal law!"—into a principle for moral discourse that says that "[o]nly those norms may claim to be valid that could meet with the consent of all affected in their role as participants in a practical discourse."[21]

By making a move from the Kantian focus on the subjective will of rational subjects to an intersubjective and communicative approach, Habermas makes his theory less susceptible to the Hegelian critique that the categorical imperative remains without practical relevance because it is in no way connected to the ethical life—the *Sittlichkeit*—of the societies to which it is meant to apply. Since the idealizations drawn from the logic of language use play an important role in the consensus-oriented modes of deliberation characteristic of democratic societies, discourse ethics cannot be said to be practically irrelevant in this sense.[22] However, it is true that the formal principle of discourse cannot in itself show what should count as a legitimate conclusion of moral argumentation. Therefore, Habermas complements it with a second rule: "For a norm to be valid, the consequences and side effects of its general observance for the satisfaction of each person's particular interests must be acceptable to all."[23] This is in fact a principle of universalizability, which should be understood as a moral rule for argumentation. It mandates that the consent of a person to a certain rule be given voluntarily and rationally, that is, that it not be motivated by fear, by dependence, or by ignorance, but by rational argument alone. Second, it stresses the fact that consent to a particular rule should not be based on egoistic motivations; rather, it should be a morally motivated consent: a consent in which the needs and interests of others are taken into account.

In recent years, Habermas has recognized that his initial formulation of the basic idea of a discourse ethics did not sufficiently account for the different meanings that the question What should I (we) do? takes on in practice. He now holds that his principle of discourse is a general principle that specifies how norms can be impartially grounded, while the principle of universalizability is a general rule for moral argumentation. In his theory of law and democracy, he supplements these principles with a principle of democracy that states that "only those statutes may claim legitimacy that can meet with the assent (*Zustimmung*) of all citizens in a discursive process of legislation that in turn has been legally constituted."[24] This principle articulates the normative expectations that underlie the liberal-democratic idea of the social cooperation of free and equal persons. It does not aim to show how communicative action is possible. It rather presupposes this, and articulates the normative assumptions underlying democracy, understood as a political complement to the idea of communicatively integrated life worlds. And contrary to the principle of universalizability, it does not only concern moral questions.

I said that Habermas discerns several meanings regarding the practical question, What should I (we) do? This question will be posed in situations that call for either pragmatic, ethical, or moral deliberation; such situations call for specific uses of practical reason.[25] When confronted with a pragmatic question—for instance, the question as to how to repair a broken car, or how to travel from point A to B in an unknown area—agents will look for strategies or techniques to solve the problem before them. The goal of pragmatic discourses is to "relate empirical knowledge to hypothetical goal determinations and preferences and to assess the consequences of (imperfectly informed) choices."[26]

The aims of practical reason change once the question, What should I (we) do? takes on an ethical dimension. What is at stake is not the adoption of strategies that will help individuals succeed in reaching a practical goal.[27] The question is which goals they have to set for themselves in order to lead good lives. Here, Habermas follows Charles Taylor's notion of "strong evaluation."[28] Taylor accounts for the ability to evaluate immediate desires and given activities in order to clarify what one really wants. Ethical questions ask for forms of critical self-evaluation that enable one to arrive at a self-understanding that is not merely contingent, but with which one can identify in the light of a personal conception of the good life.

Ethical questions can take on political significance. Such questions concern the collective self-understanding of the citizenry. The aim of "ethical-political" deliberations is not so much to aggregate opinions and to find compromises, but rather to learn, in an "actively tolerant" mode, from each other's views concerning the good life, in order to criticize and to renew received ideas of individual and collective identity (think of recent debates on multiculturalism, the Christian and humanist roots of Western civilization, a "politically correct" canon of literature in higher education, etc.). Habermas is correct when he emphasizes the fact that such questions cannot simply be decided (in a pragmatic mode) by representative voting in parliament. Rather, their treatment requires decentered and open forms of deliberation within the public sphere of society, in which every citizen should be able to participate and in which these questions are discussed until an identifiable—though always fallible—public opinion emerges that may, if this should prove necessary, be brought into the official political circuit.[29]

According to Habermas, the pragmatic and ethical use of practical reason do not have to stand the test of universalizability we discussed earlier. They are both necessarily undertaken from an egocentric perspective or, in ethical-political questions, from a perspective of a particular collective.[30] Impartiality of judgment is not a criterion for the reasonableness of their outcomes. On the contrary, both kinds of questions can only be properly addressed so long as the actors involved recognize that their pragmatic or ethical interests determine both the problematic nature of the situation they find themselves in and the aim to come up with solutions to problems given with this situation. And these solutions will primarily have to serve their interests. It is only when the moral point of view is called for that the test of universalizability, the aim for impartiality, becomes central to practical reason.

A moral question concerns the general permissibility of a certain principle or action. As Habermas puts it, it is the question "whether we all could will that anyone in my situation should act in accordance with the same maxim." This question, he maintains, breaks with "all of the unquestioned truths of an established, concrete ethical life, in addition to distancing oneself from the contexts of life with which one's identity is inextricably interwoven."[31] What the moral point of view stipulates is that we should be critical of received opinion and subjective interests, and deliberate on what would be in the interest of all concerned. Moral-practical questions are questions in which neither the aggregated will nor the ethical-political self-understanding of a particular community can count as a decisive factor. Here, the aim is to reach conclusions that each person could voluntarily accept in the light of the principle of universalizability. Questions of justice are moral questions. Constitutional issues, the formulation of basic rights, questions of judicial review, and the evaluation of forms of civil disobedience and the claims of political pressure groups typically call for the moral use of practical reason. Furthermore, moral-practical directives set limits to the pragmatic and ethical use of practical reason. Pragmatic plans and ethical orientations that clearly harm the legitimate needs and interests of others will be discredited from the moral point of view.

We have seen that Habermas claims that his moral theory is free of substantive assumptions and that it must therefore be considered neutral toward competing comprehensive worldviews. The Achilles heel of his theory lies in its assumptions about the conditions of moral argumentation in the modern world. Moral deliberations may be said to fulfill the requirements of modern and "postmetaphysical" or "posttraditional" thought if the participants in these deliberations accept the fact that pragmatic and ethical questions are of a fundamentally different nature than moral questions or questions of justice, and that the moral point of view alone should govern such questions. Under conditions of postmetaphysical thought—conditions, that is, under which a subjective belief in the metaphysical truth of a particular ethical (religious or philosophical) conviction is not a sufficient reason to consider it morally true for all people—it is, according to Habermas, impossible to make a conception of justice "contingent on the truth of a worldview, however reasonable it may be."[32] In the next section, I will argue that it is impossible to ground a conception of justice without any recourse to controversial worldviews. I will do so by investigating the conditions of moral character that deliberative democracy presupposes. But first, let me prepare the ground for what I want to say there.

The idea that people should deal with practical questions by argument rather than by relying on received opinion or hierarchical social relations is, in a way, farfetched. Even in the most egalitarian settings we can conceive of—certain friendships, discussion groups, seminars, institutions of representative democracy, and so on—factors such as experience, fame, talent, power, efficiency, and dependency play a sizable role in the outcomes of discussions. Habermas does not deny this. His point is that participants in practical deliberations should, often counterfactually, assume that all people concerned with the issue at stake participate as equals in a cooperative "search for the truth" that is guided by the idea of the force of the better argument, and that the institutional settings in which such deliberations take place should favor this assumption. Habermas has labeled this form of deliberation "discourse." One could describe it as a condensed form of practical reasoning, which has been reduced to its normatively rich characteristics: "Practical discourse is an exacting form of argumentative decision making. . . . [I]t is a warrant of the rightness (or fairness) of any conceivable normative agreement that is reached under these conditions."[33]

This definition of practical discourse again raises the question of the generality of communication. Of course, the communicative coordination of human interaction can only become a genuine possibility for societies if, in principle, the formal logic of language use allows this type of action coordination. And I think that Habermas has shown that it does.[34] In this sense, then, his approach is sound. Yet, we also have to acknowledge the fact that the analytic distinction between, on the one hand, formal aspects of communicative action and, on the other hand, substantive convictions and factual states of affairs is ultimately inspired by a substantive conviction. When it comes to the use of practical reason in situations that call for problem assessment, the normative force of rational deliberation should be considered more valuable than prevailing substantive convictions and states of affairs. This conviction, it seems to me, cannot be justified by the factual circumstance that both formal validity claims and substantive convictions play a role in social reality. Rather, it presupposes a nonneutral judgment as to the interest people have in being genuinely critical of received opinion and established social relations. This cannot be made intelligible by means of a formal analysis of the procedural logic of rational language use alone. Rather, it can only be adequately understood if we ask why we think it is necessary to undertake such a formal analysis in the first place.

It enables us to understand what it means to be willing to learn from experience and to take our social fate in our own hands. It is only because we have an interest in understanding ourselves as free and equal persons that it makes sense to defend the idea that the use of practical reason should be guided by fair conditions of rational deliberation. In this sense, then, it seems hard to maintain that these conditions have universal validity. For they appear as conditions that will primarily be valued by individuals and groups who feel that they have an interest in rational deliberation. Therefore, it seems wise to understand the notion of practical reason Habermas defends as one that has instrumental value for certain social groups. These are groups that have an interest in living under conditions of freedom and equality. Their idea is that if we want to live together under such conditions (understood in a liberal-democratic sense), then we have to let our practices of settling the pragmatic, ethical, and moral issues that divide us be guided by this or by a similar notion of practical reason.

Of course, this reading of Habermas's idea of rational deliberation makes its defense more complicated. For it implies that, in practice, the ideal notion of rational deliberation makes sense only if it is sustained by social forms that express an interest in rational deliberation. Habermas is aware of this problem. He now holds that "any universalistic morality is dependent upon a form of life that *meets it halfway*. There has to be a modicum of congruence between morality and the practices of socialization and education."[35]

So is Habermas's theory primarily an articulation of the deep structures of the substantive egalitarian and democratic morality of particular emancipatory movements, or do these movements rather adequately live up to the procedural notion of morality that is always already given with the socio-ontological constitution of humans in sociolinguistically structured forms? There are good reasons to maintain that his theory draws on both sources. However, Habermas prefers to remain silent on the historically contingent cornerstone of his theory that is founded on the substantive convictions and ideals of emancipatory democratic movements.[36] The main reason for this, I think, is that—at least as seen from his theoretical perspective—a full acknowledgment of this normative source of his theory would force him to give up the universalistic foundational strategy of his theory. For it would force him to admit that his formalistic and procedural notions of morality and of justice are contingent on assumptions as to the moral truth of substantive worldviews which—through their allegiance to egalitarian ideas of justice and democracy, nondogmatic notions of toleration, pluralism, the value of personal autonomy, and so forth—have been among the primary forces in the process of Enlightenment that he so deeply cherishes. His theory would then appear to be biased against certain worldviews. Paradoxically, the cognitivist claim to the truth—not just the acceptability—of the communicative notion of practical reason does not allow Habermas to seek an additional foundation of his practical-political thought in the truth or correctness of egalitarian worldviews that respond to this notion.

Discourse ethics, moral character, and pluralism

I want to take a closer look at the substantive assumptions of discourse ethics in terms of its expectations of the moral character of participants in rational deliberations. To begin with, there are deliberative democrats who readily admit that the procedural principle for moral deliberation does presuppose some substantive values and convictions. Seyla Benhabib, for example, makes it quite clear that the purpose of discourse theory is to "develop a model of public dialogue such as to demystify existing power relations and the current public dialogue which sanctifies them."[37] This cannot be made intelligible without recourse to some substantive assumptions as to the nature of moral character and moral argumentation.[38] Although the principle of discourse and the principle of universalizability are defined in procedural terms, their exact meaning can only be understood from a substantive moral perspective. I follow Benhabib in claiming that this perspective must entail the following ideas: first, "the moral idea that we ought to respect each other as beings whose viewpoint is worthy of equal consideration" and, second, the idea that "[w]e should treat each other as concrete human beings whose capacity to express this viewpoint we should enhance by creating, whenever possible, social practices embodying the discursive ideal." Benhabib labels this perspective "egalitarian reciprocity."[39]

Surely, this perspective does not depict practices in which egalitarian reciprocity is always realized. Rather, the perspective is an ideal: the discursive ideal. Deliberative democracy stands for an ideal that is meant to guide the actions of those who engage in public deliberation. And it understands public deliberation as a social and political practice in which pragmatic, ethical (-political), and moral questions are addressed in such a manner that proposals for their solution are evaluated in light of the aim to let the interest of all citizens in leading a good life matter equally. This, again, is a substantive aim, which embraces postmetaphysical or posttraditional worldviews that affirm the value of individual choice, the ability to take one's social fate in one's own hands by questioning the dependencies that contingently determine it. To this extent, the conceptual framework of deliberative democracy is well suited to make sense of the liberal aim understood as a progressive and radical aim.

Although the idea of discursive deliberation is more tolerant than politically liberal and liberal-perfectionist views are with respect to the possibilities to bring controversial claims into public debate, it is in no way undemanding. Amy Gutmann and Dennis Thompson make the illuminating point that while the principles of preclusion of deliberative democratic theories are less exclusionary than those of mainstream liberal theories, their principles of accommodation are very demanding. Principles of preclusion, they say, "serve the . . . purpose of determining which policies deserve a place on the political agenda in the sense of being a legitimate subject for legislation." Principles of accommodation, on the other hand, "govern the conduct of the moral disagreement on issues that should reach the political agenda."[40] If we emphasize the open character of the discourse principle (understood as a principle of preclusion), and realize that deliberative democrats believe that unconstrained deliberations concerning the legitimacy of the most basic organizational structures and substantive assumptions underlying the public order should not be shunned but rather encouraged, then deliberative democracy readily appears as a political theory that bears no dangers of excluding anybody. But as soon as we accept the fact that the procedural principles that govern the idea of rational deliberation are an articulation of the moral and political ideals of specific social and political movements, we can no longer make this idea fruitful for political theory as a tolerant principle of preclusion alone. Rather, we have to ask ourselves under what social and motivational conditions—that is, under what socioculturally embedded principles of accommodation—its tolerant procedural principle of preclusion could begin to fulfill its promise. Here, Gutmann and Thompson point to the importance of the virtue of mutual respect, which presupposes a "reciprocal positive regard of citizens who manifest the excellence of character that permits a democracy to flourish in the face of (at least temporarily) irresolvable moral conflict."[41]

Gutmann and Thompson discern two sides to the virtue of mutual respect as a condition of rational deliberation. As seen from the perspective of the individual, what is at stake here is the recognition and affirmation of the moral status of one's own position and that of others.

1. Principles of mutual respect presuppose a certain "moral or characterological integrity." First, participants in moral and political deliberations should genuinely espouse their moral positions. Second, they should articulate, defend, and act from their position in a consistent and sincere manner. ("Those who oppose abortion out of respect for fetal life should be equally strong advocates of policies to ensure that children are properly fed.")[42]

2. Principles of mutual respect also concern the way in which we confront others in moral and political deliberations. First, it is imperative that one acknowledge that differences of opinion do not necessarily prove that one of the parties to a conflict does not espouse a position that could be of value for attempts to come to a moral agreement (which, in my view, implies that one has to acknowledge the value, not just the fact of pluralism). Second, discussants should be open to the possibility that debate will prompt them to accept (aspects of) the reasons that others give, and in consequence the possibility that they transform their beliefs and act on these new, rather than on their old beliefs. "We should be seeking a balance between holding firm convictions and being prepared to change them if we encounter objections that on reflection we cannot answer."[43] Third, citizens should be willing to look for consensus or compromise in a way that minimizes rejection of the position they oppose. That is, they should not bend the limits of a moral agreement beyond what is necessary: although in democratic debate it is a virtue of all parties to be open to a change of opinion, the refutation of comprehensive worldviews one cannot accept should not be seen as a goal in its own right. Here, showing respect consists in finding the delicate balance between changes of belief (moral transformations) that are really necessary in a liberal-democratic order, and those that go further; the latter could easily result in intolerance— which can never be the aim of discussants who try to cooperate on terms of mutual respect.

In articulating these characterological requirements of moral deliberation, Gutmann and Thompson show that the principles of accommodation of discourse ethics and deliberative democracy are rather demanding. Indeed, it is clear that they presuppose an affirmation of the value (not just the fact) of pluralism and of the value of personal autonomy. For without such an affirmation, it becomes impossible to live up to the demands of the virtue of mutual respect. Although Habermas would agree with the sketched notion of mutual respect, he would certainly ascribe a different status to it in his theory than Gutmann and Thompson. As we have seen, Habermas introduced the idea of a substantive life form that meets a universalistic morality halfway. This undoubtedly consists of forms of mutual respect. But the very expression that it will meet morality "halfway" suggests that he considers such rationalized life forms to be independent of the more fundamental concept of communicative action that is always implicit in everyday linguistic practices.

By solely focusing on the formal and procedural aspects of rational deliberation, Habermas is able to suggest that his theory is free from the exclusionary effects that mainstream liberal theories are confronted with. But we should not forget that this theory could not have been formulated from any other than liberal-democratic ideals; in fact, it is a radicalized interpretation of such ideals. Therefore, the notion of mutual respect should not just be understood as favorable to, but rather as constitutive of deliberative modes of social interaction. Practically speaking, this means that the deliberatively democratic promise of a society in which there is more room for critical voices in public debate than politically liberal and liberal-perfectionist societies would allow, is dependent on egalitarian social conditions under which the virtue of mutual respect will flourish. The criterion of moral acceptability spelled out by the principle of universalizability will most easily be accepted by individuals who aim to live up to the substantive postmetaphysical or posttraditional virtues of moral character that this principle silently presupposes.

The virtue of mutual respect demands that people be willing to judge their personal beliefs, the beliefs of others, and states of affairs in society from a perspective that at least aims for some sort of impartiality. Habermas's understanding of moral deliberation adequately lives up to this demand. Second, however, it demands that people respect the individuality and personal conceptions of the good life of all participants in moral deliberations. We saw that this second demand presupposes an understanding of pluralism that stresses its value, not just its factual givenness. Although Habermas's work exhibits a thorough respect for individuality, it does not and cannot embrace pluralism as a substantive value on which it rests. For the celebration of pluralism rests on assumptions concerning the truth or correctness of particular worldviews that necessarily contest other worldviews that are opposed to moral pluralism.

Yet, paradoxically, Habermas's silent celebration of a pluralist postmetaphysical worldview must be understood as one of the main factors that inspire his rigid distinction between the moral use of practical reason and its ethical use. For if he did not make this distinction, either there would be no limits to the postmetaphysical moral scrutiny of personal convictions, or morality would be totally usurped by widespread ethical convictions. If Habermas were more logical in his reasoning, he would admit that, at the level of establishment of communicative forms of social interaction at least, the ethical and moral use of practical reason presuppose each other in a nonhierarchical sense. Yet, for him, at this level, the moral use of practical reason trumps its ethical use, which necessarily remains tied to subjective and often comprehensive perspectives. Indeed, as we have seen, Habermas holds that the rationalization of life forms should first and foremost be equated with the capacity of their members to address questions of morality and justice from an impartial perspective that abstracts from given patterns of evaluation of an established ethical life. However, this is a one-dimensional view, because it does not sufficiently account for the necessary dynamics between, on the one hand, competing ethical and, on the other, ethical and moral perspectives that make it necessary to look for universalizable moral norms in the first place. The motivational force of these dynamics can only be situated on the subjective side. For the rationality of moral norms and principles of justice can only be assessed from subjective ethical perspectives which, on principle, acknowledge the validity of such norms and principles in terms of their contribution to the sustainment of a pluralist social world. In this sense then, a firm affirmation of the validity of worldviews that embrace the value of pluralism is a necessary condition for Habermas's moral theory. Christoph Menke even goes so far as to maintain that a responsive and tolerant shaping of morally valid (just) norms toward ethical convictions cannot be explained in terms of the universalizability of these norms, because universalizable norms always already presuppose such a responsive and tolerant attitude. In other words: it is not because valid notions of justice are universalizable that they give room to ethical pluralism. Rather, they should be universalizable because according to ethical pluralism principles of justice treat each individual as worthy of equal concern and respect.[44]

So it seems that discourse ethics should be understood and defended as a moderately perfectionist moral theory that defines the conditions and requirements of moral argumentation for a postmetaphysical or posttraditional world characterized by a widespread acceptance of the value of pluralism. In such a world, individuals would recognize the outcomes of public deliberation for the sake of the contribution these outcomes make to the sustainment of a pluralist world. And the members of such a pluralist world would recognize that individuals and groups whose ideas concerning valuable forms of personal freedom differ from their own have similar needs for justice as they themselves have. For they would understand that these needs should ultimately be understood as needs that spring from their interest in leading a good life within a pluralist world. We may conclude that Habermas's moral theory rests on (a) a rather substantive notion of the purposes of moral argumentation under postmetaphysical or posttraditional conditions; (b) an affirmation of personal autonomy and the value of pluralism, and (c) demanding expectations of moral character. In the next chapter, we will discuss what this means for Habermas's theory of law and democracy and for the possibility that this theory overcomes liberalism's tragic predicament.

6

~

Law, Democracy, and Deliberation

Until now, I have not said much about the political theory of deliberative democracy. The reason for this is that, basically, this theory is an application of discourse ethics to questions of justice and democracy.[1] Jürgen Habermas's theory of law and democracy starts, again, from a certain characteristic of rational language use. He concentrates on the tension between facticity and validity always inherent in it. We have seen in chapter 5 that validity claims are necessary idealizations in communicative interaction. But the limits of what can be reached in social interaction are defined by other factors as well. Validity claims are always confronted with the "facticity" of convictions, states of affairs, and reigning norms and principles they call into question. According to Habermas law should be understood as both an effective factual force in social coordination and as a normatively rich medium. This explains why it is possible to take on both an objectifying and a performative attitude toward law: "Depending on the chosen perspective, the legal norm presents a different kind of situational element: for the person acting strategically, it lies at the level of social facts that externally restrict her range of options; for the person acting communicatively, it lies at the level of obligatory expectations that, she assumes, the legal community has rationally agreed on" (31). Of course, this does not mean that communicative actors should always view positive law as a medium that effectively guarantees their well-being. After all, positive law can be unjust. It rather means that, in principle, law should be legitimized by rational procedures of democratic lawmaking. Insofar as it is, it generally enables citizens to respect the law.

107

And to the extent that it is not, its legitimacy may be called into question.

Law and deliberative democracy

Habermas fuses two traditional starting points for reconstructing the idea of law. The first concentrates on the liberal idea of "natural" subjective rights and liberties. The second concentrates on the republican ideal of popular democratic sovereignty. According to Habermas, it is wrong to choose only one of these ideas as the starting point for a normatively rich theory of law and democracy, as he—in a somewhat simplifying spirit—claims liberals and republicans have done until the present day. His claim is that, in modern law, private autonomy—the negative liberty warranted by subjective rights—and public autonomy—the political freedom warranted by forms of popular democratic sovereignty—are conceptually co-original (*gleichursprünglich*). The normative core of modern law can be adequately understood only if one accepts the fact that it is the chief placeholder of public order in society and that it enables citizens to claim both subjective liberties and the right to engage in public practices of democratic lawmaking through which the critical interpretation and evaluation of the distribution and effects of subjective liberties becomes possible (122–23).

From this general account of the normative structure that constitutes what he calls the system of rights, Habermas derives several categories of basic rights that roughly follow the famous triad of civil, political, and social rights (122f.). Indeed, this understanding of basic rights is not as original as Habermas's general account. This should not surprise us. The aim of his theory is not so much to formulate an alternative canon of basic rights, but rather to present a more complete conceptualization of the functional necessity of these rights in discourse-theoretical terms. The main difference with more conventional liberal theories is that he stresses the essentially democratic or deliberative nature of the system of rights. A considered account of the role of democracy in the liberal constitutional state makes it possible to understand that, and why, the liberal system of rights should not be seen as an ahistoric and rigid set of dogmas derived from either a subjective-rights doctrine or from an account of the central values of "our culture," but rather as a set of always fallible intersubjectively legitimized rules for social coordination that citizens of a particular community define through the public use of reason.

In order to discuss how his discursive approach might be translated into a convincing account of a democratic practice he first introduces an account of the constitutional state that defines how legitimate forms of political and juridical power should be generated and exercised. Second, he presents a notion of "procedural democracy," which defines the rules that should govern the democratic process of opinion formation and lawmaking. Third, Habermas introduces a complex account of how relatively unorganized public debates in civil society should be linked to "official," institutionalized political procedures.

As to the first step—which concerns the generation of law—Habermas stresses the fact that different forms of argumentation play a role in institutionalized processes of lawmaking. First, and as a general rule, participants in democratic discourses should always try to reach an understanding as to the options for action available in different situations. Furthermore, not all politically relevant questions require the same mode of consensus-seeking or acceptance. This is where Habermas distinguishes between questions that ask for pragmatic compromises concerning the self-understanding or identity of the citizenry and moral-practical questions concerning universally binding guidelines for action.

It is important to stress Habermas's sensitivity to different types of political argumentation because he is often presented as treating all political and legal questions as moral issues to which universally acceptable, strictly consensus-based answers should be sought.[2] In his theory of law and democracy, however, he explicitly emphasizes that the legitimacy of law should neither be wholly subordinated to the moral use of practical reason, nor be understood in one-dimensional instrumentalist (pragmatic) or ethical-political terms. The idea is that the legitimacy of law should be understood in terms of its ability to combine these various uses of practical reason in legal and democratic practices that can meet with the assent of all citizens. Furthermore, it is remarkable that Habermas breaks with a strictly representative view of democracy. This is, of course, consistent with his aim to develop a decentered understanding of democracy. The very nature of discourse, he claims, makes it clear that the principles of the constitutional state should be complemented with a normative notion of the public sphere: "The political will-formation organized as a legislative branch of government would destroy the basis of its own rational functioning if it were to block up the spontaneous sources of autonomous public spheres or shut itself off from the input of free-floating issues, contributions, information, and arguments circulating in a civil society set apart from the state" (183–84).

As to the second step, a proceduralization of the democratic process means that democratic societies should give shape to the rights of public and private autonomy by making possible the various types of practical discourse through careful institutional design.[3] The idea is that such discourses should be structured in such a way that their outcomes can be expected to be rational. For that purpose, institutionalized discourses that affect the democratic process of opinion formation and decision-making have to answer to certain procedural criteria, the most important of which is the principle of democracy we encountered earlier: "Only those statutes may claim legitimacy that can meet with the assent (*Zustimmung*) of all citizens in a discursive process of legislation that in turn has been legally constituted" (110).

Three characteristics of Habermas's notion of procedural democracy stand out. First, it stresses the fact that the three modes of political argumentation (reaching compromise, and ethical-political and moral-practical argumentation) have a logic of their own and that their conduct can be guided by carefully designed procedures of opinion formation and decision-making. Second, it stresses the fact that voting on the basis of given convictions alone is hardly ever the correct way to settle political issues. For this way of looking at democracy misunderstands the role that subjective convictions play in social interaction. Subjective convictions (preferences), Habermas maintains, should not be thought of as isolated and unalterable building blocks of an aggregated will; rather, they should be thought of as fallible starting points for processes of opinion formation and decision-making in which they may be altered in the light of new perspectives. For convictions can be incorrect, incomplete, forced upon individuals by powers that they cannot rationally recognize, and so on. Through democratic discourse, such investigations into the reasonableness of given convictions can take place. Third, it is a necessary condition for legitimate democratic institutions that these discourses be guided in a rational—genuinely communicative—manner. For only then will it be reasonable to assume that their outcomes can count as rational—even if, as will usually be the case, not all people concerned with the issue at hand will have participated in their definition. In deliberative politics, according to Habermas, "the *discursive level* of public debates constitutes the most important variable" (304).[4]

As to the third step, Habermas is well aware of the very demanding character of his notion of procedural democracy. On the one hand, he acknowledges the difficulties facing the democratic process that spring from the functional differentiation of modern societies into semiautonomous systems such as the economy and, despite its essentially democratic constitution, administration. Empirically speaking, these systems have a strategic logic of their own—directed at economic gains and at the stabilization and legitimation of power, respectively—which do not combine easily with the task of deliberative politics to identify, articulate, and settle issues of public concern that cannot be settled in informal communicative interaction (352).[5] On the other hand, he acknowledges that a deliberative politics also suffers from a great many internal problems, such as a lack of time and information when political decisions are needed, the inertia of bureaucratic institutions associated with parliamentary democracy and law, hidden agendas of participants in political debate, and the willingness and ability of the citizenry to engage in democratic discourses (326). A theory of deliberative democracy that does not just aim to be an ideal model, but that claims to conceptualize the normative presuppositions of a political practice implicit in the institutions of liberal-democratic societies, will have to find an answer to the question as to how, despite these factual forces, communicatively generated forms of political power can successfully be implemented (354).

In order to address these issues, Habermas again concentrates on strong institutionalized procedures. He introduces a model of the political process originally developed by Bernhard Peters.[6] This model separates the "center" of the political process from its "periphery," conceptualizes the relation between them in terms of "sluices," and distinguishes between two modes of political problem-solving (354). In the center of the political process, the legislature, judiciary, and administration are found. They each have their own function and control each other. But they should not be seen as wholly autonomous. Rather, through such institutions as local administration, interest groups, political and other associations, and religious institutions, they should be tied to the infrastructure of civil society, which Habermas describes as the periphery of the political process. The idea is that processes of decision-making in the center can only count as legitimate if they are guided by "communication flows that start at the periphery and pass through the sluices of democratic and constitutional procedures situated at the entrance to the parliamentary complex or the courts" (356). The "sluices" should be understood as discourses that filter merely power- or money-based reasons out of the democratic process, thus ensuring the quality of its outcomes.

They should provide an institutional stronghold against the occupation of the democratic process by merely strategic forces.

Here, Habermas distinguishes between two modes of political and juridical problem-solving. First, routine plays an important role in the adequate treatment of points on the agenda. Noncontroversial issues can and should be handled in this (pragmatic) way in the center, because this is an effective and efficacious way to handle them. But second, in cases of new themes on the agenda—themes that might spark conflicts of interpretation both in the center and on the periphery of the political process—the political responsibility of parliament and of the courts to treat issues in a normative mode is thematized. Here, the relationship between center and periphery is of the utmost importance. The latter should be able to bring problems that call for political treatment to the center in such a way that they call for treatment in a normative mode, which may result in restoration of sound social relationships. Therefore, the members of civil society should be able to identify and thematize issues that ask for political problem-solving, and to control effectively the way in which these issues are treated in the political center (359). In fact, this is the main idea of the practice of deliberative democracy.

It may be clear that the model relies heavily on decentered public spheres in which public opinion is generated through communicative practices. These public spheres consist of a diffuse public of authors and readers, spokespersons, and the groups for whom they speak, who are affected by problems that call for normatively legitimated treatment. Public spheres are not given identifiable arenas. Rather, they are created in response to a felt need for identification, thematization, and solution of concrete problems. But public spheres are not only occupied by citizens who aim at the articulation of such problems in a communicative mode. Interest groups, party-political, and economic organizations often use public arenas to lend power to their own strategic aims. But from a normative point of view, Habermas maintains, they are able to do so only because modern societies comprise communicatively structured public spheres whose primary aim is to articulate problems that affect the integration of society as a whole (364). Seen from this perspective, public spheres are understood as a communication community of private persons with unique life histories who are, as members of society, always potentially concerned with such problems because they can and often will affect their lives (365). Public spheres play an essential role in the identification and thematization of individual experiences that point to problems relevant to the legitimate integration of society as a whole.

At the same time, they control the effects of the collective decisions made in the center of the political process by, again, identifying and thematizing their consequences for the lives of individual citizens. In a functioning liberal democracy, the public sphere can adequately defend itself against its occupation by merely interest-based contributions to public debate by this same modus operandi (372–79).

The limits of deliberative democracy

Much more than the liberal theorists we studied in part 2, Habermas has an open eye for the importance of procedures that anchor the normative potential of the idea of public deliberation in the institutional heart of society: law and democracy. I think that he is correct in his assumption that these institutions should protect the discursive level of the use of practical reason in democratic politics. He also proposes a valid theory, that is, that democratic lawmaking is not primarily a matter of gathering individual votes based on subjective preferences, but rather a matter of well-informed opinion formation in what he calls the center and periphery of the political system. His emphasis on the importance of civil society is realistic and consistent with his aim to decentralize democracy. It explains how pragmatic, ethical, and moral questions that are posed in everyday life may be brought into the political process. And it gives us strong reason to believe that the possibility of "moral transformations" of given conceptions of the good life for individuals and collectives should not by definition be kept off the agenda of liberal politics. Still, some of the conceptual and practical problems that confront discourse ethics are problems for the discourse theory of law and democracy as well. Most importantly, the account of the relation between public and private autonomy is wanting, and the focus on the proceduralization of communicative action generates problems that Habermas tends to overlook.

Habermas's stress on the internal relation between private and public autonomy serves the purpose of explaining the legitimacy of law neither exclusively in terms of negative liberties, nor exclusively in terms of popular democratic sovereignty. It is important to understand that private autonomy is not personal autonomy. As we saw earlier, personal autonomy designates an idea of positive freedom by which the individual is seen as the ultimate authority in questions concerning her conception of the good life in a pluralist world that fosters this idea of freedom. It is interesting to look at Habermas's rather unusual definition of private autonomy as a "liberation from the obligations of . . . 'communicative freedom'" (119). It "extends as far as the legal subject does not have to give others . . . publicly acceptable reasons for her action plans" (120). Private autonomy, as it is defined in terms of subjective rights, gives individuals the opportunity to shape their personal freedom in terms that do not have to be assessed from the moral perspective of their universal acceptability. Private autonomy enables individuals to drop out of the practice of rational reasoning that is given with their socio-ontological constitution as communicative actors.

The idea of private autonomy can easily be expressed in terms that are more current in liberal thought. Habermas clearly follows neutralist liberal intuitions which, as I said before, are in no way external to his perspective. In fact, his theory begins by accepting the fact that the right to subjective liberties is constitutive of the very idea of law (121). But Habermas maintains—correctly, I think— that only the principle of democracy enables citizens to shape and to evaluate the legitimacy of the legal forms that protect private autonomy. This explains his emphasis on the importance of political rights that enable citizens to participate in rational and discursive procedures of opinion formation and lawmaking. In a legitimate liberal-democratic order, the "liberation from the obligations of communicative freedom"—that is, private autonomy warranted by subjective rights to negative liberty—will, paradoxically, solely be justified from the public perspective of communicative rationality.

Again we find that, according to this theory, the legitimacy of intersubjective norms (in this case legal norms) should ultimately be judged from the allegedly ethically neutral perspective of communicative rationality. Both private and public autonomy are ultimately explained and evaluated in terms that are derived from the idea of communicative rationality. It is true that, at first sight, the silent celebration of pluralism implicit in Habermas's discourse ethics is no longer a silent one in his theory of law and democracy. After all, this theory exhibits a thorough awareness of the fact that the evaluation of the legitimacy of the system of rights by means of the exercise of the political and moral autonomy of participants to "communicative freedom" is contingent on the concrete experiences of private citizens. Yet, it would be false to conclude that the problems that I think confront discourse ethics have been overcome in the discourse theory of law and democracy.

According to Habermas, the tensions between, on the one hand, ethical well-being and self-realization and, on the other hand, political self-determination call for an understanding of law that could control and possibly even overcome them. But the legitimacy of law is not explained in terms of its contribution to a pluralist social world in which ethical pluralism is regarded as a value in its own right. Again, only the fact of pluralism is recognized. It is explained in terms of a process of rationalization by which "received practices and interpretations of ethical life were reduced to mere conventions and differentiated from conscientious decisions that passed through the filter of reflection and independent judgment" (95). In other words: pluralism is a contingent consequence of a noncontingent communicative rationalization of individuals. Although pluralism makes it necessary for individuals to take responsibility for their contingent ideas as to ethical self-realization in light of their conceptions of the good, this is understood as a consequence of, not a fundamental force in, the historical emergence of communicative reason and of the procedural criteria for legitimate norms inherent in it.

In chapter 5 I have argued that we should revise the discourse-theoretical understanding of the legitimacy of moral norms and conceptions of justice. Because the idea of communicative rationality is, among other things, an interest-based notion of practical reason, Habermas's understanding of the legitimacy of norms is not ethically neutral. This revision of the understanding of the legitimacy of legal and moral norms grounds the discourse-theoretical approach not in an abstract understanding of the logic of rational language use, but rather in the substantive purposes and ideas of the good of (large) social groups who have an interest in living under fair conditions of freedom and equality in a pluralist liberal-democratic world. What we need is not an independent notion of practical reason that meets these social groups "halfway" but a conception of well-being or the good life that helps explain why the moral and political vision of these groups can be said to be more reasonable, or even more true, than the vision of others.

Of course, a revised account of the moral foundations of deliberative democracy along these lines has important consequences for the focus on rational procedures of law and democracy. Citizens who adhere to worldviews that do not allow the unconstrained questioning of, on principle, all normative-practical imperatives may be expected to have a hard time looking for the moral point of these procedures. These procedures claim to be both rational and free of substantive assumptions. At the same time, they provide citizens with a point of view that obliges them to, in principle, be ready to question all their substantive conceptions of morality and justice. If some citizens reply that they cannot do this because it would be immoral, then the purely procedural answer has to be that such an attitude is irrational. Indeed, the answer is that rational action coordination is action coordination according to rational procedures. What my revision of the moral foundations of deliberative democracy calls for is that this tautology be sidestepped by means of an articulation of the substantive values on which the procedural understanding of rational deliberation rests.[7]

If the theory of deliberative democracy were to choose this strategy, it would still stand a much better chance of developing an adequate understanding of the important aim of neutrality it so dearly cherishes than the liberal doctrines we studied in the previous chapters. The strength of the notion of public deliberation for which deliberative democracy stands is that it at least enables all citizens to bring their controversial comprehensive ideas of the good into political debate. As we saw in our discussion of the virtue of mutual respect, rational discourses demand of their participants that they acknowledge the value of individual perspectives, that they be open to the possibility that the convictions of others may motivate them to revise their own beliefs, and that they do not understand the refutation of controversial comprehensive views as a goal in its own right. These imperatives of moral character oblige individuals and groups that adhere to liberal-democratic ideals to respect and to be open to the convictions of individuals and groups who do not wholeheartedly embrace these ideals. The main reason for this is that if we value rational deliberation because of its contribution to the sustainment of a pluralist and autonomy-embracing world, we must respect individuality, understood as a necessary condition of the capacity to act autonomously, unconditionally.

Indeed, it is perhaps wise to stress that my claim that—at the level of justification—deliberative democracy presupposes an affirmation of pluralism and personal autonomy should not be understood as a plea for a liberal society in which subjective rights are straightforwardly being used as tools to coerce citizens into accepting liberal values and virtues. If my account is correct, then for deliberative democrats private autonomy—understood in terms of negative liberty—is valuable because it creates conditions for leading a personally autonomous life within a pluralist social environment. It enables citizens to decide for themselves how to shape their lives within a legal framework that grants them freedom of thought, religion, speech, association, and so forth. And it is precisely because of its adherence to the values of personal autonomy and pluralism that deliberative democracy will, despite its substantive assumptions, not coerce citizens into accepting it. Rather, it will advocate its own views by trying to gain legitimate political power that will be used to shape cultural conditions under which egalitarian, communicatively integrated life worlds will flourish.[8]

When it comes to the further question as to how the substantive assumptions of deliberative democracy could—in practice—be recognized as valid assumptions, deliberative democracy will—just like political liberalism—have to look for ways in which it could go back and forth between, on the one hand, its more or less comprehensive ideal notion of consensus-seeking and its demands on moral character and, on the other, the conceptions of the good life and of justice of individuals and groups that adhere to worldviews that contest the acceptability of the deliberatively democratic outlook. Here, a brief reflection on Rawls's "two-stage path" to an overlapping consensus is in order.

Remember that our discussion of the path from Rawls's "constitutional (modus vivendi) consensus" to an "overlapping consensus" led to the following conclusion: what has to be changed in political liberalism's understanding of the "political" is its understanding of the reasons that should matter in public debate. Political liberalism will have to acknowledge that comprehensive and partly comprehensive notions of the good life do in fact play an important role in public discourses. As long as its own political doctrine is no more than a picture of an ideal end state of public deliberation, it should not make the mistake of understanding public deliberation in terms that fit this end state rather than the realities of societies in which this end state has not been reached. The substantive content of political liberalism as it is fully articulated at the second stage (that of the overlapping consensus) is too controversial and at the same time too rigid to dictate public deliberation in the pluralist world we inhabit.

Although it cannot claim to be a neutral doctrine, the deliberatively democratic perspective offers all participants in public deliberations an understanding of the use of public reason which, in principle, gives them equal chances at introducing controversial perspectives into debates concerning the legitimacy of the basic structure of society. In this respect, deliberative democracy should be welcomed to liberal thought. Yet, we have also seen that the formalist and proceduralist foundations of Habermas's work make it impossible to explain the value—and therefore the point of the principles of accommodation—of the public deliberation in substantive terms. And this may be expected to generate serious problems for those who cannot agree to its substantive assumptions. In my interpretation of deliberative democracy, however, deliberative democrats will readily admit that their understanding of fair deliberation is inspired by substantive assumptions that some individuals may not accept; it is also characterized by rather demanding expectations as to moral character. This acknowledgment of the nonneutrality of their strategy is exactly the starting point that we are looking for. Despite the nonneutrality of the deliberatively democratic expectations as to the proper use of practical reason, a modus vivendi between the parties to a "constitutional consensus" will readily be reached in pragmatic terms that look for compromises. From such compromises, which will result in granting rights to subjective liberties, further debates on the meaning and value of ethical pluralism, moral consensus, and the idea of public deliberation can then be initiated.

Again, out of respect for the individuality of all participants, deliberative democrats cannot coerce individuals into accepting their basic assumptions. Interestingly enough, this may prove to be a strong argument. For it makes it clear that worldviews that are conducive to liberal-democratic ideals will, in an actively tolerant mode, respect and take seriously the beliefs of others, and that deliberative democrats are open to the possibility that these beliefs may be valid, and ask for a revision of the understanding of rational deliberation and for the substantive values it presupposes. In other words, although the deliberatively democratic notion of public deliberation should not from the outset be understood as a framework that all individuals and groups in society accept, it can (if it changes its theoretical self-understanding) in principle be open to the value of the views of those who cannot or do not wish to live up to the requirements of posttraditional reason.

I hope that I have made it clear that the deliberatively democratic understanding of public deliberation should be considered a more promising substantive proposal than the political-liberal one. Contrary to what Habermas claims, I do not believe that the strength of any notion of public deliberation should be explained in terms of its lack of substantive assumptions. On the contrary, it should be explained in terms of the value of these assumptions, which we can only hope will gain popular acceptance. I have tried to indicate how Habermas's account could be revised in light of my findings. I will not pursue this line any further, because it is not my aim to solve the problems that deliberative democracy is confronted with. It has only been my aim to show that while deliberative democracy presents us with a notion of public deliberation which, in terms of access to the public domain, is more tolerant than that of political liberalism, this notion cannot avoid some substantive and indeed perfectionist assumptions as to the correctness of worldviews that embrace the values of pluralism and personal autonomy.

Another revision of key concepts of liberal thought

Before I return to the thesis of the tragedy of liberalism in the next section, I want to return to the basic concepts of liberal thought that were discussed in part 2. To what extent does the theory of deliberative democracy motivate us to revise our understanding of this concept?

Autonomy—We can still maintain that autonomy is both a capacity of liberal citizens understood as persons who engage in public deliberations concerning the validity of the general rules that govern social cooperation and an ideal central to more personal social practices and life-styles. However, more than liberal theories, theories of deliberative democracy make it clear how both capacities are related. Public and private autonomy are capacities that presuppose each other. Both notions are necessary conditions for a communicative reproduction of shared life worlds. And at the level of "second-stage" (substantive) liberal-democratic ideals of the reproduction of shared life worlds, the same goes for public and personal autonomy. According to this ideal notion, public and personal autonomy enable individuals to lead their personal and political lives in a controlled mode that is critical of autonomy-frustrating power constellations, that is, in ways that enable them to reassess given patterns of expectation in the light of new experiences. In this sense, deliberative democracy is a truly emancipatory theory, which focuses on the rationality of the social forms that constitute the conditions of people's lives. Although rational deliberation can only take place within social forms that are conducive to it, the theory of deliberative democracy stresses the fact that the understanding of autonomy-enhancing capacities that these social forms foster should remain open to better, more acceptable interpretations. It is this characteristic of the deliberatively democratic perspective that distinguishes it most from the liberal accounts of autonomy we studied earlier. The theory of deliberative democracy succeeds in showing that substantive expectations and interpretations of the autonomy of persons need not be presented as uncriticizable starting points for a normative political theory. Its value is presupposed, but its interpretation remains open to better views.

Reasonableness—Reasonableness is a virtue of liberal citizens and liberal institutions. Deliberative democracy presupposes, just like the liberal theories we discussed earlier, a reasonable pluralism. But unlike liberal theories, deliberative democracy explains how such a reasonable pluralism could be sustained and that respect for the beliefs of others should not be equated with silence on controversial issues. The communicative notion of practical reason gives us strong reason to believe that, by definition, controversial issues— issues that confront us with the shortcomings of prevalent expectations—are those issues which have to be at the center of public debates. Only if issues are controversial, are there genuine reasons to engage in discursive attempts to settle them—either by solving the problems at issue or by reaching an agreement to disagree.

Is Habermas right in claiming (disagreeing with Rawls) that reasonableness is a predicate for the validity of moral judgments rather than a predicate for a reflective attitude of enlightened tolerance? I think it is both; however, I do not believe that the deliberatively democratic understanding of the validity of moral judgments can be understood in a rigid truth-analogous way. I would prefer to reach an understanding of minimum requirements for leading a good life. For questions concerning the validity of moral judgments can only be assessed in terms of the substantive purposes and goods that the normative framework within which these judgments are made serves.

Pluralism—Communicative practical reason presupposes pluralism understood as a value, not only as a fact. Pluralism is a characteristic of societies in which overarching comprehensive notions of what is good and what is right are not assumed. Communicative practical reason aims to settle the dilemma—how can such societies be integrated in ways that are both morally binding (guaranteeing a minimum form of social unity) and that foster the pluralism on which communicative practical reason thrives? However, I have argued throughout that deliberative democracy is not neutral toward pluralism. To this extent, deliberative democracy is a moderately perfectionist doctrine that stands for a pluralist social world that is conducive to both personal and public autonomy.

Toleration—In the previous chapter, following Joseph Raz, we found that toleration is in fact controlled intolerance. Further research is necessary in order to find out how toleration, thus understood, could benefit liberal societies. Deliberative democracy stands for "militant" or "active" toleration, "in which difference is not only tolerated, but in which individuals seek to understand one another in their differences and arrive at a morally-reasoned solution to the controversy in question."[9] This idea is also expressed in the "other-regarding" demands of mutual respect as defined by Amy Gutmann and Dennis Thompson. Deliberative democracy does not understand differences of opinion as fixed states. Rather, it holds that convictions as to what is right and good can be mistaken, and that the virtuous citizen understands this and is willing to reflect on the adequacy and validity of her own convictions. To some, this may sound slightly utopian and illiberal. They may prefer John Rawls and J. Donald Moon's view that the burdens of judgment for even reasonable people are of such a type that it is in fact unreasonable, even under favorable circumstances, to expect that they will reach a firm public consensus. Here, from a deliberatively democratic standpoint, while this may often be true, there is no reason to assume that this skeptical view is always the right one.[10]

Militant toleration is closely related to the discursive ideal. And although the application of this ideal to concrete questions will always have to be guided by a commonsense understanding of what can be realistically aimed for in the situation at hand, militant toleration does have advantages over more modest liberal ideas of toleration. It motivates parties to deliberation to take the assertions, recommendations, and needs of all parties seriously. It does not a prioristically ban controversial private beliefs from deliberation. And this does seem to be a step in the right direction. Provided that it recognizes the value, not just the fact of pluralism, it motivates parties to conflicts to take seriously those who want to lead a good life.

Conceptions of the good—In the previous chapter we concluded that we have to go beyond objectivism and subjectivism and opt for a more intersubjectivist approach in order to arrive at a convincing understanding of tolerable conceptions of the good life. In studying Habermas's deliberatively democratic approach, we have become familiar with the intuition that this can only be answered in ethical, ethical-political, and moral deliberations in which the defensibility of given beliefs and needs is tested. Here, the understanding of "other-regarding" demands of mutual respect can help us formulate some essential attributes of permissible conceptions of the good life. First, such conceptions should enable those who embrace them to judge their own beliefs, the beliefs of their fellow citizens, and states of affairs in society from a perspective that transcends egoism. In other words: permissible conceptions of the good are able to live up to the moral point of view. But within a liberal-democratic framework, moral impartiality has its limits. It is a form of impartiality that affirms the value of pluralism and that respects in a special way the individuality and the conceptions of the good life of participants in ethical and moral deliberations. First, permissible conceptions of the good life recognize the priority of public reason when questions of justice are at issue. It follows from this that, second, permissible conceptions are those that are willing to "test themselves" in light of the moral and ethical claims of others. In other words, permissible conceptions are not immune to the possibility of the "moral transformation" of given beliefs, according to Seyla Benhabib. Third, permissible conceptions recognize that the value of pluralism that they affirm forbids coerced moral transformations. For such transformations would harm the respect for the capacity of autonomy that is at the basis of every defensible account of liberal-democratic thought. Liberal-democratic citizens and government prefer a society in which some conceptions of the good life survive that do not foster the liberal understanding of autonomy and well-being over a society in which such conceptions are being overruled in the name of liberal ideals. The latter option is not open to liberal-democratic thought because it would make a mockery of the very ideals on which liberal-democratic thought is built.

Neutrality—The theory of deliberative democracy stands for a substantive political outlook that is not independent of implicit assumptions regarding the value and permissibility of comprehensive worldviews. In this respect, it does not differ that much from other liberal theories. Yet, its notion of practical reason is more convincing than politically liberal and liberal-perfectionist ones. For this reason, the theory of deliberative democracy still has a great chance of developing a promising understanding of at least the aim for neutrality. This should be understood in light of our conclusion that pluralism mandates that moral norms and principles of justice treat individuals, not just politically autonomous citizens, as worthy of equal concern and respect. To the extent that they do, we call such principles universalizable. In part 4, we will find that, precisely for this reason, liberal theories—including that of deliberative democracy—should never treat as mere preferences the ideas of authentic individuality of persons who do not fit easily into the liberal framework.

Conclusions to Part 3

To what extent might the theory of deliberative democracy help us deal with liberalism's tragic predicament? In order to answer that question, let me return to my hypothesis.

> 1. Because liberalism has a purposive structure—that is, it's not an ethically neutral doctrine—there are normative conflicts in which its aim to let the interests of *all* citizens in leading a good life matter equally cannot but generate tragic conflicts.
>
> 2. In generating tragic conflicts, liberalism sometimes undermines notions of the good that it aims to tolerate; and (thereby) its own aim to let the interests of all citizens in leading a good life matter equally.

I have argued that the deliberatively democratic interpretation of liberal ideals is purposive because its conceptual framework presupposes the validity of certain ethical and moral purposes. More precisely, deliberative democracy rests on (a) a rather substantive notion of the demands of moral argumentation under postmetaphysical or posttraditional conditions; (b) an affirmation of an autonomy-enhancing understanding of pluralism; and (c) demanding expectations of moral character. A society that lives up to the normative theory of deliberative democracy will be a pluralist, posttraditional society in which the values underlying this theory will be sustained and fostered. Yet, in the real world, no society lives up to the demands of deliberative democracy.

First, not all notions of the good and social practices are autonomy-enhancing. The liberal theories we discussed in part 2 start from rather a prioristic assumptions that seriously undermine their chances of overcoming normative conflicts. Deliberative democracy can mitigate this problem, but not overcome it. In principle, its notion of public deliberation is more open to nonliberal voices. Yet, it is confronted with the problem that as long as it does not admit of its substantive assumptions, it will have to choose the strategy of arguing for the rationality of its procedures without taking recourse to any notions of the good life at all. However, it seems to be far more promising to articulate the notions of the good life that these procedures for conflict resolution presuppose. For only then will it become possible to understand to what extent the "impartial" rationality of moral norms and principles of justice can be accepted from the "sub-jective" rationality of members of pluralist societies. What we find here is a collision of substantive notions of the right and the good that both are necessary aspects—indeed irreducible building blocks—of a pluralist world. My interpretation of the theory of de-liberative democracy calls for a firm acknowledgment of the inter-dependency of these two cornerstones of a pluralist world.

The tragedy of liberalism presents itself as a tension between these two poles of a pluralist world that deliberative democracy tries to, but cannot resolve. As long as we follow Habermas's strategy, the tragedy of liberalism cannot really become intelligible. For his trust in the strong neutrality of his procedural understanding of practical reason ultimately motivates him to characterize conflicts that I would label "tragic" as conflicts between a higher and a lower form of rationality. As seen from this perspective, those who—because of their adherence to ethical values—choose not to live up to the de-mands of communicative action coordination cannot be said to act rationally. However, as soon as we acknowledge that the burden of proof is not only on the subjective side, but also on the side of com-municatively generated norms, the tragic character of some norma-tive conflicts becomes visible. For it then becomes clear that some ethical convictions that liberal-democratic societies admit compel their bearers to be true to values that simply do not fit into the post-traditional expectations of moral character implicit in procedures of rational consensus-seeking. Then, deliberative democracy has to admit that its necessarily nonneutral aim that gurantees equal op-portunities for all members of pluralist societies cannot but generate tragic conflicts.

A second point of importance is that tragic conflicts may also occur among individuals and groups who all affirm the value of plu-ralism and personal autonomy. Earlier, I used the example of reli-gious individuals who recognize these values but who have other obligations that still may collide with the outcomes of public deliber-ations. Here, the deliberatively democratic strategy has great ad-vantages over the politically liberal one. Because it does not ban controversial comprehensive beliefs from public deliberation, it at least allows of a full articulation of the colliding values that consti-tute the tragic conflict. And thereby, it prepares the ground for an in-terchange of perspectives that may (or may not) result in a change of those perspectives. Again, deliberative democrats will have to admit that their convictions (including their ideas as to procedures of deci-sion-making) are not ethically neutral. They will ultimately realize that they are genuine parties to the conflict, not representatives of an independent and uncontroversial idea of rationality that people can only reject at the risk of abandoning the very practice of rational reasoning.

> 3. The tragic predicament of liberalism seems to be related to its explicit aim to promote moral unity when it comes to the use of public reason and public deliberation; and to its implicit aim to promote key components for "private" conceptions of the good life such as the ideal of personal autonomy and the affirmation of ethical pluralism.

After all that has been said, a brief answer to this hypothesis is in order. As long as we ground our understanding of deliberative democracy or, more generally speaking, our understanding of liberalism in an allegedly independent notion of communicative rationality, we generate expectations of the possibility of moral unity that are both unrealistic and—because they are founded on a misunderstanding of the nature of pluralism—blind to the tragedy of liberalism. Here, it is important to remember that although it is highly likely that despite the fact that the logic of rational language use allows communicative action coordination, it is only from a substantive interest-based perspective that we can choose this type of action coordination. This substantive perspective is characteristic of worldviews to which the ideal of personal autonomy and the affirmation of pluralism are crucial. There is nothing wrong with defending such a situated normative perspective. On the contrary: it is only if we do so that we come to understand that the tragedy of liberalism is ultimately a consequence of the tensions that spring from the defense of a situated and controversial normative perspective that ultimately stands for universalistic ideals. In the remainder of this book, I will go into some of the many questions that spring from this idea.

PART IV

~

Liberal Community, Mutual Recognition, and Citizenship Virtue

Introduction

In the preceding chapters, it has been argued that liberal public reason and practices associated with personal and collective conceptions of the good life can and sometimes do conflict. Insofar as such conflicts emanate from what we might call the normative priority of liberal public reason, they are relevant to the thesis that liberalism is confronted with a tragic predicament. My aim will no longer be to work my way through normative theories that I think overlook the tragedy of liberalism. Rather, I will ask what implications follow from a firm acknowledgment of the tragic predicament of liberalism: To what extent might liberal theories (and liberal societies) become more liberal by accepting the fact that the very defense of liberalism cannot avoid generating tragic conflicts?

In chapter 7, I will start by making my understanding of tragic conflicts more specific. I will discuss Christoph Menke's perceptive typology of four instances of tragic conflicts in modern societies between liberal public reason and conceptions of the good life. Tragic experiences must be related adequately to the idea of a liberal community and to its developmental potential, that is, to its potential to respond to, and possibly learn from, the occurrence of such conflicts. Subsequently, the concept of a liberal community will be discussed. We will find that we need a language to account for interpersonal relations that is more substantive—more closely tied to situated human experience—than the notion of liberal public reason can provide us with.

In chapter 8, following Axel Honneth, I will examine the interpersonal relations characteristic of a liberal community in terms of mutual recognition. A theory that understands egalitarian reciprocity and the virtue of mutual respect in terms of mutual recognition is well-suited to articulate the substantive assumptions inherent in social patterns of expectation and evaluation. Moreover, it has the potential to explain how feelings of a lack of well-being may be related to reigning patterns of expectation and evaluation and how such feelings might motivate individuals and groups to change such patterns. Next, I will introduce the notion of the tragic to social theories of recognition. This will enable me to further develop my understanding of the heuristic value of tragic conflicts in order to gain a critical understanding of the limits and scope of liberal ideals.

In chapter 9, I will argue that theories of recognition reveal the meaning of core concepts of liberal thought in a way that is well suited to gain an understanding of the responsibilities of liberal governments and citizenship. This highlights the fact that capacities and values such as personal and public autonomy, reasonableness, moral pluralism, and toleration help governments and members of society cope with the constitutional vulnerability of social cooperation. I will argue that an account of the vulnerability of people should be central to any liberal political ethics.

7

~

Liberal Community and the Normative Potential of Tragic Conflicts

In chapters 7–9, I will examine to what extent my arguments can be translated into a more specific understanding of tragic conflicts. Most importantly, I will develop an account that shows that liberalism can—both in theory and in practice—actually benefit from taking such conflicts seriously. In order to do so, it seems helpful to bracket off the demands of liberal public reason for a while, and understand such conflicts in terms of individual experiences. I will focus my attention on whether conceptions of the good, desires, and obsessions that cannot be reconciled with the perspective of liberal public reason can still be said to have a certain validity that liberalism should take seriously. Later, I will investigate how these relate to the idea of a liberal community.

Christoph Menke's typology of tragic conflicts

The individual is not only the anchoring point of public reason; she is also responsible for making personal decisions concerning her conception of the good life. Of course, it is true that access to valuable ideas of the good life is dependent on existing social forms. But modern ideas of freedom imply that, in relation to such social forms, only I can decide what is good for me. In comparing modern notions of freedom with the ancient polis idea of freedom, Menke speaks of a revolution in the dependency of the individual on the ethical life of society as a whole.[1] He shows that the modern outlook has brought about a reversal of this dependency through an ironic understanding of individuality that is closely tied to a specific understanding of freedom. This designates the ability of the individual to stand back from prevalent beliefs and decide for herself whether or not she—as the person she is or aims to be—can embrace them. "A general determination [of the good] can provide one with the content, but never with the right reasons for an authentic notion of the good: what is good for us can also be good for me—but not *because* it is good for all of us."[2]

The fundamental idea of democratic self-determination is that citizens find out, through public deliberations on questions that concern them all, what, upon reflection, all concerned could voluntarily and autonomously agree to be an acceptable or just way to handle the question at hand. Ultimately, the normative priority of liberal public reason is grounded in the ability and in the willingness of socially responsible, cooperating individuals who accept that this priority is to the benefit of society as a whole. Yet, Menke points out that individuality as it concerns finding a personal conception of the good life goes one step further in granting authority to ironic freedom. Whereas ironic self-determination through the use of public reason is ultimately directed at a common understanding of what would be good or just for all concerned, attempts at ironic self-realization (the finding and shaping of personal freedom) are directed at determining what would be good for the individual. In assessing this latter question, the individual's options are—at least at the level of personal experience—not necessarily restricted by the boundaries that public reason sets. For attempts at self-realization do not oblige individuals to search for a collectively validated determination of the good life. Rather, the very idea of self-realization presupposes that the individual stand back from prevalent beliefs and expectations, even those that were generated through the public use of reason.[3]

Menke's analysis of personal freedom understood as self-realization is not meant to undermine the idea of public reason. Rather, his aim is to make clear that the ideals of, on the one hand, individual self-realization and, on the other, democratic self-determination through the use of public reason, can collide in ways that generate tragic conflicts. He distinguishes between four types of tragic conflicts to illustrate his point.

The sacred—Menke understands a religious conviction, in terms of positive freedom, "as [the conviction] that is central to the identity of an individual; as a determination of what is good for him, for his authenticity."[4] The sacred—or rather a conception of the sacred in terms of the idea of God(s), sacred objects, living things, places, rituals, and so on—gives meaning to the life of the religious individual.[5] It constitutes her experience of what is ultimately valuable in life and shapes her normative-practical outlook on life. It shapes her individuality to such an extent that the impairment or the destruction of what is sacred will be a direct blow to her very individuality, to her personal sense of self.[6]

Menke is surely right in stressing that the sacred cannot be reduced to a merely symbolic framework that concerns the "private" freedom of an individual alone. Rather, the sacred constitutes a framework that has a normative-practical force in many, if not all, situations in which religious individuals find themselves. And this may well conflict with the central values and principles of liberal public reason. For it is likely to impose more obligations on individuals than liberal public reason. The very idea that liberal public reason allows the questioning of the validity of some substantive beliefs—unconditional respect, even for unborn life, the holiness of certain objects and spaces, and so on—that necessarily remain unquestioned (cannot be questioned) in the sacred order the religious individual lives by, may well be an unspeakable disgrace to her. Since (the conception of) the sacred constitutes the very personal sense of self of the religious individual, the question to what extent she can respect or even embrace the principles (and outcomes) of liberal public reason is up to her to decide. Her de jure status as a citizen of a liberal society does not guarantee a de facto outlook on life that is conducive to liberal public reason. Individuality cannot be adequately understood in terms of the demands of liberal citizenship alone. It can—and should—be bounded by adherence to public reason, but this is a matter of prudent self-restraint in a pluralist world, not a matter of being true to the "given" higher rationality of public reason.

Community—Menke sees at least two conflicts between liberal public reason and authentic self-realization as it is dependent on membership of particular communities. The first conflict is between liberal public reason and traditional nonegalitarian communities. While liberal public reason ideally stands for equal opportunities for all citizens, traditional communities ascribe different and often rather unquestionable roles to their members. This is a problem for liberal justice, but it need not be a problem for the members of these communities so long as they wholeheartedly embrace this role as defining their authentic personal sense of self.[7] Yet, traditional communal values will inevitably clash with liberal understandings of the true needs and interests of human beings, if only because the normative-practical directives of the traditional community concerning, for instance, role-specific modes of conduct, the distribution of (political) power, and claims to territory, do not fit in well with the egalitarian normative-practical directives of liberal public reason. A focus on individual rights and liberties, democratic lawmaking, and private property, for example, is likely to impair the worldview and (the social conditions of) the self-understandings of members of traditional communities.

Menke points to another potentially tragic conflict, which concerns liberal communities. Inherent in the liberal tradition is a tendency not to restrict the demands of public reason to liberal societies alone. Indeed, as seen from a moral point of view, it seems unjustifiable not to extend egalitarian liberal ideals to all human beings. But this confronts the liberal individual with a new problem, one with which we are all familiar. In order to lead a good life in Western societies, she cannot avoid adopting a life-style which, if only because of the financial costs associated with it, must appear as deeply immoral when compared to the fundamental needs of many members of, particularly, Third World countries. However, she cannot wholly avoid the seemingly immoral requirements of the good life in Western societies because this would make it practically impossible for her to lead an authentic life in her own cultural environment (community).[8]

The forms of self-realization associated with the sacred and communal belonging appear most frequently in the literature on (tragic) conflicts between liberal public reason and nonpublic conceptions of the good life. It is understandable why this is so, for in both cases we find rather easily identifiable conflicts between a categorical identification with shared ideas of the good life on the one hand, and the categorical claims of the egalitarian good of public reason, which aims to guarantee the conditions of liberal interpretations of well-being, on the other.[9] Furthermore, liberals who take their own ideals seriously will tend to feel sympathy toward individuals who try to remain true to communal goods. They will—at least in a rudimentary form—recognize a socially responsible attitude in the beliefs and actions of such individuals. For they orient themselves, as liberals do, to a normative-practical set of beliefs that defines the conditions of being good and acting justly in terms of social obligations and intersubjectively shared directives. It is probably because of this formal parallel that so many contemporary liberals try to bridge the gap between their own ideas concerning social responsibility and morality and those of others.

This sense of obligation often rapidly fades when liberalism is confronted with forms of individuality which, at least as seen from the perspective of liberal public reason, do not aim at social and moral defensibility because they concern highly personal (private) questions. Menke identifies two ideals of authenticity that are in this category.

Character—Orientations to the sacred and to community consist to a large extent in wholeheartedly embracing socially pregiven and often (at least within a certain context) widely recognized notions of the good life. This is much less the case for individualistic orientations to the categorical obligations of one's own character. Personal ideals, desires, and obsessions may lead to tragic conflicts with the reign of liberal public reason. Here, examples vary from principled forms of civil disobedience to the control of sexual desire. It is remarkable that Menke illustrates the orientation to character solely with examples taken from literary fiction, such as Don Juan and Faust's obsessive orientation to evil. At first sight, this may seem to pose the question as to whether more concrete empirical examples would not be in place. But upon reflection, this approach has its merits. In literary imagination, the attempts of individuals to be true to traits of character that clearly clash with prevalent values in society can be much more clearly captured than by looking at "empirical cases." For in "real life," these attempts will usually be much more bounded or even oppressed by the demands of social order than they are in the imagination. The reign of both law and "decent" or "prudent" social expectations are strong forces in practice. They force us to restrain our character and to conduct ourselves in ways that are not threatening to our fellow human beings.

Of course, literary imagination can be understood as an effective means to control controversial desires. As a doctrine of personal freedom, liberalism is not at all opposed to this strategy of self-control—precisely because of the relatively nonthreatening rationalizations of threatening desires that literary imagination may be said to provide. Furthermore, we must remember that, more often than not, literary imagination captures real predicaments. One need only think of sexual orientations such as pedophilia or more cruel variants of sadomasochism. If not controlled by demanding forms of self-restraint, such orientations may well harm the rights and the physical and mental integrity of others, and therefore conflict with public reason and law. Yet, as character-bound orientations, they may well be of existential importance to individuals. It is the aim of every normative theory to account for the legitimacy of the restraints that public reason lays on our personal lives. But the public legitimacy of such restraints does not (cannot) guarantee that on the personal side of the public moral calculus a tragic sense of loss, a personal sacrifice so huge that one feels deeply estranged from oneself and society, will not be experienced.

The experiment—Forms of authenticity that find their anchoring point in experiments with various identities lack the idea that one's character is something that is more or less pregiven and unalterable.[10] Contrary to the three forms of authenticity just mentioned, they do not relate to a categorical obligation: "For the idea of the experiment leaves no room for any certainty that *these* plans and desires are categorical and fundamental for an individual; that will have to be found out first through experimenting."[11]

Menke rightly observes that this kind of orientation to personal freedom is often understood as being conducive to a flourishing liberal culture.[12] For the "hypothetical" and undogmatic (noncategorical) form of experimenting with one's "private" identity seems to leave much more room for compromises between individuality and liberal public reason than the three other models. Yet, as Menke shows in a discussion of "excessive" experiments with (the limits of) individuality, controversial "private" experiments necessarily relate to the public ethos—based on respect for the freedom and equality of each individual—of a liberal society. Every experiment—whether social, ethical, moral, sexual, or aesthetic—which crosses the boundaries set by this notion of respect, finds its self-definition partly through the negation of the socially and politically acceptable, and risks being curtailed for doing so.[13]

So liberal public reason can conflict with personal conceptions of self-realization and the good life in quite different ways. On the one hand, we encounter understandings of authentic individuality that find their anchoring point in collective practices that conflict with the collective practice of democratic self-determination through liberal public reason. On the other, we find understandings of authentic individuality that are highly personal and clash with the idea of limiting unbounded individuality in the name of collective demands (whether liberal or nonliberal) as such. In all cases, we find a conflict between the collectively validated good of public reason and forms of individuality that are constitutive of the comprehensive self-understandings of persons and collectives.

Again, it is important to note that this tragic constellation is not external to liberalism. On the contrary, it springs directly from liberalism's purposive structure. Yet, it enables us to be perceptive of the occurrence of tragic conflicts. In all of the cases, what is harmed (or at least frustrated) are conceptions of the good life and ideals of self-realization. The liberal presumption of equal value of such ideals obliges liberals to take such ideals seriously even when they conflict with demands of public reason. Where it is clear that such "ideals" are in fact potentially harmful desires or obsessions, as in the case of pedophilia, liberals will at least have to take seriously the identity-formative force of these desires and obsessions for the person in question—especially so because she will often not be able to control her desires and obsessions.

At a more general level, the incongruity of liberal public reason and personal ideals of self-realization might well be a necessary condition for a flourishing liberal society. Indeed, it may well be the case that our understanding of what the perspective of public reason demands and can tolerate changes constantly because individuals and collectives confront the public claim to legitimacy with its exclusionary and possibly tragic effects—in these cases, the effects it has on ideas regarding ideals of self-realization. This conjecture fits in well with the conclusion in the previous chapter that the acceptability of notions of public reason should primarily be understood in terms of their ability to treat individuals, not just politically autonomous citizens, with equal concern and respect. It may well be that the possibility of emancipation of both suppressed groups and individuals and our understanding of what liberal public reason demands exists only because of the painful but unavoidable incongruity between the two perspectives. It is important to keep this point in mind. It gives us a first glimpse of an understanding of the tragic that liberalism could actually benefit from.

Toward an understanding of liberal community

I now turn to the concept of community, because we are in need of a concept that can be used to describe the overall social setting in which practices of self-detemination and self-realization have their place. I propose that we use the concept of "liberal community" to take on that task.

In recent years, much has been said about the notion of a liberal community. As a reaction to the communitarian critique of liberalism, which was highly influential in the 1980s, many authors have tried to show that liberalism is not the political theory of mainly self-interested, disenchanted individuals communitarians often purport it to be.[14] This is a worthwhile attempt, and the present study aims to do something similar. My critique of liberal neutrality, my refusal to understand public autonomy and reasonableness in formal and procedural terms only, and my focus on human aspirations that cannot be fitted into the liberal framework have certainly been inspired by the work of such communitarian authors as Charles Taylor, Michael Sandel, Alasdair MacIntyre, and Michael Walzer.[15] However, I try to remain on the liberal side of the controversy.[16]

There is a simple reason for doing so. The communitarian critique of liberalism is typically directed at a dominant theoretical and practical outlook that most critics do not want to abandon. As practically all reconstructions of the communitarian critique have shown, most communitarian critics occupy a place within the broad liberal tradition.[17] Their aim is not to undermine liberal ideals but rather to gain a better understanding of the theoretical means that are needed in order to account for and defend them.[18] The recent communitarian critique has reminded the liberal tradition once again that normative political theory should not be concerned only with questions of public justice. Rather, it should make clear how claims to justice can be integrated with the demands of community membership.[19]

From a sociological point of view, the concept of community is perhaps best understood in terms of a "set of interacting variables" such as historicity, identity, mutuality, plurality, autonomy, participation, and integration.[20] The interpersonal and institutional relationships that make up a community are characterized by a sense of shared history and culture. Paradigmatic figures from the past, a cherished political tradition, victory or defeat in wars and other conflicts, and the origins and a shared understanding of a common language as well as shared purposes and virtues over time, all play a role in the generation and regeneration of a shared identity.[21] Historicity provides a community with a rich reservoir of principles, ideals, shared practices, and a collective memory. Such a reservoir of cultural knowledge is of great importance for a community's ability to react to current situations in the light of its own traditions.[22] Communal belonging plays a constitutive role in the generation of personal as well as collective identity. In the larger social setting of a community, members play specific social roles. From the perspective of the individual, such a role is perhaps best understood as a balance between loyalty and authenticity, between adherence to shared values and practices (the perceived identity of the community), and an affirmation of one's own identity in terms of a personal evaluation of these values and practices. The tension between collective self-determination and individual self-realization will always be inherent in this balance.

Philip Selznick stresses the fact that communities can only survive if their members gain something by their membership. He calls this a condition of mutuality. This is an important point, because it breaks with the (once) widespread liberal tendency to view communal belonging, almost by definition, as a threat to personal freedom.[23] Furthermore, this idea stands in relation to the tragic idea that if one does not sufficiently gain by one's membership, then great losses may emanate. Community, Selznick maintains, begins with interdependence and reciprocity, and can develop into "solidarity, and from there to fellowship."[24] This understanding of mutuality as a basis of community is inspired by both a socio-ontological and a normative perspective. The socio-ontological perspective sees community as an ontological "fact." People are born into communities and benefit from the condition of mutuality that is implicit in all social relations. From a normative point of view, this is then interpreted as a characteristic of social relations that enables individuals to find out whether given communal relations shape the condition of mutuality in ways that they can agree with. A liberal community is a community from which members gain something on the basis of what was earlier called egalitarian reciprocity. It must be conducive to aspirations of self-realization and self-determination and to a use of public reason that frustrates individuality as little as possible, and that distributes the burdens and advantages of community membership in egalitarian ways.

A similar normative point of view can be discerned in Selznick's remarks on plurality, autonomy, and participation. A good community values a pluralism of social forms. It allows a "healthy differentiation of institutions and of personal, family, ethnic, locality, and occupational groups," which exist together within a shared "framework of legitimacy."[25] He sees such groups as "intermediate associations"; their modus operandi is to ensure that members of larger communities enjoy security, orientation, political influence, belonging, love, work, competition, self-realization, and so on. He explicates his ideas further in discussing autonomy: "[T]he worth of a community is measured by the contributions it makes to the flourishing of unique and responsible persons."[26] Here, Selznick uses an argument that resembles the idea that autonomy and pluralism presuppose each other. Autonomy can only be exercised in a social environment that provides individuals with a range of valuable options.

And such an environment can only be upheld through autonomous action. Through acting autonomously in pluralist social environments, people participate in the life of a community, attain a sense of self, and help shape their community.

Selznick primarily concentrates on forms of communal participation concerned with what he calls "the basic continuities in life": family, work, and friendship.[27] He sees these as the basis of participation in broader social contexts such as politics and religion. I subscribe to a similar view, because the prepolitical realm of social cooperation must be understood as the multifaceted "place" where valuable social practices are located. So to the extent that the exact value of politics and religion is best experienced through the basic continuities that Selznick identifies, I agree with him. Yet, participation in a liberal community should also be understood at a fundamental level, in political terms. Through articulating concerns that are often best experienced through basic continuities in life (the freedom and prospects of one's family, one's work, and one's social life) people benefit their community; they motivate the community to reflect critically on the legitimacy of its social and political directives and the many patterns of social expectation related to them. In this sense, political participation, or rather political awareness, which begins at a prepolitical level (i.e., a level not immediately associated with democratic institutions), is as important to a liberal understanding of the community as are the other forms of participation. Political awareness is the awareness that members of the community should be free to participate in processes of the reproduction of the conditions under which they try to reach individual and collective well-being. In relation to the concept of public reason, the important thing to remember is that the notion of the community makes clear from the beginning that social and political participation is closely tied to a sense of belonging. Participation should not be measured only from a perspective of collective self-determination, but also from a perspective that values the situatedness of individuals in concrete social forms that foster their individual and collective conceptions of what it means to lead a good life.

Finally, many social theorists stress the fact that communities play a role in processes of social integration. The substantive characteristics of a flourishing community—which are defined by the specific understanding of the elements of community just discussed—have a strong hold on the lives of community members. They find their expression in institutions, norms, beliefs, and practices (among them, democratic practices of public reasoning) and, through them, integrate individuals into shared social forms. This may seem to be a rigid, deterministic view, but it is not. Communities may suppress the values of autonomy and free self-realization, but they may also foster them. As long as historicity, identity, mutuality, plurality, autonomy, participation, and the need for integration are understood in terms of respect for the integrity of persons, there is no need to be overly wary of the concept of community as a central element of a liberal political theory.[28]

This last remark is directed at liberal theorists who equate the concept of society with justice through public reason and the concept of community with traditional nonegalitarian social forms that are not sufficiently controlled by public reason.[29] Of course I do not want to deny that there are many cases in which appeals to liberal justice have had and continue to have a liberating force over communal patterns of social expectation. But this in itself is no reason to think that liberal thought can do without the concept of community. This refers to the shared life form, the "ethical life"—comprising all social, cultural, economic, and political practices and institutions associated with the constitutional state and with civil society—of liberal societies. A liberal community aims to be highly inclusive; it includes all citizens of liberal societies on the premise that their often very different interests in leading a good life should be treated equally. To this extent, liberal community is closely tied to the idea of liberal public reason. But whereas liberal public reason refers to the narrow and problem-oriented task of critically evaluating matters of public-political concern, a liberal community refers to the much broader shared practices and life forms that constitute the experiential and motivational basis of public reason. In the light of my earlier findings, the use of liberal public reason must be understood as one of these practices. Members of liberal societies need security, belonging, love, work, competition, self-realization, and so on. These needs cannot be satisfied through the use of public reason alone.[30]

A liberal community is an ideal notion, a vision on an anticipated ideal situation. It depicts an ideal understanding of the ethical orientations; the forms of self-restraint; and the common practices, rights, and obligations of citizens who agree to the basic egalitarian premise upon which the idea of a liberal community rests. Because it is an ideal notion that articulates nonneutral normative expectations, we cannot reasonably expect that the idea of a liberal community will not be controversial. The notion of a liberal community does not offer an adequate description of current states of affairs in liberal societies. Rather, just like John Rawls's idea of the overlapping consensus, the notion of a liberal community refers to an anticipated end state of social cooperation. Yet, from a normative point of view, the ideal of a liberal community is as real and as necessary for our understanding of our social and political aims as existing states of affairs. For we can only judge the value of existing conditions from an ideal notion that articulates our highest aims in social coopera-tion, and we can only successfully hold onto or change our ideal no-tion by confronting it with given states of affairs.[31]

A convincing notion of a liberal community must encompass the understanding of autonomy, reasonableness, pluralism, the good life, and toleration we have developed in the preceding chapters. As virtues of the practice of public reason they also are crucial for an understanding of the ethical life of liberal societies as a whole. It is not surprising, then, that the most influential accounts of a liberal community that have recently been developed spell out lists of virtues and accounts of practices to which these virtues are crucial.[32] In chapter 9, I will take a closer look at some of these virtues and practices. But for now, I want to pose a more fundamental question, how community membership relates to the personal experience of individuals. This is important because it motivates us to find out to what extent experience is indeed shaped by community member-ship, and to what extent the given conditions of community mem-bership are shaped by the articulation of individual experience. Here it is in order to study an argument developed by Charles Taylor.

Taylor's argument starts from a phenomenological account of emotions. It shows that, upon reflection, "raw" emotions such as shame and spite are never simply given in an objective and uninter-preted way. Rather, they are always experienced in relation to prop-erties of a particular human subject.[33] According to Taylor, this "subject-referring" quality of emotions points to a very fundamental characteristic of life. It shows that we can explicate some of our most basic feelings and actions only with reference to frameworks of meaning that explain their bearing for us: "[T]he (linguistic) mean-ing of 'shameful' can only be explicated with reference to a subject for whom these (emotional) meanings have weight, and if there were no such subjects, the term itself would lack sense."[34] This amounts to saying that the frameworks of meaning that constitute human expe-rience provide humans with evaluative standards that in attempts to make sense of their experiences and actions can only be neglected at the cost of no longer being able to understand these actions as ac-tions of subjects of experience. Our emotions help us understand that situations bear a certain moral "import" for us and that this import can only be explained in terms of the frameworks of meaning we (aim to) live by—frameworks that define us as rational, moral beings, with a professional ethic, as creatures of God, and so on.[35]

Through the articulation of our subject-referring feelings, we discover pictures of our moral predicament, pictures that help explain what matters to us qua subjects.[36] These articulate which insights are constitutive of our responses to, and interpretations of, the situations we find ourselves in. An articulation of such insights is an interpretation of our feelings. But it can never be an interpretation of "raw feelings." In our experience, the variation possible is not that between interpreted and noninterpreted feelings. Rather, the terms chosen to arrive at an adequate articulation of our feelings can vary: "Our feelings incorporate a certain articulation of our situation, that is, they presuppose that we characterize our situation in certain terms. But at the same time they admit of—and very often we feel that they call for—further articulation, the elaboration of finer terms permitting more penetrating characterization. And this further articulation can in turn transform the feelings."[37]

Now, the relevance of this argument for the notion of a community is that the articulation of our feelings presupposes the use of language. Language is by nature intersubjective; it exists and is maintained within a language community.[38] The language by which an individual articulates her own point of view is always related to the common language of the community. This is not to say that a common language necessarily wholly and precisely determines the way in which she will articulate her own framework of meaning; it is just to say that language provides her with the ability to make sense of the world because she is, first, being brought up with frameworks of meaning communicated through language and, second, at later stages in life, able to stand back from and contest these frameworks by directing her attention—again in dialogue—to other, often competing frameworks, and to find articulations that adequately help her respond to the plurality of options and experiences in life that she is confronted with. In this sense, Taylor maintains, language use is a transcendental condition of human subjectivity. And because language use is always situated within certain traditions, practices, and, indeed, intersubjectively shared frameworks of meaning, it can be said that the communal aspect of human existence is a transcendental condition of human subjectivity as well.[39]

I have said earlier that we need to find out to what extent individual experience is shaped by its situatedness in common life forms. Of course, Taylor's argument does not provide us with a comprehensive answer. Still, it does enable us to see that individual experience is determined by, on the one hand, the use of substantive common languages that provide people with evaluative standards and, on the other hand, emotions, feelings, which reveal to them the value or adequateness of these standards for them. This is a dialectical understanding of human experience that goes back and forth between, on the one hand, given standards of evaluation (including social and political directives for action) and, on the other, personal experiences that motivate people to (partly) affirm or dismiss the value and adequateness of such standards.

Individual experience is shaped by and in turn shapes many different, although often overlapping common languages. People may be members of familial communities, political communities, ethnic or religious communities, occupational communities, neighborhoods, and so forth. These communities provide people with different, sometimes irreconcilable standards of evaluation. For our purposes, it is important that we differentiate between three aspects of the situatedness of individuals in common life forms:

> 1. Individuals are situated in concrete communities, such as the family, occupational communities, associational communities, the political community, and ethnic communities. Such communities are characterized by standards of social expectation and evaluation that individuals either (feel they can) live up to, or not. Insofar as these standards aim to let the interests of all members in leading a good life matter equally (and do so according to the interpretation we have given to this aim), they are liberal standards of expectation, characteristic of liberal communities.

> 2. Liberal communities encompass specific practices and institutions that are directed at public problem-solving through the use of public reason. This serves the task of identifying and solving problems that frustrate the well-being of citizens. Through the use of public reason, the collective self-understanding of liberal communities may gradually change.

> 3. Within liberal communities, individual experience plays a special role. It is the experiential touchstone of both individual self-understanding and of the substantive directives of liberal communities, including their understanding of public reason.

This threefold distinction makes it clear that it is not enough to work with the simple dichotomy "liberal public reason versus community." Liberal public reason is a function of liberal communities. Yet, it is a necessary function: in a pluralist society, liberal public reason and communities presuppose each other. Liberal communities shape the social world because they encompass liberal understandings of historicity, identity, mutuality, pluralism, autonomy, participation, and social integration. To the extent that questions concerning these aspects of liberal communities are in need of political or judicial treatment, the use of public reason becomes necessary. In such cases, the use of public reason may change the perception of questions and problems that liberal communities are confronted with. Individual experience is the experiential touchstone of the legitimacy of social relations within liberal communities. The dialectics of individual experience and prevalent standards of expectation and evaluation are—both in public deliberation and in other social and personal matters—a fundamental force in the critical reproduction of life forms and in the standards of evaluation that they incorporate. This is not to say that we have to abandon the normative priority of liberal public reason. As a justificatory strategy for a liberal order, a normative priority has to be ascribed to liberal public reason. It is characteristic of flourishing liberal communities that their members trust in and sustain practices of public reasoning. But the normative priority of public reason should not lead to an unquestionable belief in the adequateness of prevalent understandings of public reason. By articulating individual experiences—which may be related to conceptions of the sacred, of community, or to demands of one's own character—and transforming them into social and political claims, members of liberal societies may succeed in making it clear that prevalent understandings of public reasoning and, more generally, prevalent standards of social expectation and evaluation do not live up to the legitimate needs of some groups of citizens, and therefore to the liberal aim.

8

~

Struggles for Recognition
and Tragic Conflicts

It seems necessary to dig deeper into the dialectics of given standards of expectation and evaluation and individual experience. First, a more thorough understanding is needed to demonstrate how standards that define the substantive characteristics of particular communities affect personal experience, and how they can foster or frustrate the individual and collective well-being of their members. Second, the question arises, how can feelings of a lack of well-being motivate individuals to change given standards? These questions arose in the previous chapter, where it was said that conflicts between the standards of liberal public reason and the felt need to be true to the sacred, to community, or to (experiments of) character are not just frustrating, but could well be a necessary condition for a flourishing liberal society that learns from these tensions. It was conjectured that our understanding of what liberal public reason—and more broadly, liberal community—demands and can tolerate changes continuously because individuals and collectives confront generalizing claims to the legitimacy of certain ideas and policies with their possibly exclusionary effects, that is, their effects on personal freedom. What we need is a theory that accounts for the logic of this continuous struggle, understood as a social struggle for the individual and collective well-being of members of liberal communities and societies.

Confronted with this theoretical need, several authors have proposed to concentrate on concrete experiences of social injustice and on various forms of disrespect.[1] Such approaches introduce a dynamic of ideal notions of justice and respect and concrete experiences of injustice and disrespect to political theory. Experiences of injustice and disrespect always occur in social settings. Whether liberals talk about political or economic opportunities or the sociocultural perception of certain individuals and groups whenever they say that people are being treated unjustly, they mean that the attitudes of certain people, or the performances of certain institutions, prevent certain people from leading their lives under conditions of freedom and equality. But what does this mean? Why is it wrong? It's because unjust or demeaning situations are situations in which people will ultimately lose their self-respect. This approach goes one step further than (public-reason) approaches that state that a just society should guarantee conditions of egalitarian reciprocity to its members. For it tries to articulate, in terms of personal experience and conditions of well-being, not just in procedural terms of equal access, why egalitarian reciprocity is a condition of a just social world.

Axel Honneth's theory of recognition

In my view, the most interesting attempts that have recently been undertaken to go this one step further are formulated in terms that stress the importance of social recognition of the identity, social roles, and legal status of individuals. Theorists of social recognition usually differentiate between several modes of recognition that are understood as prerequisites for the well-being of individuals. Axel Honneth has thus far presented the most comprehensive contemporary theory of social recognition; therefore, I will concentrate on his work.[2]

Honneth differentiates between three modes of recognition: emotional support, cognitive respect, and social esteem. He relates them to different dimensions of personality: needs and emotions, moral responsibility, and concrete traits and abilities of persons (92ff.). These are related to specific social settings within modern societies. The paradigmatic setting in which emotional support is given is the setting of primary relations (relations of love and friendship). The setting of cognitive respect—unconditional respect for the integrity of persons—is primarily that of legal relations (of rights). And the setting for recognition of concrete traits and abilities of individuals (related to work, gender, culture, ethnicity, etc.) is provided by "communities of value"—the aggregate of cultural self-understandings (122)—of a particular society.

By means of an empirically informed analysis of the three modes of recognition, Honneth develops an understanding of the practical "relations-to-self" they foster. His basic idea is that coming to understand and trust oneself as a separate and unique individual entitled to respect always involves the experience of being recognized as such by others. In other words: one's relation-to-self is always dependent on one's relation-to-others. Studies in developmental psychology and psychoanalysis by, among others, Donald Winnicott and Jessica Benjamin show that forms of mutual recognition between parents and children, friends, and lovers generate a form of basic self-confidence. In relations of love and friendship, the emotional neediness of persons plays an important role. They are, except for the early months of a child's life, relations that border on the symbiotic—relationships in which one is "oneself in another" (100; see also 37ff.)—but in which people are still separate, that is, people who have their own distinct emotional and physical needs and identities. Indeed, following Winnicott, Honneth maintains that bounds of love—particularly those between parents and children— are characterized by a struggle for recognition of the physical and emotional boundaries of individuals' distinctive ways of being themselves. In order to successfully share one's needs and emotions with others, one must have the capacity "to be alone in a carefree manner," that is, one must be able to self-confidently trust on the continuing love and care of a parent, a friend, a lover, even when she is not there (103f.). According to Honneth, the self-confidence-generating mode of recognition characteristic of relations of love and friendship are "both conceptually and genetically prior to every other form of reciprocal recognition" (107).

Honneth makes much of a methodological approach that identifies experiences of injustice or—in the vocabulary of the theory of recognition—disrespect. Therefore, it does not come as a surprise that he makes his case by looking at instances in which people are withheld the recognition that they are entitled to. In the realm of the emotional relation-to-self labeled self-confidence, the most fundamental forms of disrespect affect the physical integrity of an individual. What is affected by forms of physical injury such as torture and rape—and, one might add, pure neglect—is not only the body, but also, and perhaps even more importantly, "the feeling of being defenselessly at the mercy of another subject, to the point of feeling that one has been deprived of reality" (132) Such forms of disrespect, Honneth observes, rob people of the basic trust in their ability to "autonomously coordinate their own bodies" and of the "reliability of the social world" (133f.). Thereby, they gravely affect the important capacity to be alone with oneself in a carefree manner. The physical, psychological, and social consequences of instances of physical injury such as torture and rape show—*ex negativo*—how important due recognition of the need for physical and emotional integrity is for the basic self-confidence of individuals. According to Honneth, it is no less than a necessary condition for free self-realization of the individual in any community.[3]

Mutual recognition is a prerequisite for social and individual well-being not only in primary relationships of love and friendship. Honneth turns to two much-used terms related to the vocabulary of recognition—*respect* and *esteem*—and is able to differentiate between their meanings by pointing to structural traits of modern societies. He starts from a general thesis concerning legal forms of recognition, which states that "with the transition to modernity, individual rights have become detached from concrete role expectations because they must, from that point on, be ascribed in principle to every human individual as a free being" (110). There is no doubt that this thesis is widely accepted. Legal recognition is not conceptualized hierarchically, in terms of the esteem that individuals are thought to deserve by virtue of their specific social roles and characteristics, but rather in terms of unconditional respect for these individuals, understood as bearers of individual rights. In modern societies, the idea of legal equality sets limits to the power of conventional systems of esteem. For this reason, Honneth seems to be quite right in separating modes of recognition characteristic of the context of law from modes of recognition found in more concrete communities of (associational, occupational, cultural, and ethnic) value.[4]

Within the context of law, Honneth turns to the Kantian idea that every subject must be considered an end in itself. This idea articulates universal respect for the freedom of the will of people, that is, for their capacity to act autonomously. Earlier, we have seen that it is by no means easy to conceptualize this. Honneth takes on this task by looking at the legitimation of modern law. First, following deliberatively democratic intuitions, he notes that the idea of rational agreement that lies behind virtually every account of modern law suggests that the autonomy or moral accountability of citizens is presupposed by modern law. Second—and this time in a Hegelian, not Kantian vein—he makes it clear that it cannot be decided once and for all how this capacity should be thought of because it will always be dependent on historically contingent ideas of what rational agreement means (114). Consequently, in a third step, he tries to reach an account of (public or political) autonomy and legal recognition that is true to current ideas of citizenship and rational will formation.

For this purpose, he turns to T. H. Marshall's famous study of the expansion of civil, political, and social rights in England from the eighteenth century onward.[5] What interests Honneth most in Marshall's study is that it shows how the initial idea of equal civil rights for a relatively small elite in early modern societies generated a "developmental pressure" that—in hindsight—simply had to result in social struggles for the granting of such rights—and their political and social counterparts—to ever more previously excluded groups.[6] Honneth envisages this in the sheer strength of legal recognition as a prerequisite to individual self-determination and self-realization in societies in which such forms of recognition have social validity. This movement toward the universal granting of full citizenship rights, was—by definition—accompanied by the decoupling of rights and status. The idea of legal equality was, and still is, the primary focus in the political struggle for recognition by excluded groups: "Each enrichment of the legal claims of individuals can be understood as a further step in fleshing out the moral idea that all members of society must have been able to agree to the established order on the basis of rational insight, if they are to be expected to obey the law" (117). This enables Honneth to account for the substantive characteristics of contemporary ideas of legal recognition and citizenship. For given the historical development of the idea of citizenship in liberal-democratic welfare states, people can be expected to participate in society in a morally responsible manner only if they are granted civil liberties (legal protection from unlawful interference in the private sphere); political rights (the formal status of a citizen participating in democratic processes); and social rights (the minimum guarantee of a standard of education, health care, and economic security needed to take on the dignity of citizenship in more than just a formal way). Today, Honneth concludes, legal recognition means something other than it did, for instance, two centuries ago because both the content of rights and the class of rights holders have been enormously extended. As the struggle for the legal recognition of social rights indicates, changes in the understanding of what it means to be a morally accountable citizen are closely tied to historical changes in ideas concerning the social prerequisites of autonomy. Today, being respected as a citizen means that one is understood, and—as a matter of relation-to-self—that one understands oneself, as being not only a bearer of civil and political rights, but also as someone who has the right to claim a certain standard of living, care, and education that enables her to fully participate in society.

In a society in which the vast majority of citizens can make claims to the tripartite scheme of civil, political, and social rights, those who are wholly or partly excluded from full citizenship—say new and possibly illegal immigrants or, as a classic case, slaves—will have a hard time respecting themselves as full participants in society. Without legal protection, without the right to participate in the public life of society, and without basic social rights, life becomes particularly harsh. Most notably, it becomes virtually impossible to act in autonomous and—according to the standards of expectation and evaluation characteristic of the society one lives in—morally responsible ways. Because of the immense influence of legal institutions, individuals who are not legally recognized as full citizens are likely to lose part of their self-respect (134).[7] In a sense, they are socially dead individuals.[8] Theories of recognition not only enable us to understand which social relations and relations-to-self constitute the dominant social patterns of expectation within society; they also enable us to understand how these relations are connected to mechanisms of inclusion and exclusion that have—although not always in these terms—been the topic of the discussions of various political theories in the preceding chapters.

Finally, Honneth goes into the conditions of what he calls social esteem and self-esteem. As we have already seen, social esteem concerns modes of recognition that enable individuals to "relate positively to the concrete traits and abilities" characteristic of them as members of society (121). A major sociological problem Honneth is faced with in his attempt to present an adequate contemporary account of this mode of recognition is given with the much-discussed gradual demise in late capitalist societies of dominant group-related forms of social dignity such as those associated with work, class, and religion. As long as the dignity of people is primarily measured in terms of the "predetermined worth of traits that are attributed, as types, to entire groups" (125), the social world is relatively easily surveyable. But once particular life histories—made up of all kinds of past and present allegiances to professions, communities, gender, cultural and ethnic groups, and so on—become the main point of reference in questions of social esteem, things get more complicated. From that point on, Honneth states, one or other form of value pluralism must constitute the "cultural framework of orientation" within which social worth is assessed (125). Within such a framework, individual achievements, traits, and abilities—socially recognized or disrespected forms of self-realization—become the measure of social worth.

But still, even in pluralist societies, the evaluation of the worth of forms of self-realization presupposes a general normative framework from which such evaluations derive their validity. According to Honneth, modern law cannot provide such a framework, because—by definition—it recognizes (and thereby values) only general capacities of people—their autonomy, their reasonableness, their capacity to develop a personal sense of freedom, and so forth, not individual traits and achievements. Honneth conjectures that the evaluative framework of social esteem will have to include abstractly defined goals of society—most importantly, a form of solidarity that is true to the characteristics of the community at large. However, it is to be expected that such abstractly defined goals will always remain controversial because, inevitably, they will have consequences for the social esteem and the relations-to-self of particular individuals and groups (127).

From a liberal perspective, the aim of such struggles must ultimately be the development of a "community of value" in which each individual is recognized for her particular traits and abilities and will therefore be able to arrive at the relation-to-self that Honneth labels "self-esteem." This would make possible pluralist forms of "postconventional solidarity," in which mutual estimation "means to view one another in light of values that allow the abilities and traits of the other to appear significant for shared praxis." This form of solidarity would be accompanied by forms of active toleration, that is, "felt concern for what is individual and particular about the other person" (129).

Struggles for recognition and the tragedy of liberalism

At the beginning of this chapter, I brought up two questions concerning the dialectics of individual experience and the situatedness of individuals in given social forms. First, how do standards that define the substantive characteristics of a particular community affect personal experience, and how might they foster or frustrate the well-being of its members? Second, how could feelings of a lack of well-being motivate individuals to change given standards? Honneth's theory of recognition provides us with the terms in which we can now begin to answer both questions.

In answer to the first question, Honneth's theory has lent us an empirically informed insight into the sheer power of given standards

of social expectation. Whether we talk about the situatedness of individuals in families and in other relations of love and friendship,
their membership in the legal and the political community, or their
concrete traits and abilities as members of society, the theory of
recognition makes it clear that standards of social expectation are
rather directly related to the sense of self and to the opportunities
and individual well-being of individuals. In order to see oneself as a
competent member of the community, one must be recognized as
such by at least a sufficient number of fellow members. Otherwise, it
is highly likely that one's well-being will be affected. Against this
background, egalitarian reciprocity must mean that a society that is
both just and good would distribute the conditions of due recognition, in all three spheres, in fair ways.

In answer to the second question, the importance of struggles
for recognition, which have not been properly discussed yet, should
be emphasize. If it is true that interpersonal relations of recognition and disrespect both affect the sense of self and the opportunities
and individual well-being of people, then transformations in such relations may be expected to change the sense of self and the opportunities and individual well-being of people as well. But how could
such transformations come about? Here, Honneth asks how "experi-
encing social disrespect can motivate a subject to enter a practical
struggle or conflict" (135). On the side of disrespected individuals,
feelings of shame, rage, hurt, or indignation may exist. Such feelings, Honneth conjectures, "are, in principle, capable of revealing to
individuals the fact that certain forms of recognition are being withheld from them" (136). Therefore, they may motivate them to engage
in social struggles for the forms of recognition that they feel are un-
justifiably being withheld from them.

Honneth concentrates on "moral emotional reactions," "emotional excitations with which human beings react to having their actions unexpectedly repelled owing to a violation of normative
expectations" (137). Here, it is important that he follows John
Dewey's account of emotions that was developed within the context
of a pragmatist psychology and theory of action.[9] It is characteristic
of pragmatist theories that a shared life world is understood as a set
of often implicit moral and technical expectations that guide the actions of those who inhabit this life world. From such a perspective, a
"violation of normative expectations" does not necessarily occur explicitly. Rather, implicit normative expectations—for example, "I
have a right to be treated with equal concern and respect"—may be
violated in concrete situations in which one feels that such expecta-

tions are not being fulfilled—as in "We do not give you legal protection because you are a foreigner." Furthermore, it is characteristic of this pragmatist approach that feelings of guilt, which spring from one's own violation of a norm one recognizes, or feelings of moral indignation, which spring from the experience that others violate valid norms, are understood as containing cognitive components which, in principle, can be opened up (137). Through the moral indignation one feels when fair treatment is being withheld from one, one may become able to positively articulate the violated norm(s) in question ("foreigners should have a right to adequate legal protection"). Emotions can reveal moral intuitions. And moral intuitions can in turn be further articulated and defended by means of social and political activism. Struggles for recognition of moral intuitions, intuitions as to the need for certain types of recognition can then be engaged in.

Honneth's reflections on the motivational sources of struggles for recognition fit in well with Charles Taylor's dialectical understanding of human experience that was discussed in the previous chapter. Taylor makes the point that given standards of expectation and evaluation—which we can now interpret as substantive patterns of recognition and disrespect that govern human interaction in particular communities—both shape the experience of individuals and often call for redefinition insofar as they do not fit in well with the felt needs of individuals who are subject to them. Yet, much more than Taylor does, Honneth makes clear that individuals whose needs and interests are frustrated by reigning standards of evaluation and expectation may not have the social and political power that is needed to effectively articulate their needs and interests and thereby to change these standards. Furthermore, he emphasizes that physical and mental abuse, the denial of rights, social denigration, and the emotions that accompany them do not necessarily result in opposition. Honneth is correct in stressing the fact that much depends on the cultural-political environment in which injustices occur. Social movements, pressure groups, the media, the legal system, and democratic institutions all play an important role in shaping an environment that enables disrespected individuals and their sympathizers to identify social injustices and to change given social practices and standards through struggles for recognition (138f.).

As seen from an emancipatory perspective, a cultural-political environment that is conducive to struggles for recognition serves two goals: first, it assures that the society or community in question remains open to the possibility that grave injustices may occur in it and that such injustices should be mitigated or even overcome. For this purpose, it allows the formation of groups and movements that explicitly aim to identify injustices and restore, through social and political action, sound patterns of recognition. It may be clear that this is important for a theory that wants to gain insight into the heuristic value of tragic conflicts. In cases in which tragic conflicts can be understood as conflicts over expectations regarding the form of recognition people are due, they may be overcome or at least be mitigated through changes of prevalent patterns of recognition. And second, through the formation and activities of such groups and movements, disrespected individuals can organize themselves and can regain a sense of self-confidence, self-respect, and self-esteem. Here, many examples can be cited: the civil-rights movement, self-help groups for battered women, gay groups, nationalist groups such as the IRA, labor movements and trade unions, and so on.

This list is meant to raise several questions. Liberals will not have any difficulty recognizing the merits of the first three groups. The civil-rights movement has played a role in the establishment of a revolutionized sense of justice that can hardly be overestimated. And the same goes for the social struggles in which battered women and gays continue to engage. However, labor movements and trade unions may raise some eyebrows. For many will want to argue that theirs are primarily economic goals, not goals that concern questions of respect and esteem.[10] Here, the correct answer is that we should not be reductionist about these matters. As Honneth shows in a discussion of the work of social historians such as E. P. Thompson and Barrington Moore on social struggles by the lower classes in England and Germany, social struggles for a certain standard of living are often motivated by both material interests and feelings of moral indignation that concern the social perception of the members of these classes.[11] The lack of esteem for their contribution to the division of labor within society has often motivated workers to struggle for better wages. But the simple fact that this struggle was and remains to be one of the chief objectives of labor movements does not necessarily mean that harm to professional dignity is not among the chief motivations for such socioeconomic struggles. I think that Honneth is right in his belief that questions of recognition play a key role in concrete struggles over the distribution of material goods and opportunities (165).

Struggles for recognition of nationalist groups confront us with still other difficulties. Here, it seems unquestionable that struggles for cultural recognition and recognition of a desire for political self-determination are at stake. Yet, from a liberal perspective both the terrorist means and the specific nationalist rhetoric by which these struggles for recognition are (were) carried out are deeply problematic.[12] I do not aim to answer questions of the legitimacy of political violence and nationalist rhetoric here. Rather, I want to point to serious problems concerning the assessment of the legitimacy of concrete struggles for recognition that Honneth's theory is confronted with.

Honneth claims that the value of struggles for recognition can only be assessed from a normative framework that anticipates a provisional end state of law and solidarity in which all valid traits and abilities of individuals would be socially recognized in ways that warrant the social conditions of their individual and collective well-being.[13] The normative framework he has in mind is directed at securing a cultural-political environment in which "the three forms of recognition—love, rights, and esteem—constitute the social conditions under which . . . a person can come to see himself or herself, unconditionally, as both an autonomous and an individuated being and to identify with his or her goals and desires" (169). He argues for a postconventional morality that would foster the differentiation of intimate relationships, law, and social esteem and the diverse needs, virtues, and capacities associated with the institutions within which these relationships of recognition have their proper place. Furthermore, such a postconventional morality must be designed to "unleash the inherent potential" of each of the forms of recognition (169). It must enable individuals and groups to identify and to articulate injustices in the light of the normative potential inscribed in legitimate institutions and to treat all members of postconventional societies as being in need of these forms of recognition. The normative framework he has in mind, Honneth claims, "lets an objective-intentional context emerge, in which historical processes no longer appear as mere events but rather as stages in a conflictual process of formation, leading to a gradual expansion of relationships of recognition" (170).

It is one thing to state that an ideal understanding of the ethical life of liberal societies can be formulated in terms of relations of mutual recognition, but it is quite another to state that struggles for recognition that can be reconstructed with this ideal in mind point to an "objective-intentional context" that puts struggles for recognition in a surveyable historical perspective of social and moral development. Honneth's normative conception of the ethical life of a just society combines an ethos of legal concern and respect for all members of society with a pluralist sensitivity to particular traits and abilities of individuals and to the social conditions under which these traits and abilities can be properly exercised and valued. He even holds that his conception of ethical life is sufficiently formal "to avoid raising the suspicion that they embody particular visions of the good life" (174). But this claim cannot be upheld.

As we have seen earlier, Honneth's postconventional conception of ethical life is designed to sketch the contours of a society in which fundamental conditions of personal integrity are sufficiently protected. Insofar as only early parent-child relations are at issue, it may be true that "the integration of love into the intersubjective network of a posttraditional form of ethical life does not change its [love's] fundamental character" (176). This claim seems to be problematic for intimate relationships and friendships among adults. The expectations of egalitarian reciprocity implied in these relationships have most certainly been influenced by normative transformations of the realms of law and social cooperation. It therefore seems neither possible nor desirable to present the ideal conception of ethical life as being neutral with respect to personal or collective notions of the good life. Liberal theories are biased toward the value of pluralism (this Honneth affirms himself) and toward the value of personal autonomy. But liberal societies also respect the freedom of conscience of their members. And for this very reason, there will always be room in liberal societies for authentic choices, practices, and allegiances concerning ideas of self-realization—for instance, in terms of the sacred, of community, or of individual character—which cannot be reconciled with choices, practices, and allegiances that respond to more substantive liberal aims and goals (the defense of personal autonomy, value pluralism, toleration, liberal reasonableness, etc.). This is why I brought up the problem of radical nationalist sentiments. Such sentiments express allegiances to a strong idea of community. In principle, liberal societies can admit the existence of such allegiances. But in these specific cases, the allegiance to the community finds its definition partly through a negation of universalistic ideals of justice and membership in a political community. Although radical nationalist sentiments may wither away in just liberal societies, there is no guarantee that they will. It all depends on the possibility of overcoming tragic conflicts between competing normative frameworks and, ultimately, between the formation of a shared normative-practical outlook. The problem is that Honneth's harmony-oriented notion of solidarity makes it virtually impossible for him to see a real conflict here. Although a notion of solidarity in terms of pluralism is of prime importance for the integration of society, I have difficulties with the focus of this theory on a form of postconventional solidarity in which "individual competition for social esteem would acquire a form free from pain, that is, a form not marred by experiences of disrespect" (130). Honneth's implicit suggestion that an ideal notion of postconventional solidarity could do away with such experiences altogether seems to be too optimistic.

Honneth's views notwithstanding, we have to distinguish between, on the one hand, an ideal of solidarity that can help us explain how certain forms of disrespect destroy the dignity of people and, on the other hand, the empirical lack of forms of solidarity that are all-inclusive. On the former level, the social theory of recognition explains a lot—it sketches the contours of a highly desirable ideal—but on the latter level it jumps to conclusions. Honneth's notion of solidarity paradoxically suggests that, in practice, genuine forms of solidarity will only be realized after the struggles for recognition he puts at the center of his theory have been successfully completed. The idea is that, in principle, all valid beliefs and practices in modern societies could be reconciled in an overarching posttraditional form of solidarity. He rightly observes that "the formation of community-generating value horizons" is subject to normative limitations set by the idea of permissible forms of individual self-realization implicit in modern law (177). Starting from this idea, he then argues that, in liberal societies, modes of self-esteem fostering self-realization will be generated only through those forms of interaction that respond to these normative limitations. From a normative perspective, this argument is convincing. But because Honneth cannot adequately conceptualize forms of group-based solidarity or individual self-esteem that are based on the refusal to answer to these limitations—based on obligations that may spring from allegiances to the sacred, to community, or to (experiments of) character—his theory makes it difficult to understand the struggle for recognition of such groups and individuals as possibly valid struggles.

So it seems that, at least as far as its normative expectations are concerned, Honneth's model is not really susceptible to the tragic character of struggles for recognition. He might evade this problem by considering the possibility that his understanding of the "objective-intentional context" of struggles for recognition is a normatively rich interpretation of objective social processes. As seen from this perspective, struggles for recognition are objectively given social phenomena. Yet, the intentional aspects of these struggles may or may not point in the direction of a liberal-democratic notion of ethical life. As far as they do, liberal societies will be hospitable to these struggles. Furthermore, starting from a presumption of equal value, liberal societies aim to take seriously all claims that are expressed through struggles for recognition. But given their bias toward a substantive, nonneutral conception of ethical life, liberal societies cannot tolerate the substantive goals of all struggles for recognition.

My critique of Honneth's ideal conception of ethical life makes it necessary to rethink the contours of a provisional end state of social struggles in which competition for social respect and esteem can acquire a form "not marred by experiences of disrespect." In the course of the present study, I have discussed some theories that aim for rather far-reaching forms of ethical-political harmony within a neutral moral framework—the theories of John Rawls, Jürgen Habermas, and now Honneth—and some that doubt whether harmony through neutral moral procedures will ever be attained—the theories of, for instance, Christoph Menke, J. Donald Moon, and Joseph Raz. All theories that take the former route anticipate an ideal end state of social and political cooperation to which the idea of ethical harmony is critical. A difficult question that these theories are confronted with concerns the normative force of their anticipated ideal end states in societies in which these end states have by no means been reached. Rawls, Habermas, and Honneth all use similar strategies to deal with this problem. They start from given normative intuitions and moral needs, reconstruct them in theoretical terms of "reasonable social cooperation," "communicative action," or "struggles for recognition," and discern, in Honneth's terms, an objective-intentional structure in the practices associated with these terms that point to an envisioned ideal end state.[14] In all cases, this is a liberal end state. And in all cases, it is maintained that the objective-intentional context liberal institutions and ideals provide citizens with is sufficiently neutral with respect to different ideas of the good life. Although Rawls, Habermas, and Honneth all acknowledge the fact that some ideals of self-realization and self-determination do not seem to fit into their "neutral" normative frameworks, they trust in the adequateness of their reconstructions of prevalent normative ideals and expect that—through social struggles—ever more people and cultural frameworks will meet their normative frameworks "halfway." The implicit suggestion of this strategy is that once people have morally embraced these frameworks, they will—in retrospect—understand that the beliefs and allegiances they sacrificed for the greater goal of a just and reasonable liberal order were not that essential to their individual well-being after all.

Theories that take the latter route are more sensitive to the occurrence of tragic conflicts. They acknowledge that liberal normative frameworks are—both with regard to their moral foundations and to their practical effects—not neutral and that they may clash in irreconcilable ways with other values. Raz's perfectionism makes it clear that liberalism stands for a substantive nonneutral ethics of pluralism. Although he tends to reify the liberal outlook to such an extent that its cherished social forms become rather uncriticizable, he at least makes it clear that liberalism is not a political tradition that transcends all social conflicts and can give all parties to such conflicts their proper place and equal opportunities within a liberal order. Liberalism itself struggles for recognition in a social world that encompasses many comprehensive doctrines that engage in such struggles. To the extent that it gains political power and social adherence, liberalism is able to lend social, legal, and political credibility to its ideals of political and personal freedom, self-determination and self-realization, toleration, moral pluralism, and so on. To the extent that this struggle is controlled by the use of public reason, this is not necessarily reprehensible. But the fact that it is controlled by the use of public reason does not warrant that personal losses may not be experienced by those who do not fit in well into the liberal scheme.

The use of public reason calls for self-restraint and sometimes the transformation or even the disciplining of given allegiances—and this not only as an "admission fee" to liberal-democratic society. Rather, learning to live with ethical and political conflicts, sacrifice, loss, toleration of the intolerable, and (therefore) with demands of self-restraint and self-transcendence is a daily reality of social life in even the most tolerant pluralist societies. For this reason, competition for social esteem that is "free from pain" seems to be an impossibility. For more or less autonomous, self-reflective citizens of pluralist societies, the demand of ego-demarcation that Honneth stresses as a demand only of early childhood never comes to an end. Throughout their lives, individuals have to choose in favor of some values and against others. And they have to endure tragic and irreparable sacrifices, including the experience of being denigrated by others, which necessarily accompany such choices. Furthermore, autonomous and self-reflective individuals do not all make the same choices. Out of respect for each other's autonomy, they have to respect the choices that others make—even if they cannot possibly give their esteem to the values and practices of others. Yet, other people may prefer being true to themselves while challenging the boundaries of the legally and socially acceptable to gain what they feel is only the false esteem of others. Indeed, I fear that a value horizon in which competition for social esteem acquires "a

form free from pain" would do away with individuality altogether—
that rebellious, self-determining and self-realizing, often erring, but
still most important source of invention and social criticism that provides the theory of recognition with its normative foundation and its
practical possibilities.

Of course, liberal theories that are perceptive of tragic conflicts
are also loosely inspired by a conception of an ideal end state of social and political struggles. Since they are liberal theories, they hold
that the notions of the right and the good liberalism has to offer are
worthy of everyone's respect. And they would welcome a world in
which everyone would embrace them. Yet, this alternative conception of liberalism stresses the fact that the path to a more liberal society will be paved with tragic conflicts over allegiances to the
sacred, to community, and to individual character. And it fears that
this is not just a contingent phenomenon, but a necessary consequence of the conceptual tensions at the heart of liberalism. To put it
bluntly: the path to a more liberal society will be paved with tragic
conflicts and losses because—for all we know—the liberal ideal will
always remain vulnerable to tragic conflicts.

It is important to understand that this tragic view is meant to
be more than a politically correct footnote to liberal literature. My
claim is not just that liberalism is confronted with tragic conflicts,
because that could still be rationalized by pointing to the greater
good of a just and good liberal society. Rather, I want to argue for the
much stronger claim that the theories I have discussed in the present study can only be said to be liberal theories insofar as they acknowledge their tragic predicament. Either implicitly or explicitly,
every normative political theory tries to sketch a route to an ideal
end state. Theorists who take the former route just indicated, the
route that follows an allegedly objective-intentional path through
history, tend to judge the character of normative conflicts that occur
along this historic path solely from the perspective of the ideal end
states they anticipate. What is alarming about this strategy is that
it puts a lid on the presumption of equal value, that is, it is not sufficiently open to the ideal end states that inspire the actions and beliefs of those who question the liberal route. For as seen from this
perspective, these end states must appear to be deeply mistaken—
that is, as hopelessly out of touch with the objective-intentional path
through history. The alternative conception I advocate warns
against the theoretical reification of ideal end states. Although it understands that it is not possible to engage in normative argumentation without anticipating such an end state, it holds that open-ended

conflicts are as important to the continuous reevaluation of conceptions of ideal end states as the latter are to the evaluation of concrete normative conflicts.

So paradoxically, once liberalism admits that it is not a neutral doctrine but just one party to social struggles over questions of justice, social esteem, and self-realization, it becomes less dogmatic and more tolerant to difference and to the tragic conflicts that may spring from it. Furthermore, it becomes more liberal, because it is able to take the moral claims of marginalized groups within liberal societies much more seriously than versions of liberalism that keep trying to prove that there is an objective-intentional route to a just society that will benefit the legitimate needs of all—understood as individuals, not just as politically autonomous citizens. Although there is no doubt that the authors who disagree with this argument often look for ways in which their theories could respond to this criticism, my claim is that they will not succeed in their attempts as long as they conceptualize their aim for neutrality in the wrong way. We may conclude that Honneth's answer to the first question of this chapter, how given standards of expectation and evaluation affect personal experience, is well taken. His answer to the second question, how feelings of a lack of well-being could motivate individuals to change given standards, is too optimistic. Although it seems valid that such feelings can form a motivational basis for social critique, Honneth's claim that the value of given social struggles can be sufficiently assessed from the perspective of an objective-intentional context of life is not well founded. For this reason, it seems to be more practical to propose that Honneth's normative point of view articulates the requirements of ethical life that are crucial to the best articulation of liberal-democratic visions of solidarity we can give today.

9

~

Vulnerability and Responsibilities of Liberal Citizenship

After the discussion of the need for recognition, the question becomes important of how—in a positive vein—standards of evaluation and expectation affect the ability of individuals to perceive themselves as autonomous, reasonable, pluralist, and tolerant. As we have seen, this is dependent on several types of emotional, legal, and social recognition. It must be the aim of both liberal institutions and social practices to guarantee these substantive forms of recognition to all members of societies. So long as we primarily concentrate on public reason, we can only—rather tautologically—state that the capacities for autonomy, reasonableness, respect for pluralism, and toleration should be protected and fostered because they are prerequisites for the flourishing of a just society that is coordinated through the use of public reason. But once we understand that this is contingent upon modes of recognition that are prerequisites for individual and collective well-being, we can see that they ultimately derive their value from the fact that they are capacities and virtues that help us cope with our highly vulnerable, recognition-dependent social nature.

Vulnerability and responsibility

In the history of political philosophy, much has been said about the protection of vulnerabilities.[1] John Stuart Mill's harm principle, which starts from the fact that we are vulnerable to what others

163

may inflict on us, comes to mind. The harm principle states that "the only purpose for which power can be rightfully exercised over any member of a civilized community, against his will, is to prevent harm to others."[2] According to this principle, three aspects of human liberty should never be harmed: first, liberty of conscience (involving liberty of thought and feeling, of opinion, "moral and theological sentiments," and freedom of expression). Second, liberty of "tastes and pursuits; of framing the plan of our life to suit our own character" as long as others are not harmed by this liberty. And third, the "freedom to unite, for any purpose not involving harm to others."[3]

Mill correctly stresses the fact that action as well as inaction may harm the liberty of others, thus inaction as regards the failure to provide members of society with the social prerequisites for these three liberties must be understood as morally wrong.[4] In this sense, and to the extent that they can, governments as well as individuals have a duty to provide members of society with these prerequisites. If they do not, they are likely to cause harm to others. On the action side of the argument, the harm principle is usually understood as preventing both the government and individual citizens from using forms of coercion against individuals who stand for ideas of personal excellence or social and political projects that many think are repugnant, but are not necessarily harmful to others. In this sense, the harm principle protects the negative liberties of citizens of pluralist liberal societies. Here, it may seem that we are confronted with a problem. Throughout the present study, I have argued that liberalism is a moderately perfectionist doctrine; that liberal societies and citizens cannot and should not aim to be neutral as regards the value of autonomy, reasonableness, pluralism, and toleration. Yet, at least in one possible interpretation, the harm principle seems to suggest that it would be wrong for liberals to defend these values. For in liberal societies, the social and political power of these values sets limits to the options of individuals. To be sure, they do so in special ways; ways that foster a liberal order. But we have seen that such an order is still likely to affect negatively the liberties of individuals and groups that do not easily fit the liberal scheme. Must the conclusion be that even the most ideal liberal order must be rejected because it is likely to harm the liberties and the individual or collective well-being of some of its citizens?

It would be wrong to interpret the harm principle in this way. "Causing harm" means, by definition, to act wrongly. But this presupposes that anyone who says that harm is being caused in a particular situation speaks from a moral position that is guided by certain standards of expectation and evaluation from which stems her understanding of what is wrong. As Joseph Raz puts it: "Without . . . a connection to a moral theory the harm principle is a formal principle lacking specific concrete content and leading to no policy conclusions."[5] Anyone (members of government, individual citizens, etc.) who claims that harm is being done implicitly states that the moral standards of expectation and evaluation from which she speaks are justified. Liberal standards of expectation and evaluation regard the protection of the integrity of the individual, the protection of the practices of self-determination and self-realization that govern her life, as their highest moral purpose. For liberals, causing harm is equivalent to showing a lack of respect for the integrity of individuals who are in need of specific conditions of well-being. Practices of public reasonableness, justice, pluralism, and toleration are designed to protect individuals from preventable vulnerabilities, that is, avoidable harms to (the conditions of) their well-being.

This substantive interpretation of the harm principle does not prevent liberal governments and citizens from moderately perfectionist strategies that foster conditions of integrity and autonomy in light of liberal ideals. But it is important that such strategies do not undermine liberal ideals. First, thoughts, feelings, and utterances that do not harm the capacity for autonomous action may not be harmed. Second, ways of life, practices related to ideals of personal excellence that respect the capacity for autonomous action may not be harmed. And third, associations of individuals that respect these limits may not be harmed. Yet, this reformulation of the harm principle is not a straightforward recipe for action. Most importantly, the harm principle should not be understood as a permit to directly coerce people into leading personally autonomous lives. Since respect for autonomy implies respect for individuality (understood as the locus of the capacity for autonomous action) liberal governments and citizens have a duty to seek on a case-by-case basis a balance between the legitimate claim of a liberal order that its values should be respected and sustained and the demand that individuality should be respected as a value in itself.

Liberalism promotes the conditions for personal integrity in terms of autonomy by defending an understanding of public reason along the lines I have sketched and by protecting and fostering forms of recognition that are conducive to liberal understandings of personal integrity. This aim of liberalism is justified insofar as it prevents individuals from ending up in vulnerable situations; situations that make it impossible for them to be recognized as, and to understand themselves as, full persons in the emotional, the legal, and the social sense, who are worthy of equal concern and respect by their fellow human beings and by the government. Yet, the tragedy of liberalism implies that the strategy to prevent individuals from ending up in vulnerable positions will sometimes backfire: the reign of liberal public reason and virtues cannot always avoid harming the personal integrity of individuals who aim to live their lives according to obligations of religion, community, or character that conflict with liberal ideas of the good. Here, liberal governments and citizens have special responsibilities that concern the toleration of "difference" in liberal societies. These responsibilities can best be understood if we tie them to the understanding of the dynamics of ideal liberal end states of justice and solidarity and concrete normative conflicts we developed earlier. This ideally encompasses three elements:

> 1. Prevalent liberal beliefs as to the demands of liberal justice and public reason and the demands of allegiances to the sacred, to the community, and to individual character. Such beliefs are inspired by liberal conceptions of an ideal end state of justice and solidarity, in which these sometimes conflicting demands are balanced.

> 2. Prevalent nonliberal beliefs as to the demands of justice and public reason and demands that emanate from allegiances to the sacred, to the community, and to individual character. Such beliefs are inspired by different conceptions of a balanced ideal end state of justice and solidarity that may conflict with liberal ideas.

> 3. Attempts by both parties to reach compromises or even forms of consensus that could help resolve the conflict in question.

For the sake of the argument, I assume that these conflicts occur in a society in which liberal beliefs are predominant. They have been accepted by the majority of citizens and govern, at least to a large extent, legal and political thought in this society. In such a society, it is likely that the normative conflict will be put on the social and political agenda by (sympathizers of) a group of people who feel that the liberal order harms their emotional, moral, and social dignity. Now, in a liberal society, such a claim will be taken seriously because it at least suggests that the liberal order does not live up to its highest aim. As seen from a liberal perspective, several outcomes of the debate over the issue are possible:[6]

1. The claim turns out to be justified.
2. The claim turns out not to be justified.
3. The claim turns out to be undecidable.

In the first case, prevalent liberal beliefs and the conception of an ideal end state of justice and solidarity that inspire them, will be altered. Some examples are provided by the once hot issues of political rights for the working classes and for women. A little over a century ago, it was possible for a respected liberal member of the English House of Commons, Robert Lowe, to state the following: "Because I am a Liberal . . . I regard as one of the greatest dangers . . . a proposal . . . to transfer power from the hands of property and intelligence, and to place it in the hands of men whose life is necessarily occupied in daily struggles for existence."[7] The ideal end state of justice and solidarity that Lowe envisaged clearly did not include suffrage for the working classes. And we can easily imagine how similar arguments against suffrage for women were being put forward. Meanwhile, the social struggle for universal suffrage has changed things for the better. The important thing is that, with this struggle, our understanding of what liberalism means and demands of us has changed. Claims to justice by individuals who were excluded from full participation in society have gradually been recognized as fully valid and have considerably changed the practices and ideals of liberalism as it exists today.

In the second case, prevalent liberal beliefs and the ideals that inspire them will not or will not considerably be altered. Here we may think of extremist right-wing parties that claim that they have a right to fully participate in the democratic process. In this case, the beliefs and ideals of contenders of the liberal order are so totally at odds with the liberal outlook that by recognizing their claims, a liberal society would endanger its own survival. It would legally validate a political point of view that explicitly aims not to respect all citizens (and to overthrow democratic institutions in the process). Liberalism cannot tolerate such a point of view. However, it can and should try to understand why such points of view are attractive to some citizens. Here, it will probably find that extremist right-wing parties prey on feelings of discontent or moral indignation among the population that liberal parties should be more sensitive to (they usually concern unemployment and questions of race and immigration). In this indirect sense, liberalism can learn from deeply immoral claims, but it should not be tolerant to these claims themselves because they represent threats to the integrity of persons and to the conditions of autonomy and moral pluralism that liberalism defends.[8]

The third case is the category in which tragic conflicts abound. Many controversial claims concerning the integrity of traditional communities, religious beliefs, and (experiments of) character come into these categories. Here, parties to the normative conflict should first try to find out to what extent the liberal order harms the integrity of other parties and to what extent the perspectives of the contending parties harm the legitimate needs and interests of citizens who wholeheartedly identify with liberal values and practices. In order for this to be possible, the parties will have to take each other's substantive convictions seriously. Most importantly, they should try to understand to what extent the state of affairs that triggered the normative conflict creates a situation in which individuals become highly vulnerable to the actions of others. The assessment of their vulnerability should first and foremost be undertaken in terms of the conditions of their physical and mental integrity. If it turns out that the liberal order harms conditions of integrity in unjust ways—that is, in ways that could be avoided without endangering the well-being of other citizens—then legal or social aspects of the liberal order in question will have to be changed. Yet, it cannot always be expected that the normative conflict will be wholly overcome by such an approach. Liberal societies may (and usually should) democratically decide not to leave questions of abortion and euthanasia totally up to individuals to decide (e.g., by mandating that an independent physician check whether there is sufficient reason for abortion or euthanasia), not to chastise pedophiles solely for their feelings (and to educate and possibly punish individuals who discriminate against them); or to grant indigenous or national groups a certain measure of cultural autonomy or political self-government. By doing so, they can partly meet the wishes of individuals whose obligations to the sacred, to character, and to community cannot be fully met within a liberal society. But liberal societies can only go so far as their aim to protect the integrity of individuals allows them to. They cannot meet every individual demand for justice for the simple reason that liberal conceptions of justice and the good do and always will conflict with some conceptions of justice and the good that do not fit into the liberal scheme.

Tragic conflicts do not only occur in the third case I just discussed. They occur in the first one as well. Struggles for equal legal recognition by the working classes, women, and other excluded groups have had and sometimes continue to have tragic aspects. An individual who engages in such struggles may be tormented by the tension between, on the one hand, her respect for many aspects of the law and social standards that (at least to some extent) recognize her as an individual worthy of respect and esteem and, on the other hand, her felt need to object to prevalent social expectations and interpretations of the law that might motivate her to actually break the law (e.g., through civil disobedience, which might result in her being punished for an action that at a later point in time will be understood as morally legitimate). The difference between the first and the third cases is not absolute. In the first case, normative conflicts that once had a tragic character eventually turned out not to be irreconcilable after all—although this does not mean that the tragedy of the situation was, at the time it occurred, not there. In the third case, it might well be that future liberal societies will find ways to deal successfully with normative conflicts which, in the here and now, seem to be irreconcilable and tragic. This remains an empirical question that no normative theory can answer. As to the "tragedy" of the second situation, it would be a mistake to claim that the strictly personal predicament of a deeply immoral person who cannot freely exercise, for instance, her racist obsessions is a tragic one. I have argued throughout that a willingness to relate to others on the basis of equal respect and a presumption of equal value is a precondition for a moral search for commonality. Acknowledging the tragedy of a situation from a normative point of view presupposes that one recognize that a morally valid, or at least tolerable feeling or belief has to be sacrificed because of other such feelings or beliefs. The predicament of a deeply immoral person does not fall within this category.[9]

This analysis of normative and possibly tragic conflicts enables me to go into the responsibilities of liberal governments and citizens of liberal societies.

1. Liberal governments and citizens will have to evaluate normative conflicts in the light of the aim to let the interests of all citizens in leading a good life matter equally. They should understand, however, that this aim is not a ready-made recipe for resolving normative conflicts. For what is at stake in such conflicts is precisely the question concerning notions of the right and the good, and of which practices as-

sociated with them can be tolerated in a liberal society. The
outcome of the debate that goes back and forth between contested ideal notions and given conceptions of what is of value
will possibly change the liberal understanding of what is
just, what is good, and what an ideal end state of law and
solidarity would look like.

2. Liberal governments and citizens will have to enter the
debate on the premise that they, or rather the social order
they identify with and uphold, may be responsible for the
predicament of the contending parties. Out of respect for individuality and conditions of autonomy and pluralism, they
will have to consider the possibility that much value must be
ascribed to the feelings, beliefs, and ideals, of these parties.

3. As a consequence of the second point, certain institutional conditions for a fair and unconstrained debate about
the conflict at hand must be guaranteed. Liberal governments have a special responsibility here, because they have
the means to see to it that these conditions are being met. In
trying to live up to this responsibility, they should acknowledge that the shaping of institutional or procedural conditions will itself be a hot issue in which many aspects of the
colliding convictions that eventually led to the tragic conflict
will already be articulated.

4. The conflict must first and foremost be assessed in terms
of avoidable vulnerabilities that the parties to the conflict
are subject to. Such vulnerabilities can best be assessed by
discussing the social conditions of personal well-being (in the
emotional, the legal, and the social sense) that shape the experience of the parties to the conflict. This is where things
become complex, because here the normative expectations of
the parties will clash most strongly. We may even expect battles of interpretation over what it means to be vulnerable to
the (in)action of others. For the liberal party to the conflict,
the aim must be to create a situation in which the needs of
the other parties will be harmed as little as possible. Yet, liberals cannot go so far as to indiscriminately recognize every
claim to justice; they are subject to limits set by their aim to
sustain and promote a pluralist social and political order in
which people can live autonomously. They cannot and should
not coerce all members of liberal societies into leading au-

tonomous lives, but they may legitimately create a social order in which it is easier to lead an autonomous life than one that turns its back on the demands of (liberal interpretations of) personal autonomy.

Virtues of liberal citizenship

Finally, it seems necessary to tie this understanding of the responsibilities of liberal governments and citizens with respect to tragic conflicts to recent debates over virtues of liberal citizenship. After all, a society will only be as liberal as the civic virtues of its members allow. Contemporary liberal thought often seems allergic to the idea of citizenship virtues. This is understandable. Pluralist societies cannot easily be conceived of from an integrationist perspective that envisages a narrowly defined set of virtues for all citizens. Yet, we have seen that liberal thought has certain moderately perfectionist traits. With this comes an understanding of virtues conducive to the functioning and flourishing of a liberal society.

Autonomy, reasonableness, the affirmation of value pluralism, toleration, and sensitivity to the vulnerability of individuals are virtues of those who are willing and able to question their own interests and beliefs and those of others. These virtues presuppose a certain adherence or loyalty to the main institutions of liberal society. But inherent in this is the expectation that citizens should not just accept these institutions as they are. Rather, the liberal citizen is characterized by a critical loyalty. The liberal citizen understands that liberalism is not just about granting equal rights, but rather about defending an understanding of the right and the good that is responsive to claims that emanate from individual conceptions of self-realization and self-determination.

These virtues may be called general virtues of liberal citizenship. But virtues characteristic of the various domains of mutual recognition should also be considered. It may be clear that citizens should be able to restrain their own interests and needs insofar as these could harm the needs and interests of others. The virtue of self-restraint is important in intimate relations, legal relations, and within communities of value.[10] Individuals who do not restrain themselves within intimate relationships—who use their loved ones and friends as means, not as ends, so to speak—not only risk being abandoned by them because even bonds of love and friendship have their limits, but also, more fundamentally, risk harming the physical and mental integrity of their loved ones' and friends' (and probably also their own) ability to articulate their needs in a self-confident manner. This is fundamental for the development and sustainment of a person's well-being within other spheres of society. Because children are future citizens, and because adult loved ones are either full citizens or are otherwise worthy of concern and respect, it is imperative that in intimate relationships one restrain oneself in such a manner that the basic self-confidence of one's significant others will not be impaired. And mutatis mutandis, the same argument goes for the two other domains of recognition we discussed. In legal relations, the citizen should restrain herself in such a manner that the rights and therefore the self-respect of her fellow citizens will not be harmed (this of course presupposes that these rights are legitimate, that they do not inflict preventable harms on rights holders or on others). Within communities of value, self-restraint is necessary because liberal democratic solidarity presupposes that we act on the presumption that our fellow human beings are in principle worthy of equal esteem. Here too, the aim of the virtuous citizen is to treat others primarily as ends, not just as means.

The virtue of self-restraint requires that one be able to transcend one's own interests and needs and to take into account the interests and needs of others. This brings us to the virtue of toleration, one that is stressed by all liberal theorists, even by those who normally are very reluctant to speak in terms of citizenship virtues. Of course, toleration is a heavily contested concept. Quite different attitudes are associated with it. Some think of toleration merely as the capacity to live with moral pluralism in a "live and let live" sense. Yet, in our understanding of citizenship, toleration presupposes that citizens not only accept pluralism but affirm it. Being a tolerant individual implies that one respects not only the rights and liberties of others, but also their choice for forms of self-realization that one would not choose for oneself, but that can legitimately be made within a liberal-democratic framework. Furthermore, being tolerant in this sense implies that one recognize claims for equality and liberty by individuals and groups that are illegitimately discriminated against by the law or, more generally, by received standards of expectation and evaluation. The virtue of critical loyalty to liberal institutions and practices presupposes this "active" or "militant" notion of toleration.[11]

As to explicitly political virtues, Stephen Macedo has conceptualized such virtues analogous to the classic separation of powers into judicial, legislative, and executive powers. This is a fine proposal, especially because it makes perfect sense to understand this separation of powers as the institutionalization of a valuable "division of labor" within the use of practical reason, the instances of which are all necessary moments of a fair balance in the self-government of a liberal society.

Judicial virtues enable people to judge states of affairs from an "impartial" standpoint. This is of course related to the basic terms that define what should be considered just and fair; it is not (cannot be) a totally detached impartiality. The virtue of impartiality stands for the ability to respect the rights of others, and to weigh their social and political claims from a presumption of equal value. Attachment to principle is another judicial virtue, which stands for the "reluctance to bargain and compromise where rights and liberal fairness are at stake."[12] Judicial virtues are virtues of justice and active toleration; they enable citizens to identify injustices that concern themselves and others, and that weigh them in the light of principles of justice they accept.

Legislative virtues concern the ability of citizens to engage in processes of opinion formation and will formation. The good citizen is able to engage in dialogues with others in order to reach compromises or even consensus in affairs that concern them all. In part 3, we saw that a citizen is expected to articulate and defend her beliefs in a consistent and sincere way and to act consistently on these beliefs. Furthermore, she is expected to acknowledge the authenticity of the beliefs and claims of others and the possibility that others might articulate points of view that could prompt her to reevaluate and to possibly transform her own beliefs. Finally, she understands that a plurality of opinions does not necessarily have to be overcome so long as this plurality does not threaten the social and political order and legitimacy of a liberal society.[13]

Finally, executive virtues enable citizens to act effectively on insights gained and decisions made by the exercise of judicial and legislative virtues. Executive virtues such as perseverance and independence of thought enable people to reach for certain goals in ways that are both effective and principled. Members of interest groups and voluntary associations in civil society in particular exhibit these virtues. They change the broad public opinion and put particular themes on the official political agenda (Greenpeace, Amnesty International, emancipation groups, etc.). And perhaps more moderately, executive virtues may inspire citizens to participate in local programs (varying from participation in official local politics to voluntary work in shelters for the homeless and for refugees, environmental programs, etc.).[14] Generally speaking, these virtues enable citizens to stand firmly for what they believe in.

Macedo makes the important point that, just like in the institutions of the constitutional state, a stable balance between these virtues of practical reason in moral character is necessary. None of the three virtues should overwhelm the other two. "Detachment without engagement," "tolerance without discrimination," and the pursuance of own goals without regard for others will harm the balance that is needed to let social relations flourish.[15]

A liberal order may be expected to function and even to flourish if a considerable number of citizens act on these virtues. However, the very logic of the liberal framework makes it impossible to legally enforce many of these virtues. The liberal state cannot oblige its citizens to act virtuously, for this would entail the state violating the very conditions of autonomy and responsibility it seeks to foster as prime values in social cooperation. To come to terms with this, it is wise to differentiate between legal obligations that are absolutely necessary to avoid the occurrence of apparent injustices from voluntary virtuous behavior that may be expected to sustain and strengthen society and the well-being of citizens in a farther-reaching sense. Often, legal obligations come with rights—although legal obligations to respect animals, the environment, and cultural communities show that these obligations do not necessarily spring from the rights of the beings or entities we should respect. In these cases, the justification of legal obligations is less immediate and may be given in terms of decency, the prevention of cruelty, or the collective well-being of particular groups within society. But if we stick to the perspective of individual rights and legal obligations, it is safe to say that this protects individuals from avoidable vulnerabilities and guarantees opportunities for them to flourish as individuals. In a social world governed by rights, it is obligatory that citizens respect rights—particularly basic rights such as freedom of speech and conscience, rights to association, legal protection, due process, passive and active political rights and rights to education, health care, and social security. A liberal society should prevent such basic rights, which protect human dignity on a fundamental level, from being distributed in ways that make some individuals or groups more vulnerable than others.

Up to a point, the virtues of self-restraint and self-transcendence are legal obligations. In our pursuit of individual aims, we may not harm the physical or mental integrity of others, nor may we harm their integrity as rights holders. We need to restrain ourselves in order to respect the rights of others and we often need to transcend our subjective convictions and desires in order to be pluralists who remain open to the value of the convictions of others. Beyond the realm of legal obligations, the virtues of self-restraint and self-transcendence should govern the conduct of individuals who want to take seriously the tragic predicament of liberalism. These virtues are of tantamount importance for reaching a sense of self by means of which the tensions between individuality and the demands of public reason can be endured.[16] For if the perspective that I have developed and defended in this study makes any sense at all, we must conclude that liberalism is a highly demanding normative doctrine that asks individuals to internalize two normative perspectives that can hardly ever be totally reconciled. In order to live up to the requirements of liberal public reason and the limits legitimate law imposes on the personal freedom of individuals, individuals have to restrain themselves. They have to subject their personal convictions to the more impartial perspective of public reason in order to make pluralism possible. This also calls for self-transcendence in the light of the legitimate needs of others. It is true that for some the exercise of these virtues will be more easy than for others. And it is also true that, in practice, individuals who cannot or do not wish to restrain or transcend their subjective perspectives will often be forced to do so. But whether self-restraint and self-transcendence are engaged in on a voluntary basis or not, losses will be felt. The capacity of individuals to endure such losses and still remain actively tolerant, is tacitly presupposed by every theory that holds out the liberal promise of justice, equality, and personal freedom for all.

Conclusions to Part 4

In the preceding parts of this book, it was argued that the tragedy of liberalism is a noncontingent, indeed unavoidable predicament of liberal normative theories. In this part, it has been asked what theoretical and practical consequences spring from this fact. A deepened understanding of the irreducible value of individuality and the tensions—and dialectical interaction—between individuality and the demands of public reason and, more generally, the demands that spring from membership of pluralist liberal communities is the result. By embracing an understanding of social relations in terms of mutual recognition and disrespect, it becomes possible to elaborate the idea that liberalism rests on substantive assumptions as to the value of moral pluralism, the ideal of personal autonomy, and various demands of moral character in diverse settings of modern societies. A firmly articulated liberal-democratic conception of relations of mutual recognition should be seen as an attractive starting point for debates on the acceptability of this conception in pluralist societies. Yet, it is important to differentiate between an ideal conception of liberal-democratic society and the role that this conception may legitimately play in the assessment of normative conflicts in the here and now, that is, in societies that cannot be said to live up to the ideal conception. An ideal conception of ethical life should be understood as an attempt to articulate the expectations as to the nature of legitimate law and solidarity in an ideal end state of social cooperation that adherents to the ideal anticipate in their normative thinking. Yet, normative theorists should realize that the often controversial nature of their ideal conceptions is a good reason to take seriously the claims of those who cannot agree to them. For at least some of these claims may be expected to articulate normative perspectives that liberals should take seriously—precisely because they may motivate liberals to change their very understanding of an ideal end state of justice and solidarity. Such an approach makes it possible to sketch a rudimentary yet not unpromising picture of the heuristic value of tragic conflicts that the liberal outlook is a party to. Liberalism can learn from tragic conflicts as soon as it recognizes that it plays a role in their generation. For this reason, liberal theories and societies that take the tragedy of liberalism seriously may be expected to become more liberal by doing so. For recognizing the tragedy of liberalism mandates that one be sensitive to the vulnerable positions into which variants of liberalism that are too self-assured about the reasonableness and neutrality of their normative perspectives may maneuver individuals. Only such a sensitivity will enable liberalism to recognize and to repair avoidable harms to forms of individuality that may not perfectly fit into the liberal order, but that do not necessarily harm the integrity of others. Since I have argued throughout that the acceptability and indeed the generalizability of moral norms and principles of justice must be judged from their contribution to the sustainment of a pluralist world in which individuality and not just formal citizenship is to be respected unconditionally, this consequence of my interpretation of liberalism provides us with a strong indication of its general worth.

Still, I concede that my interpretation only seems to have value for assessing the question as to how we could learn to live with—not how we could totally overcome—the tragedy of liberalism. But then again, given the character of most contemporary liberal theories, the first question may at the moment be more important for the revision of liberal political philosophy. It is true that I have not offered more than preliminary remarks that require much more research. But I do believe that an interesting ethics of citizenship could be developed from the idea that we need to understand how individuals could learn to endure the tragedy of liberalism by means of forms of self-restraint and self-transcendence that are based on an affirmation of the value of pluralism and personal as well as public autonomy.

Let me now return to my hypothesis and arrive at a conclusion to the theoretical core (parts 2, 3, and 4) of this study.

> 1. Because liberalism has a purposive structure, that is, it is not an ethically neutral doctrine—there are normative conflicts in which its aim to let the interests of all citizens in leading a good life matter equally cannot but generate tragic conflicts.

> 2. In generating tragic conflicts, liberalism sometimes undermines conceptions of the good life that it aims to tolerate; and (thereby) its own aim to let the interests of all citizens in leading a good life matter equally.

These two hypotheses still hold. Yet, the most important conclusion is that our insights into the tragedy of liberalism do not condemn us to resignation when we are confronted with tragic conflicts. Although it seems highly likely that tragic conflicts will always occur in pluralist liberal societies, the possibility that at least some of them may be overcome should not be ruled out in advance. This is a reassuring conclusion, one that provides us with a strong reason to recognize and to endure tragic conflicts. It also provides us with a strong reason to openly articulate the purposive structure of liberalism. Only one step is required to make such an articulation acceptable: liberalism should openly admit that it is a normative doctrine that does not transcend but very often is a party to normative conflicts that occur in modern societies. Generally speaking, reasonableness is not a capacity that only characterizes liberal individuals. Every worldview that articulates normative-practical directives defends a conception of reasonableness. And it is in finding out what reasonableness could mean for adherents to different worldviews that liberal understandings of reasonableness are confronted time and time again with their own limits. For although liberal doctrines offer strong normative perspectives on the conduct of pluralism, they cannot transcend the competitive pluralism and the social struggles to which they are, and probably always will be, parties.

It would be slightly redundant to reevaluate in detail all the findings of the preceding parts in the light of our findings in chapters 7, 8, and 9. Yet, some points are significant. The moderately perfectionist strategy for public deliberation that I presented in part 3 still seems to offer a promising perspective on liberal attempts to come to terms with concrete tragic conflicts. It should be supplemented with an understanding of the heuristic value of tragic conflicts. Here, it is particularly important to acknowledge that public deliberation must be understood as a justificatory strategy that presupposes the validity of demanding relations of mutual recognition. These relations are far more substantive and historically situated than initially suggested by a mere acknowledgment of the rationality of procedures for deliberation. Axel Honneth's theory of recognition derives its understanding of the moral and deliberative autonomy of individuals from an anthropological—not from a formal-linguistic—account of their socio-ontological constitution. I find this to be a more promising approach. First, the moral psychology it rests upon helps us understand why individuals are motivated to articulate experiences of injustice in the first place. Second, it provides us with a clear (although ideal-typical) account of the social mechanisms that may be held responsible for various forms of injustice. And third, it at least in principle provides us with a language in terms of which we can better understand the nature of tragic conflicts. It is true that, because of its concentration on an "objective-intentional path" that would guide struggles for recognition in the modern world, Honneth's theory is not sufficiently perceptive to the occurrence of such conflicts. But I hope to have shown the perceptiveness of this theory to such conflicts. All that is needed is a clear distinction between the substantive normative perspective that the theory is guided by and the given struggles for recognition it reflects on (that may or may not respond to this perspective).

> 3. The tragic predicament of liberalism seems to be related to its explicit aim to promote moral unity when it comes to the use of public reason and public deliberation; and to its implicit aim to promote key components for "private" conceptions of the good life such as the ideal of personal autonomy and the affirmation of ethical pluralism.

This hypothesis also still holds. Yet, we have found that it should not be the primary aim of liberal theories to overcome the tensions that spring from this aim by means of a prioristic conceptual frameworks that claim to overcome them from the outset. Indeed, we have found that liberalism should be ready to endure these tensions, because our understanding of what liberalism requires is heavily—and noncontingently—dependent on the insights that tragic conflicts between the two moments of this aim confront them with. The phrase "seems to be related" in this hypothesis is much too weak, then. As a conclusion to the theoretical core of this study, we may reformulate this hypothesis into the confident assertion that the tragic predicament of liberalism springs from liberalism's attempt to articulate a purposive understanding of moral unity—based on an affirmation of the values of pluralism and autonomy—for a pluralist world. In this world, this understanding of moral unity will always remain controversial. But a correct understanding of the moral foundations of liberalism makes it clear why liberals are obliged to revise their understanding of moral unity whenever members of the pluralist world come up with valid reasons for them to do so. Here, valid reasons are reasons that show that the current liberal understandings of (the conditions of) pluralism and autonomy—and the conceptions of justice and the good life they inspire—illegitimately discriminate against conceptions of justice and the good life that deserve to be respected in a liberal order.

PART V

~

Liberalism and Multiculturalism

Introduction

From the theoretical conclusions arrived at in this study many practical questions arise. What limits does the tragedy of liberalism set to social policies of welfare states? Is there a tragic conflict between the conditions for leading a good life and the demands of the liberal market? What does the tragedy of liberalism mean for the application of law to individual cases? Could feminist theory benefit from the thesis of the tragedy of liberalism?[1] It has not been the aim of this study to answer these questions. Still, it seems to be a good idea to try to at least tentatively find out what advantages my interpretation of liberalism could have over other perspectives in assessing such questions. For this purpose, I want to discuss some questions of multiculturalism.

Given the interests of this study, it may not come as a surprise that I will concentrate on the topic of multiculturalism. More than any other debate in recent years (except perhaps for the debate over communitarianism that preceded it), the debate over multiculturalism has prompted liberalism to reevaluate its central concepts in the light of new social and cultural developments. In multicultural societies—societies in which certain groups are perceived and often present themselves as cultures with distinct identities—pluralism seems to be more visible than in the (largely nonimmigrant) European societies in which liberalism originated. This is not to say that these societies were not characterized by pluralism before the post-World War II period of mass migration to Western European

181

countries; it is just to say that pluralism—which in the debate over multiculturalism is primarily understood as cultural pluralism and the many possibilities (of a flourishing pluralism) and fears (of social fragmentation) that are associated with it—has only recently become an issue of public concern. It is not that societies that previously were homogeneous have suddenly become very pluralistic; it is just that the character of pluralism has changed. On the one hand, cultural differences are greater than they used to be because immigrant cultures have—both in size and in social and political organization—become more visible. On the other hand, there is a trend toward stressing the importance of cultural belonging as a prerequisite for leading a good life. Both trends press liberalism to reflect on questions of multiculturalism. For if it is indeed true that cultural belonging is a prerequisite for leading a good life, then liberalism has the difficult task of fostering cultural belonging in a society characterized by cultural pluralism. Against this background, the question of multiculturalism must be understood as a question of the amount of cultural diversity and cultural authenticity a liberal society can allow of without undermining its own ideals of public justice and individual well-being.

I do not aim to design an agenda for the treatment of policy questions concerning multiculturalism; rather, I want to concentrate on two partly overlapping, partly conflicting ideals that play an important role in the philosophical debate over multiculturalism: first, the ideal of being true to one's own values, cultural allegiances, practices, and so forth, and second, the general ideal of justice, peace, and mutually advantageous social cooperation among those who inhabit pluralist societies. Of course, today the debate over the conflicts between these ideals takes place in terms that are highly contemporary. Until recently, the ideal of being true to one's own cultural identity was very often associated with an anachronistic shortsightedness that longs for former (imagined) times of complete cultural authenticity, while the second idea of universal justice was presented as the most enlightened and just view imaginable.[2] But in the last decade or so, things have changed. I aim to find out to what extent the two often conflicting ideals can be taken seriously from a liberal perspective.

In chapter 10, I will introduce the specific (meta)questions of multiculturalism I want to address: What is a culture? Is it a fixed context that has a normative priority over the individual, or should it primarily be understood as a prerequisite for individual flourishing that is to be judged from the perspective of the freedom of the individual? Subsequently, I will discuss Charles Taylor's influential analysis of conflicts over multiculturalism in the Canadian Province of Quebec. Taylor's "liberal-communitarian" outlook has played an important role in putting questions of multiculturalism on the philosophical agenda. It enables us to get a grasp of the problems at issue, but challenges some fundamental liberal intuitions in ways that make it necessary to look for less communitarian, more liberal answers to these problems.

In chapter 11, I will look for such liberal answers in the "cosmopolitan" alternative to multiculturalism sketched by Jeremy Waldron and the "group-differentiated rights" approach of Will Kymlicka. It will not be my aim to discuss these strategies comprehensively. Rather, I will try to find out to what extent different theoretical framings of the debate make it possible to develop a satisfactory liberal perspective on questions of multiculturalism. The group-differentiated rights approach will prove to be more fruitful than the cosmopolitan alternative. Ultimately, the aim is to show that an either implicit or explicit sensitivity to liberalism's tragic predicament is important for the assessment of questions of multiculturalism.

10

~

Multiculturalism and
Cultural Authenticity

Let us first look at the term *multiculturalism*. Just like many other
important terms in political debates and in political theory, it has
more than one meaning. In its least specified meaning, a society
characterized by "multiculturalism" is simply one in which many
cultures live together. Used in this sense, multiculturalism is mainly
a descriptive term. Yet, multiculturalism can, and very often does,
take on a more affirmative and normative meaning. It can become a
fighting creed. People who argue in favor of multiculturalism do not
just say that many cultures live alongside each other in one society
(for most Western democracies this is simply a fact). Rather, they
argue for certain forms of multiculturalism and, accordingly, for policies that enable different cultures to flourish alongside each other
within liberal societies.

The debate over multiculturalism has changed the ways in
which many liberals talk about questions of rights and social integration. Leading liberals of the 1970s, such as John Rawls and
Ronald Dworkin, put the needs of individual citizens, understood as
holders of inalienable individual rights, high on the agenda of political theory. This was understandable. Their work from this period
may be said to reflect primarily on issues such as individual freedom, equality, nondiscrimination, and civil disobedience as they
where shaped by the political struggle for equal civil rights that
dominated the 1960s. What was at stake was the equal legal recognition of all members of society. In the 1990s, liberals increasingly

talk about "collective rights," "group rights," and "cultural rights."[1] Equal rights are—at least in normative theory—no longer a hot issue; progressive and conservative theorists largely agree that—in some interpretation or other—equal rights for all citizens are a prerequisite for a just society. Yet, as soon as this consensus was reached, another question came to the fore in political debates. If the constitution and most legal and political practices in democratic societies recognize that all citizens, irrespective of their race, gender, ethnicity, and so forth, should be treated as equals, then the question emerges, what does the equality-based treatment of individuals mean for their concrete identities—that is, their identities as people who do understand themselves and others in terms that stress differences?

How (not) to talk about multiculturalism

In order to discuss properly questions of multiculturalism, it is important that we first offer a definition of culture. Here, it makes sense to look at culture from two angles, first, from a rather detached, descriptive perspective. Second, we can look at culture from our personal experiences. As seen from the detached perspective, culture may appear as "learned behavior (and its products) to which social meaning is accorded."[2] We may say that a certain group of people is characterized by certain practices, that they were brought up with the idea that it is important to sustain these practices, and that they ascribe meanings to these practices, which we then take to be critical to their cultural self-understanding. In turn, "our" (the detached onlookers') understanding of the meaning of these practices for "them" may prompt us to recognize individual members of this group of people as members of a specific culture. As seen from this perspective, formal (institutional) and informal behavioral patterns of identifiable groups ("Acting like a Hopi Indian," ". . . like a German," ". . . like a Frenchman," etc.) make up a culture. We then identify cultures by ascribing more or less objective features to them.

Of course, this is a simplified account of the "descriptive" perspective on culture. But in all its simplicity, it is not unintelligible. There is no doubt that we often look at culture in this way. In a sense, we all are early anthropologists. We travel through Mexico or regularly buy our food at a Turkish shop in the neighborhood and generalize our experiences in ways that result in descriptions of "the" Mexican or "the" (immigrant) Turkish culture. Yet, there is a well-known danger in this way of thinking about culture. It invites us to think about cultures in terms of easily identifiable closed contexts that are internally characterized by well-defined and rather unquestioned standards of expectation and evaluation. As a result, we tend to understand the social world as a patchwork of many relatively closed and therefore often incommensurable contexts of value and action.

It is only by taking seriously forms of participation and individual experience of members of cultures that we can see the limits of this understanding of culture.[3] As seen from this participatory perspective, culture is both given and continuously being (re)produced by cooperating individuals. The "given" element of culture consists in the historically produced behavioral patterns we assemble through interacting with others. Such behavioral patterns serve the purpose of bringing unity to the life of individuals and collectives: they show us how we are expected to conduct our lives in the social environments we inhabit, they enable us to understand the meanings of practices and objects, and thereby to interpret the world and act in it. This "given" aspect of culture is not something we can choose to either accept or not; a noncultural life is an existential impossibility. As Clifford Geertz puts it: "When seen as a set of symbolic devices for controlling behavior . . . culture provides the link between what men are intrinsically capable of becoming and what they actually, one by one, in fact become. Becoming human is becoming individual, and we become individual under the guidance of cultural patterns, historically created systems of meaning in terms of which we give form, order, point, and direction to our lives."[4] Thus, culture is not just a given behavioral pattern; it is rather a means to govern (patterns of) behavior. Because of this aspect of governing behavior cultures should, already at the most fundamental level, not be understood as rather static and closed entities that predetermine our actions and beliefs, but rather as means through which we guide our actions and beliefs. And as we know from experience, the guidance of actions and beliefs is closely related to reactions to many different circumstances that may prompt individuals to change the ways in which they govern their actions and beliefs and, therefore, the substantive characteristics of their culture. This brings us to the question, to what extent is culture something that individuals produce?

As a rule, a culture (here in the sense of "civilization" or "nation") is made up of many different, far more specific cultures. We can talk about "political cultures," "occupational cultures," "bureaucratic cultures," "the gay culture," "cultures of unemployment," and so on, which all fall within larger cultures such as the broad legal or democratic culture of a society.[5] If we accept the fact that cultures help individuals and groups govern their actions and beliefs, then all these cultures may be said to represent ways of organizing human action and aspiration. Through institutional design, shared symbols, forms and codes of communication, and so on, they enable individuals to govern their lives in meaningful ways. Cultures are continuously being produced and reproduced for this purpose.[6] Of course, the purposes and organizational strategies of some may conflict with those of others. Clashes of cultures are possible, and within cultures, disagreements over the adequate organization of social cooperation can and often do occur. Cultures (or rather the individuals who have cultural power) may discriminate against some of their own members or the members of other cultures. Cultures are historically constructed means of governing beliefs and actions of individuals, and they are produced and sustained with certain purposes in mind, such as securing power of certain elites, protecting and promoting ideals of personal and collective identity (as in gay or ethnic cultures), or effectively organizing instrumental rationality (as in the corporate culture of firms or bureaucratic cultures).

If all this is correct, then it may be said that, in a way, virtually every society is "multicultural."[7] The political, legal, economic, social, and familial needs of each society and its members will be served by interacting political, legal, economic, social, and familial cultures. And members of such societies usually participate in more than one of these cultures. Depending on their needs, their roles, and their status within these different cultures, they occupy a certain place within society. They may be active politicians, voters, or political outcasts; judges, criminals, or law-abiding citizens; employers, employees, or unemployed; active volunteers in social programs or social pariahs; grandmothers, fathers, children, and so on. If we consider this plurality of social roles and identities, it becomes clear that there is something wrong with ascribing a "cultural identity" to individuals solely by discerning general characteristics of "their" culture. Cultures are not monolithic entities that have a similar effect on the self-understandings, social roles, and opportunities of all their members. Rather, they organize and thereby distribute the conditions of individual and collective self-understandings and individual opportunities according to the (interaction of) always produced and alterable organizational standards of many cultures, which together make up a social order that is called *a* culture in the sense that inspires the onlookers' reifying, nonparticipating perspective.

The debate over multiculturalism is a debate over, as Will Kymlicka puts it, multiculturalism "which arises from national and ethnic differences."[8] He uses the term *culture* as "synonymous with 'a nation' or 'a people'—that is, as an intergenerational community, more or less institutionally complete, occupying a given territory or homeland, sharing a distinct language and history. And a state is multicultural if its members either belong to different nations (a multination-state), or have emigrated from different nations (a polyethnic state), and this fact is an important aspect in personal identity and political life."[9] I follow this definition of the central terms of the debate, but not without remarking that I believe that the terms *intergenerational community* and *sharing distinct language and history* are more fundamental than institutional completeness and, particularly in polyethnic states, territory, or homeland. The debate over multiculturalism starts with the firm belief of individuals that they form an intergenerational community and share a language and a history. Immigrant cultures usually do not claim territory and their cultures are usually not sustained by complete institutions; on the contrary, integration into the society they immigrated to is very often accompanied by a loss of institutional completeness of their expectations concerning the social role and purposes of politics, law, religion, and the family.

The debate over multiculturalism presupposes that ethnic groups and nations can be identified within society. Often, this is simply taken for granted. Politicians, journalists, theorists, and, perhaps most importantly, spokespersons of ethnic groups and nations, very often use such terms as *ethnicity* and *nationality*. Since we are primarily interested in finding out how liberals should think about multiculturalism, however, it is important that we understand what is being said when we use these words. How should liberals identify ethnic communities and indigenous people? By race? By behavioral patterns? By language and religion? Or by modes of self-ascription? The first three of these possibilities are problematic from a liberal perspective. As I have argued throughout, respect for personal autonomy is the cornerstone of every normative account of liberalism. Liberals who reflect on questions of multiculturalism will have to be true to this starting point even in their "descriptive" attempts to identify ethnic groups and nations within society.

Race is unfit for identifying someone as a member of an ethnic group or a nation. A black man who was born and raised in Senegal, who studied in England and France, and who now works in the Netherlands may or may not identify with ethnic or national groups in any of these or other countries. Of course, we need not be overly wary of race as a characteristic of individuals. Race does matter—it can be a huge factor in the self-understanding of people and in the ways in which they are being treated. But race alone says nothing; it is the role that people ascribe to it in assessing their own and other's capacities and characteristics that makes it the factor it very often is.[10] Behavioral patterns, religion, and language say more. Dress and associations of people in the light of cultural and religious aspirations and language often are indicative of their being members of ethnic or national groups. But from a liberal perspective, it must be the self-ascription of individuals as indeed belonging to an ethnic or national group that counts most. Such self-ascriptions will often be put in terms of race and, particularly, a shared culture or intergenerational community; an ethnic or national community is a group of people, "predominantly of common descent, who *think of themselves* as collectively possessing a separate identity based on race or on shared cultural characteristics, usually language or religion."[11] From a liberal perspective, it is important to stress the factor of self-ascription because, out of respect for personal autonomy, liberals do not want to treat people on the basis of assumed characteristics these people do not wholeheartedly identify with.[12]

Several things follow from these observations. First, liberals should not treat cultures as closed entities. In Western liberal societies, even the most closed and authentic ethnic and national cultures will always interact with political, legal, economic, educational, and health-care "cultures" of the larger society. Second, the extent to which this interaction is evaluated positively should not be left to these cultures as a whole to decide (through their spokespersons, leaders, etc.). Rather, and from a liberal perspective, this question should be left to individuals capable of autonomous action to decide. Of course, this presupposes that a liberal society should—whenever this is possible—recognize individual members of such cultures as full citizens. By doing so, it provides them with at least the minimal institutional means to decide for themselves if and how they want to strike the balance between their membership of different cultures. Yet, third—and again out of respect for the capacity for personal autonomy—liberal societies should not counteract cultural practices that do not harm the individual's well-being. Of course, here the question emerges, what does it mean to harm their well-being? This question is notoriously hard to answer. The least we can say is that if certain cultural practices are a prerequisite for an individual's opportunity to lead a good life and if these practices do not harm the legitimate needs and interests of others, then liberal society has an obligation to sustain and foster them as much as possible.

This brings us to the question as to what extent cultural belonging is a prerequisite for leading a good life. In addressing this question, it again seems important not to exaggerate the differences between cultures. Each sustainable culture has similar structural aspects; it provides individuals with the symbolic, institutional, and material means to develop a sense of self-confidence, self-respect, and self-esteem through participation in a social world to which—as far as the social and moral fabric of this world is concerned—intersubjective relations of recognition are important issues. From a liberal perspective, it is important that these relations foster certain conditions for the personal integrity of individuals. Throughout this study, I have argued that conditions of personal integrity should be understood not only in detached universalistic terms. Rather, as Axel Honneth puts it, conditions for personal integrity are contingent on both the universalistic notion of equal respect for people in the legal sense and on the recognition of their concrete traits and abilities. Individual experience and forms of critique on prevalent understandings of rights and public reason cannot be taken seriously without taking into account these latter aspects of personal integrity. Concrete traits and abilities of individuals—and therefore the chances they have of understanding themselves as, for instance, a Roman Catholic, a Jew, a Turkish immigrant, or a French-speaking Quebecois—are always socially and culturally situated. Self-understandings are contingent on social forms that either enable or discourage individuals to identify with these traits and abilities, and to be recognized or not as full persons with unique identities. It is important to remember this when discussing questions of multiculturalism. Just as members of the cultural majority in liberal societies need recognition of the social forms that are essential to their self-understanding, members of minority cultures need recognition of the social forms that underpin their feelings of self-confidence, self-respect, and self-esteem.

As we have seen in chapter 3, John Rawls understands the conditions (the social bases) of self-respect as a primary good. This is essential for a person's self-understanding as a free and equal person. If it is true that social forms that sustain and foster concrete traits and abilities of people are necessary conditions for their being able to understand themselves as free and equal persons, and if culture plays an essential role in this, then free identification with cultural identity must be a primary good for citizens of liberal societies. Later on in this chapter, I will argue for such a view.[13] And there is no a priori reason why national or ethnic cultures should not be considered valuable forms of culture; it all depends on the way in which they can be integrated into the larger culture of liberal societies.

Here, again it is important to remember that claims to cultural belonging and cultural authenticity are not new topics on the liberal agenda. Liberalism has always been a political theory that tries to respect citizens' needs for cultural belonging. Sometimes, it has somewhat naively assumed that cultural identity is an entirely private matter. But once we accept, in accordance with my interpretation of liberalism, that liberalism is a nonneutral doctrine with rich cultural presuppositions that sets demanding limits to the guidance of behavior, we can free ourselves of this naïveté. We then come to understand that multiculturalism does not so much confront liberalism with an entirely new question; it rather turns highly relevant once again an old liberal question: how to control, sustain, and foster cultural diversity within one nonneutral normative framework.

A liberal-communitarian perspective: Charles Taylor

Charles Taylor's essay "The Politics of Recognition"[14] has played an important role in putting questions of multiculturalism on the agenda of liberal political philosophy. In this essay, Taylor argues that a specifically liberal understanding of rights undermines the social and cultural conditions for the individual and collective well-being of members of cultural minorities in liberal-democratic nation-states. Partly, the attention Taylor's essay attracted can be explained by his reputation as a "communitarian." It cannot be denied that the essay exudes a thorough communitarian spirit. Taylor makes much of the social and cultural situatedness of individuality and, particularly, of the need for cultural authenticity. And he goes further than most liberal authors do in arguing for collective rights to political self-determination for national minorities, especially for the French-speaking inhabitants of Quebec. Yet, it cannot be maintained that Taylor simply discards the universalistic normative framework of modern liberal states that are usually thought to cast doubts on the desirability of greater political autonomy or even independence for national minorities. On the contrary, Taylor's perhaps most interesting contribution to the debate over multiculturalism is that he tries to make it clear that a specific understanding of liberal ideas of justice and rights that remains sensitive to the importance of cultural belonging should motivate liberal states to take seriously claims to cultural authenticity and/or political self-government by national and ethnic minorities.

Taylor sees human relations, including expectations regarding justice and rights, primarily in terms of recognition. Yet, he identifies serious tensions between the notion of equal respect for the dignity of every human being per se (which is central to most liberal theories of justice and rights) and the notion of equal respect for concrete traits and abilities or, as Taylor calls it, respect for differences. Both notions, he claims, are crucial to the cultural self-understanding of modern individuals and to their expectations regarding identity, citizenship, and just government. According to Taylor, the former notion, which has firm roots in Enlightenment thought, promotes a difference-blind universalism. Its most important early philosophical proponent was Immanuel Kant, and today this notion of equal respect is most strongly defended by such theorists as John Rawls and Jürgen Habermas. Presumably for rhetorical reasons, Taylor exaggerates the difference-blindness of these theories. Yet, he sees the real problems that confront them very clearly. Although they can justify differential treatment of individuals and groups on the ground that they find themselves in unfavored social positions (resulting in policies of affirmative action in the field of work, education, culture, etc.), they can only do so on the assumption that such measures will successfully help these individuals and groups integrate into "an eventual 'difference-blind' social space" (40). What these theories cannot adequately respond to, however, are claims to "maintain and cherish distinctness, not just now but forever" (40).

But, one might want to ask, why should claims of the latter type be taken seriously at all? Taylor seeks the answer to this question in the cultural history of modern societies, particularly in what he calls the subjective turn of modern culture, by which individuals have gradually come to think of themselves as "beings with inner depths" (29). In eighteenth- and nineteenth-century Europe, authors such as Rousseau and Herder articulated a sense of "being oneself" that was rather opposed to both calculative (utilitarian) and moral-universalistic (Kantian) Enlightenment thought. An ethics of authenticity was crucial to this sense of being oneself. Abstract moral duties toward humanity were seen as less important than a genuine moral contact with oneself, through which one comes to know one's own appropriate "measure" (29). This last idea was radicalized in the Romantic period, in which self-realization was understood as being true to one's individual originality. And it is important to see that someone like Herder applied this idea both to individuals and to (national) cultures; the Germans, the French, and so forth, were each thought to have their own distinct ways of being themselves; different cultures came to be perceived as expressing the authenticity and originality of different peoples. Taylor is surely right in noting that this was (one of) "the seminal idea[s] of modern nationalism, in both benign and malignant forms" (31).

Underlying the politics of equal dignity and the politics of difference, Taylor shows, are different notions of what it means to respect human potential. This is usually understood as respect for the rationality and autonomy of the human subject, while respect for difference is respect for the potential "for forming and defining one's own identity" (42). And one of the assumptions underlying Taylor's thought is that personal and collective identities that succeed in providing people with the means for their individual and collective well-being—even if we sometimes do not understand exactly how and why—must be presumed to have valuable aspects that are worthy of respect. If I understand Taylor correctly, his view is that the two modes of respect need not necessarily conflict. And indeed, as we have seen, modern liberal theories try to reconcile these two different notions within a single normative framework. But Taylor makes the point that respect for forming and defining one's own identity has recently often been radicalized into the principle that every personal or cultural identity, understood as springing from the potential to form a distinct identity, should be accorded equal respect or recognition. This is where the two notions of respect come into conflict.

As we have found repeatedly in earlier parts of this book, the liberal politics of equal dignity cannot respect and foster all personal and collective notions of what is valuable in life. Practically speaking, this would be an unworkable strategy. And normatively speaking, it would imply that liberalism should tolerate all kinds of individual and cultural strivings that might well have discriminatory effects on the individual well-being of many citizens of liberal societies. Yet, since equal-dignity-based strategies are not nearly as neutral as their proponents often purport them to be, it is no wonder that advocates of the politics of difference (most frequently found among spokespersons fighting for concrete causes, e.g., feminism, collective rights, and gay rights), regularly claim that, as Taylor puts it, "the supposedly fair and difference-blind liberal society is not only inhuman (because suppressing identities) but also, in a subtle and unconscious way, itself highly discriminatory" (43). In this study, I have tried to show that there is much truth in the claims of both camps; they could not exist without each other, but they often cannot be reconciled (this sounds rather like the message of a rock ballad, and perhaps this should not surprise us).[15] The two positions frequently end up in normative deadlocks that seem to be irresolvable because of, on the one hand, the valuableness and, on the other hand, the incompleteness (a lack of sensitivity to difference or a lack of a general normative theory) of both sides of the conflict.

Although Taylor does not use the term, he may be said to be highly sensitive to the tragedy of liberalism. He does not choose for one side of the conflict but stresses that the politics of equal dignity and the politics of difference presuppose each other even though they do not combine easily. The politics of difference can be fought out only in a society in which the idea of equal dignity has become part of the moral self-understandings of citizens; only if citizens feel that they should be recognized as equals per se does it make sense to claim recognition for their more concrete traits and abilities in terms of equal respect and esteem. And in most cases, claims of the latter sort are not accompanied by claims of individuals and groups that they no longer are recognized as worthy of equal dignity at all. Rather, what they look for is an interpretation of liberalism that would combine the two notions of respect in ways that are more true to the nonuniversalizable—personal and cultural—needs and interests of individuals.

Taylor tries to sketch the contours of such a liberal theory by reflecting on the normative implications of the struggle for greater political autonomy or even independence of many of his French-speaking fellow citizens of Quebec. The issue here is the following: in 1982, the Canadian Charter of Rights was adopted. It aligned the Canadian political system with that of the United States because it offered a schedule of individual rights that was meant to be the basis for judicial review of legislation at all levels of government. It was soon recognized that this schedule does not fit in easily with the collective cultural goals of French Quebecois. The aim for survival of language and culture—and claims to collective rights to self-government of cultural groups that follow from them—must appear as problematic from the perspective of the charter because it can easily frustrate the individual rights of citizens. Good examples are the Quebec policies that do not allow Francophones and immigrants to be educated in English-language schools and that oblige larger businesses to be conducted in French. It may be clear that, from a liberal perspective, such policies affect the options for choice

of individual citizens and are therefore highly suspect. Yet, many
Quebecois are willing to accept this restriction of options, and they
believe that Quebec should be recognized as a distinct society in
need of special collective rights that serve the survival of French
language and culture (52f.).

It is important to understand culture as a primary good. Should
a government actively promote allegiance to a specific culture that it
thinks is (or should be) central to the self-understandings of most of
its citizens? Or will such a policy necessarily harm the equal protection of citizens under the law and (therefore) result in unjustifiable
forms of discrimination? The mainstream liberal answer to this last
question is that it will. Therefore, the answer to the former question
is that a government should not actively promote allegiance to a specific culture, although it may promote a cultural pluralism that all
citizens will benefit from. Yet, whatever view on the issue one
chooses, political society will never be neutral between, as Taylor
puts it, "those who value remaining true to the culture of our ances-
tors and those who might want to cut loose in the name of some individual goals of self-development" (58).

One might want to argue that culture should be understood as a
public good in the same sense as clean air and green spaces. From
this view, the government has to guarantee all citizens access to
such goods, that is, these goods should be provided to citizens in
order for them to flourish. For culture, this would mean that the government should uphold cultural pluralism, and that citizens should
be free to choose which cultures they identify with in education,
work, leisure, and so on. But according to Taylor, this way of viewing
the matter misses the point. For Quebec, he claims, at issue is an attempt to make sure "that there is a community of people here in the
future that will want to avail itself of the opportunity to use the
French language. Policies aimed at survival actively seek to *create*
members of the community, for instance, in their assuring that future generations continue to identify as French-speakers. There is
no way that these policies could be seen as just providing a facility to
already existing people" (58f.).

Taylor argues for a form of liberalism that would allow policies
that let a specific culture survive, while still respecting such fundamental liberal rights as "rights to life, liberty, due process, free
speech, free practice of religion, and so on" (59). He proposes to distinguish between these fundamental rights and less fundamental
rights such as those concerning the language of commercial signs
and—although he does not mention them at this stage of his argu-

ment—compulsory attendance of French-language schools.[16] Quebec governments should be free to guarantee the survival of French-Quebecois culture, and the citizenry should have a fair amount of democratic autonomy in deciding how this goal can best be achieved. But in all this, the fundamental liberal rights of citizens of Quebec as well as those of citizens in other parts of Canada should not be harmed. For liberalism as a political doctrine, this is meant to imply the following: it should not insist on the uniform application of rights and it need not be overly wary of collective goals. The integrity of cultures and the ways in which they provide individuals with the means to lead a good life should be taken more seriously by liberal politics and liberal political theory.

It is appropriate to label Taylor's position a "liberal-communitarian" one. It respects fundamental liberal rights but is not willing to let (interpretations of) these individual rights trump collective, communitarian goals on every occasion. In a pragmatic mode, it is willing to consider the valuableness of such goals in specific cultural-political matters, and sometimes to opt in favor of cultural survival (61).

Taylor's position has been heavily criticized. Habermas, for example, has claimed that Taylor's position "attacks" liberal principles because it "calls into question the universalistic core of the modern conception of freedom."[17] What Taylor fails to understand, Habermas says, following Ronald Dworkin, is that collective goals "can only 'trump' claims based on individual rights if these goals can in turn be justified in the light of other rights that take precedence."[18] Some of these rights, Habermas acknowledges—here following Will Kymlicka—may well be "rights to cultural membership," for "the integrity of the individual legal person cannot be guaranteed without protecting the intersubjectively shared experiences and life contexts in which the person has been socialized and has formed his or her identity."[19] The solution to problems like the one Taylor discusses, Habermas suggests, can only be found by guaranteeing—through civil and political rights—that citizens can engage in ethical-political debates that concern their shared notion of the good life. Ideally speaking, these debates should be taken seriously by democratic parliaments and governments. Therefore, they may well—as part of a public notion of the good life—play a role in the "general legal order" of society.[20] But shared conceptions of the good life can never overrule individual rights.

Habermas's comment on Taylor's essay is well informed but demonstrates an overconfidence in the ability of liberal-democratic

societies to deal reasonably with questions of pluralism and multiculturalism. It seems to beg the question. Taylor's essay is a cautious
and open-minded investigation into an area that is relatively unknown to mainstream liberal theory. Although I agree with Habermas that Taylor tends to overlook the needs and rights of citizens of
Quebec who might not sympathize with the aspirations of "the"
French-Quebecois culture, I think that we should acknowledge that
Taylor does point to real problems, in particular, that members of
national groups who perceive themselves as members of authentic
cultures may genuinely feel that their particular culture should be
understood as more than just an option among many others in liberal societies. Habermas does not take this problem seriously.

As we have seen in part 3, there is a reason for this. According
to Habermas, a just constitutional order should be understood as the
logical expansion of expectations of justice that are always already
given with the deep structure of communicative action. The logic behind this way of reconstructing the rationality and adequateness of
modern law is evolutionary. And this in a teleological way: it implicitly anticipates an ideal posttraditional end state of law and solidarity in which claims to personal or cultural authenticity will always
be evaluated from the perspective of the ideal communication community, that is, a community of autonomous individuals who are all
capable of engaging in reasonable public deliberations. Habermas
applies this ideal notion of a rational life form to concrete normative
conflicts that occur in the here and now. Assuming that his understanding of rationality is correct, he states that strictly moral questions should be distinguished from evaluative or ethical questions.
Whereas moral questions should always be answered with the demand of the "generalizability of interests" in mind, evaluative or ethical questions can only be adequately answered in concrete life
contexts such as traditions and particular cultures. But simply because of the a priori characteristics of rational communication, the
generalizability of interests from a posttraditional perspective is the
greatest good.

From a mainstream liberal-democratic perspective, Habermas's
strategy results in unsurprising outcomes. If we apply it to questions
of multiculturalism, culture can be understood as a primary good.
But it will always give priority to personal and political autonomy
and individual rights, not to collective purposes and collective rights.
Of course, according to many liberals, this is an entirely defensible
position. What is wrong with Habermas's contribution to the debate
over multiculturalism is not so much its recommendations but its

justificatory strategy. As I have argued throughout, the principle of the generalizability of interests is not a neutral principle based on some all-explaining form of rationality; it is a moderately perfectionist liberal principle that defends particular values and interests. And I believe that it would be a much better strategy to openly defend it as such. The principle of the generalizability of interests is an articulation of the liberal aim to let the interests of all citizens in leading a good life matter equally. If we take that aim seriously, there is no reason to dominate debates concerning normative conflicts by means of an Archimedean perspective that can hardly take these conflicts seriously. On the contrary, we should try to be open to the possibility that the perspective we want to defend is mistaken. Taylor's careful and open-minded analysis of the claims of both mainstream liberal perspectives and groups of people who think that there is sufficient reason to argue for collective rights seems to be better suited for this task than Habermas's approach.

However, this is not to say that I agree with Taylor's view on the Quebec issue. I think that his understanding of culture and community is problematic. Throughout his essay he speaks of French-speaking Quebecois as a single-minded group of people who want to send their children to French-language schools and want to conduct their businesses in French. And because they do, Quebec policies that are directed at the survival of French-Quebecois culture must be considered valid. From a liberal perspective, I have difficulties with this way of talking about "the" cultural-political goals of "a" culture. As I said earlier, self-ascription of individuals as members of particular cultures must, from a liberal perspective, be the most important factor in deciding what cultures individuals identify with. In itself, the fact that people speak French and have intergenerational roots in French-Quebecois culture does not necessarily mean that they are in favor of sending their children or immigrants to French-language schools. And the same goes for running a business in French. Just like most citizens of modern societies, most French-speaking Quebecois will participate in many cultures. Despite their cultural roots, some of them may have good reasons for not understanding their cultural identity as the chief factor that has to be considered in making personal choices. They may aspire to move to English-speaking Canada in the future and therefore want to send their children to English-language schools. They may run a computer software company and feel that it would be advisable to run their firm in English, in order to compete on the international market. They may have immigrated to Quebec from Germany or the

Netherlands and want to give their children the opportunity to learn to speak English fluently (French, they might argue, they will learn from their friends in the street and through the media).

Taylor explicitly states that he wants to defend a liberal perspective. Fundamental liberal rights should not be harmed by this perspective. But his tendency to regard French culture as an indisputable constitutive (and therefore primary) good for all French-speaking Quebecois, let alone his implicit approval of the policy concerning the compulsory French education of all immigrant and French-speaking children, does seem to harm a fundamental liberal right—the moral right to decide for oneself how one wants to shape one's life. Of course, if Quebec were an independent state, the situation would be slightly different. Then French could be promoted as the national language—although special measures would be called for in order to protect minority cultures (English culture among them). But as long as Quebec is part of Canada, I think that an obligation to provide bilingual education is as far as one can go from a liberal perspective. The argument would be that both languages are important prerequisites for flourishing as a "free and equal" citizen of both Canada and Quebec. It would be at the discretion of the individual as to the culture and language they most strongly identify with.

There are points in Taylor's argument where it seems that he would have to agree with this view. There is a strange tension between his allegiance to the ideal of authenticity understood as the ideal of finding "my own original way of being" (32) and his remark that identity is primarily a question of "where we're coming from" (33). With this last remark he is right to the extent that we can never completely break with the values with which we were raised. Even if we despise practically everything that we were once brought up to believe, we still on occasion define our identity in relation to our old identity. On an ontological level, this is simply how things are. But the ideal of authenticity is not an ontological matter; it is a historically situated and normatively rich ideal, and it says that we should aspire to become people who wholeheartedly identify with the values, plans, and modes of self-restraint that shape our personal lives. It is unfortunate that Taylor lets his ontological assumptions determine his normative outlook to the extent that they do. If where we are coming from is mainly determined by a particular culture or community, and if culture or community is understood in reifying terms (as easily identifiable homogenous entities), then our individual identities must be understood as expressions of particular cultures or communities. The emphasis on the importance of collective rights that guarantee the survival of French-Quebecois culture in Taylor's essay springs from the fear that if particular cultures wither away, individual identities will necessarily be emptied of almost everything that made them valuable in the first place. From a liberal perspective, however, this claim is dubious.

Cultures are always evolving. They help us govern various behavioral patterns (practices) and the felt adequacy or inadequacy of these patterns may in turn prompt us to make choices that change our understandings of the cultures we participate in. I was raised in a Catholic family. The Catholicism of my grandparents was (and partly still is) very different from the Catholicism of my parents. And although I do not consider myself a Catholic anymore, my Catholic background has undeniably shaped my outlook on life. There is a certain way, my way, of relating to Catholicism and to religion in general—it expresses itself through certain crypto-religious experiences and longings; a sometimes nostalgic, sometimes frightening, sometimes amusing sensitivity to certain symbols, rituals, saints, devils, and so on. Over three generations, my family's relation to the Catholic faith has changed drastically. The Dutch state has not actively promoted the survival of Catholicism as it once existed—although some Catholics with great social and political influence have. And I have been relatively free to find my own way in all this. At times, I have sensed a feeling of loss. But I certainly have never sensed that my individuality was being emptied of almost everything I once valued. On the contrary, I make my life meaningful by participating in other cultures and practices. Through my education, my work, and my changing relations with my family and friends, I have opened up new horizons, which now play an important role in my life.

It may well be that membership of a language community or a nation has more pervasive consequences on individuality than a Catholic upbringing (that was of the typically Dutch liberal kind anyhow) has. Still, and again from a moderately perfectionist perspective, the freedom to choose one's own path in life is more important than the survival of the exact cultural framework within which one was raised. The liberal state does have the obligation to provide its citizens with a rich cultural environment. It must promote a plurality of valuable options, but these options should not run counter to the (capacity for) personal autonomy of individuals. Ideally speaking, only those options that citizens voluntarily choose will eventually survive in liberal societies. Tragic experiences may result from this—as any talk with a conservative grandmother will make clear. But tragic experiences are a fact of life. Liberalism can and should try to accommodate the needs of people whose cultural allegiances are under pressure in society. Upholding a rich cultural environment in which progressive and conservative, indigenous, majority, and immigrant groups can live together is the best general strategy liberalism can come up with to deal with such problems. But the liberal perspective will always favor particular conceptions of the good life. What is crucial is adherence to the value of personal autonomy. This is where liberal contributions to debates on pluralism and multiculturalism should draw the bottom line.

This may seem to be a harsh view, particularly so because it cannot console "dissident" groups or groups that simply cannot keep up with the pace of modernization and liberalization by pointing to a notion of rationality that justifies the losses they suffer "from nowhere." In the end, however, such consolation cannot be given. As we have seen in this study, both the moral foundations and the effects of liberal justice and reason are not ethically neutral. Taylor understands this very well, and his essay should be praised for the accuracy with which it makes this point. Yet, Taylor's implicit understanding of the tragedy of liberalism prompts him to come up with conclusions that cannot be reconciled even with a form of liberalism that is aware of its own tragic predicament. It is true that such a variant of liberalism aims to take seriously the needs and interests of those whose most deeply felt beliefs are threatened by liberal practices. But from this it does not follow that liberalism has an obligation to guarantee the survival of their cultural framework. It can only go so far as to provide them with options that enable them to struggle for the survival of this framework.

11

~

Two Liberal Views of
Multiculturalism

The discussion of Charles Taylor's liberal-communitarian outlook in
the previous chapter has made it clear that it is not easy to balance
the two ideals at issue in the multiculturalism debate. These ideals
are, first, the ideal of being true to one's own values, cultural allegiances and practices, and so forth, and second, the general ideal of
justice, peace, and mutually advantageous social cooperation among
those who inhabit pluralist societies. If it is ascribed too much importance, the former ideal poses a threat to both the normative priority of public reason and to the good of individual freedom as
inspired by the character ideal of personal autonomy and by an affirmation of ethical pluralism. Two possible alternatives to Taylor's
position suggest themselves to the liberal theorist. One may either
try to tone down the importance of the former ideal by arguing that
the survival of specific cultural settings should never be among the
aims of liberal answers to questions of multiculturalism or one may
look for ways in which the liberal framework could meet some of the
claims to cultural survival without sacrificing the normative priority
of public reason and the good of individual freedom. The former attempt has been undertaken by Jeremy Waldron, the latter by Will
Kymlicka.

Jeremy Waldron's cosmopolitan alternative

In his essay "Minority Cultures and the Cosmopolitan Alternative,"[1] Waldron comes up with an account of multiculturalism that in many ways is the exact opposite of Taylor's account. "To put it crudely, we need culture, but we do not need cultural integrity. Since none of us needs a homogeneous cultural framework or the integrity of a particular set of meanings, none of us needs to be immersed in . . . small-scale communities which . . . are alone capable of securing this integrity and homogeneity. Some, of course, still may prefer such immersion, and welcome the social subsidization of their preference. But it is not . . . a necessary presupposition of rational and meaningful choice" (135).

Waldron does not deny the fact that culture plays a constitutive role in our lives. Rather, he questions two assumptions that underlie approaches such as Taylor's. The first of these assumptions is that "the social world divides up neatly into particular distinct cultures, one to every community," and the second states that "what everyone needs is just *one* of these entities—a single coherent culture—to give shape and meaning to his life" (131). Of course, no serious theorist will phrase these assumptions in these clearly exaggerated terms. But I think that Waldron is right in maintaining that implicit assumptions of this sort do underlie some influential contemporary accounts of multiculturalism, including recent interpretations of Article 17 of the International Covenant on Civil and Political Rights of the United Nations. This article states that "In those States in which ethnic, religious or linguistic minorities exist, persons belonging to such minorities shall not be denied the right, in community with the other members of their group, to enjoy their own culture, to profess and practice their own religion, or to use their own language."[2] In itself, this Article need not appear as problematic from a liberal perspective. But I agree with Waldron that the view professed in a 1979 U.N. report stating that cultures may protect their integrity "by placing limits on the incursion of outsiders and limits in their own members' choices about career, family, lifestyle, loyalty, and exit" does seem to be problematic (111). Given my critique of Taylor's position, it may be clear that I sympathize with Waldron's attempt to question the assumptions underlying such views. However, as we will see, I think his overall conclusions are not sound.

Waldron discredits the idea of, or the longing for, cultural integrity mainly by showing that cultural integrity is not an adequate reaction to the contemporary world. He sees this contemporary world as a global society that is characterized by considerable economic, moral, and political interdependencies among different ethnic groups, nations, nation-states, and civilizations. The two "godfathers" of modern economics, Adam Smith and Karl Marx, already acknowledged the significance of global—or at least supranational—economic interdependencies, and Waldron is surely correct in emphasizing that since their times these interdependencies have only become stronger. He is also right in noting that "all advanced societies share certain general political and moral problems about property, freedom, welfare, and equality, and are aware of these problems" (125). One need only think of global problems concerning ecology, wars, refugees, human rights, and so forth to see that different countries, nations, and cultures do share many political and moral problems and that, particularly in the twentieth century, supranational institutions have been created to address them.

From the pervasiveness of our global interdependencies, Waldron derives an insight into our debt to the global community. He uses an interesting rhetorical strategy to make his point. He borrows an argument that is frequently being used by his "communitarian," "Aristotelian," and "Herderian" adversaries, and uses it for his own purposes. The argument states that we "must own up to the role that society has played in the constitution of our selves and cultivate a sense of allegiance and obligation that is appropriate to that social provenance" (128). Contemporary communitarians, Waldron maintains, tend to apply this argument mistakenly to small-scale communities (nation-states at best) only. If they were to repair this sociological failing in their thought, however, they would readily acknowledge that "in the modern world particular cultures and national communities have an obligation to recognize their dependence on the wider social, political, international, and civilizational structures that sustain them" (129). They would come to understand that responsibilities follow from dependence: most importantly the responsibility to participate in and sustain the wider—global—context in which their immediate—local—cultural surroundings are embedded. This is where Waldron straightforwardly ventilates some of his irritations with the proponents of cultural integrity: "The theoretical point is simply that it ill behoves the partisans of a particular community to sneer at and to disparage those whose cosmopolitan commitments make possible the lives that they are seeking to lead" (130).

So, paradoxically, what Waldron suggests is that it is precisely because of liberal and cosmopolitan beliefs and institutions—beliefs and institutions that acknowledge the existence of global responsibilities and celebrate cultural hybridity instead of cultural integrity—that small-scale or diffuse ethnic communities within liberal societies can remain true to their local allegiances. To a certain extent, I think this is a sound argument. In the modern world, cultural pluralism can only flourish if rules, personal motivations, and institutions can be lent credibility that recognize claims for cultural integrity on the premise that members of particular cultures should not let their moral and political outlook be dominated by obligations that spring from their local allegiances alone. We can simply translate this into a Rawlsian requirement of reasonable pluralism. Still, Waldron sometimes suggests that the reasonableness of this requirement is enough to distinguish real problems from false problems created by outdated feelings of culturalist nostalgia. To me, this seems to be a rather empty suggestion.

Waldron explicitly admits that the liberal and cosmopolitan conception of the autonomous, culturally more or less hybrid person "evokes a spirit of discernment, restlessness, and comparison. It is . . . simply antithetical to the idea that certain structures of community are to be *preserved* in their integral character" (150 n. 87). Since he makes this point—which in itself is entirely correct—it is not immediately understandable why "partisans of particular communities" should feel a sense of allegiance and obligation to the cosmopolitan understanding of culture, particularly so because the globalization of economic, political, and moral interdependencies cannot be said to have been instigated by indigenous people such as American Indians and Australian aboriginals, or ethnic minorities in Western Europe, such as Turkish and Moroccan migrant workers. Without wanting to generalize "their" experience, I think it is safe to say that their perspective has often been, and often still is, one of reacting to a cosmopolitan and liberal culture that they feel is not primarily theirs. Of course, many ethnic minorities with non-Western cultural roots came to (often were invited to) Western European countries for economic reasons that were rather directly related to global economic interests—among others, the interest of Western countries to quickly reestablish social stability and a firm status on the international market after the collapse of their industries and trade relations during and after the Second World War. But given the social and political treatment many of them have received in more or less "cosmopolitan" liberal democracies (implicit and overt discrimination in the workplace, limited access to higher education and well-paid jobs, xenophobia regarding Islamic culture, restricted political and social rights, remigration programs when unemployment struck Western Europe in the 1970s, etc.), it is not greatly surprising that we are sometimes confronted with anticosmopolitan and antiliberal sympathies held by members of ethnic minorities. If society does not recognize individuals as autonomous and responsible and does not provide them with the social and material conditions to act as such, it cannot reasonably expect them to behave in an ideal manner. On the contrary, it is very understandable that those who do not receive the full legal and social recognition that they are due retreat to their "imagined" cultural communities in order to find a stable and secure cultural environment.[3] In short, Western societies have often neglected the importance of forms of social integration that could help strike a balance between assimilation and cultural integrity by providing minorities with genuine reasons to cultivate a sense of allegiance and obligation to liberal-democratic or even cosmopolitan values. Waldron's implicit suggestion that we all have good reasons to live up to our global interdependencies and to celebrate the liberating hybridization of culture and identity is erroneous. By addressing his considerable rhetorical skills almost solely to cultural minorities that do not find it easy to celebrate cultural hybridity in the liberal and cosmopolitan environment they find themselves in, he comes very close to what might be called a strategy of blaming the victim.

Waldron could, and probably would, reply to all this that I do not understand him correctly; that his cosmopolitanism presupposes that all citizens of society should benefit from a fair distribution of primary goods in the Rawlsian sense and that adherence to liberal or even cosmopolitan ideals can only be expected if liberal or cosmopolitan societies have something valuable to offer to all their citizens (and long-term guests). Still, such a reply would not really console me, since I have difficulties with his unwillingness to regard cultural membership as a primary good. In order to explain why, I will look at Will Kymlicka's influential argument concerning the benefits of membership, and Waldron's critique thereof.

Waldron argues against Kymlicka's view that liberals should accept the fact that culture is a primary good. Kymlicka's argument encompasses six steps: (a) a liberal theory should always acknowledge that individual freedom to form and to revise one's own beliefs is "a crucial precondition for pursuing our essential interest in leading a good life"[4]; (b) some basic conditions will have to be met before individuals can be expected to exercise this freedom. These conditions are rightly called primary social goods; (c) one of these conditions is that individuals should be able to acquire a sense of self-respect which—among other things—presupposes that they have the effective freedom to examine and either confirm or reject the worth of the beliefs they actually have; (d) such freedom is only possible in a cultural environment that presents them with a range of valuable options in the light of which they can evaluate their beliefs. Such a plurality of valuable options will necessarily be embedded in a "given" cultural structure that loosely defines individuals' outlook on life. Such a cultural structure should be understood as a common language and a shared history that shows the point of various activities: "Our language and history are the media through which we come to an awareness of the options available to us, and their significance; and this is a precondition of making intelligent judgments about how to lead our lives"[5]; (e) Kymlicka states that it follows from this that liberals "should be concerned with the fate of cultural structures, not because they have some moral status of their own, but because it is only through having a rich and secure cultural structure that people can become aware, in a vivid way, of the options available to them, and intelligently examine their value."[6] This implies that liberals should regard cultural membership—membership of a "rich and secure cultural structure"—as a primary good that is crucial to an individual's ability to acquire a sense of self-respect; and (f) since liberal societies are not culturally homogeneous, it may be necessary that the liberal state grants members of minority cultures special rights to protect their cultural structure against influences by the majority culture that frustrate their chances of acquiring the minimum sense of self-respect that is needed to lead a good life.[7]

I believe that Waldron does not treat Kymlicka's argument fairly. He suggests that Kymlicka is looking for an argument that would oblige liberals to help particular communities preserve the "purity," the precise character (i.e., the predominant interpretation) of their cultural heritage (135). But this is not what Kymlicka says. In fact, just as Waldron does, he explicitly rejects strategies to preserve cultural integrity in this sense: "In one common usage, culture refers to the *character* of a historical community. On this view, changes in the norms, values, and their attendant institutions in one's community (e.g. membership in churches, political parties, etc.) would amount to loss of one's culture. However, I use culture in a very different sense, to refer to the cultural community, or cultural structure, itself. On this view, the cultural community continues to exist even when its members are free to modify the character of the culture, should they find its traditional ways of life no longer worth while" (166–67). Cultural membership in this second sense—a membership that enables individuals to understand themselves as Quebecois, Inuit Indians, Turks, Moroccans, and so forth—should be considered a primary good. But the liberal value of personal autonomy, of being free to choose one's own path in life, makes it impossible to argue for cultural membership in the first sense, for it would be an illegitimate restriction of the personal autonomy of members of cultures.

Kymlicka's view is far from unrealistic; in fact I think that it adequately fits our commonsense understanding of how cultures change and develop. It is important to all of us that we can speak and write in our native language, and that we are free to participate in institutions that shape our cultural heritage. Of course, at least from a liberal perspective, it is of tantamount importance that we are free to learn from (fragments of) other cultures. Waldron is surely right in stating that "more or less meaningful fragments, images, and snatches of stories"—Aramaic storytelling (the Bible), German folklore (the Grimm brothers' fairy tales), and Roman mythology (Romulus and Remus)—have enriched our culture precisely because their purity was not being upheld (135). But here, he is not in disagreement with Kymlicka; the latter does not shy away from the fact that we can only make the best of our lives if we have free access to both our original cultural environment and other cultural environments.

In the end, Waldron makes the same mistake as Rawls and Dworkin: he presupposes that liberal or cosmopolitan societies are, or should be, culturally homogeneous. The implicit suggestion is that we should all react to our global interdependencies in similar ways; a cosmopolitan culture will be a pluralist culture, but it will be one in its cosmopolitan values. But this is simply a false assumption, which underestimates the role that cultural identity plays in our lives. We do not start from similar cultural backgrounds in our global society and since liberals are often among the proponents of global society, they have the responsibility to look for ways in which the self-respect of those whose cultural environments do not combine easily with liberal or cosmopolitan demands they cannot evade can be secured. This is simply a matter of showing respect for every individual's capacity for autonomy. It is true, however, that some seemingly illiberal recommendations follow from this. Kymlicka states that, in some cases, cultures should be granted the right to put "temporary special restrictions on individual behavior."[8] The introduction of alcohol or modern media to communities that are not familiar with them, he says, may seriously affect the well-being of their members. They can affect the stableness and security of the cultural framework in ways that do not seem to benefit anybody. But while temporary restrictions on behavior may be legitimate insofar as they protect individuals from rapid changes to the character of their culture, the ultimate purpose of such restrictions must be to help "the culture to move carefully toward a fully liberal society."[9]

This seems to be a much better view than Waldron's. The latter believes that the fact that some of us do not need cultural integrity in a strong sense (which is true) is a sufficient reason for assuming that the contingent availability of fragments of many different cultures is enough to protect everyone's self-respect. His conclusion is that cosmopolitanism must be considered a viable alternative for everybody. But this is not a sound conclusion. The fact that it is possible to relate to culture in a seemingly detached and ironic way does not prove that this is a viable possibility for everyone. Furthermore, Waldron tends to forget that his cosmopolitan ideals are underpinned and fostered by stable and secure cultural structures that encompass, among other things, rights that protect individual liberty, media, and social institutions that celebrate liberal and cosmopolitan sympathies, a worldwide academic culture that enables some cosmopolitans to feel at home in many different societies, forms of political and legal power that are conducive to liberal and cosmopolitan life-styles, and so forth. If we remember how much a cosmopolitan life-style is dependent on such structures, we begin to understand why Waldron's argument does not show that liberals have no good reasons to argue for "social subsidization" of cultural frameworks. Even if liberals would in the end have to argue for cosmopolitanism, special provisions—special rights, subsidies, and so forth—would be called for in order not to let the well-being of those who—for cultural or other reasons—cannot keep up with social and political developments be harmed. So the special-rights interpretation of Article 27 of the International Covenant on Civil and Political Rights that Waldron vehemently argues against does not appear that unreasonable after all; it articulates a reasonable view if we remember that such special rights may be needed to handle social conflicts and feelings of loss of identity that spring from the immense differences in normative outlooks in global society.

It is true that, in my discussion of Taylor's view, I myself have made use of my personal experience that my well-being has not been negatively affected by my fragmented cultural identity. But in itself, that experience does not say much. It says that it is possible to lead a good life without being immersed in a "pure" cultural environment.

However, if we accept the fact, as Waldron does, that liberal and cosmopolitan ideals and institutions are likely to harm the well-being of those who—in this case for cultural reasons—cannot wholeheartedly embrace them, and if we conclude that these ideals and institutions seem to become ever more dominant in Western societies, then we have to conclude as well that liberals do have good reasons to protect at least temporarily the cultural environment of those who cannot keep pace with the globalization of our interdependencies. It is true that the social world does not divide up neatly into particular distinct cultures and it is also true that not everyone needs just one of these cultures to give shape and meaning to her life. For these reasons, we may conjecture that there is nothing wrong with promoting social assimilation of nonliberal cultures. But we cannot expect that assimilation to happen overnight. It is exactly because liberals and cosmopolitans are often more responsible for the globalization of social life than members of threatened cultures, that they—and the institutions they uphold—have special responsibilities toward the well-being of members of minority cultures. The tragedy of liberalism prompts us to acknowledge these responsibilities. But Waldron does not recognize the tragedy of liberalism. He evades the real conflict at the heart of questions of multiculturalism by embracing just one of its constituent poles—the fact that many people adhere to and flourish because of liberal values and practices—and by downplaying the other—the fact that other people see these values and practices as threats to their identity. This conflict need not always be tragic; through education, active toleration, and rights to cultural membership, many aspects of the conflict may be overcome. But the resolution of conflicts starts with the acknowledgment of their existence. Waldron does not offer us the means to make that first step.

Will Kymlicka's "group-differentiated rights" approach

So it seems that we need a subtler account of multiculturalism that evades the simplicities of both Taylor and Waldron's position. Although I think that there is much to be said for Taylor's basic account of the problems at stake (but not for all his normative recommendations), we have seen that this account has not been sufficiently spelled out. Therefore, we cannot adequately judge its merits and shortcomings. Furthermore, Taylor espouses a problematic notion of culture; a notion that focuses on "cultural characteristics" instead of what Kymlicka calls cultural structures.

In his recent book, *Multicultural Citizenship* (1995), Kymlicka has further developed his notion of a cultural structure.[10] The primary good of cultural membership, he now says, should be understood as membership of a "societal culture"—"a culture which provides its members with meaningful ways of life across the full range of human activities, including social, educational, religious, recreational, and economic life, encompassing both public and private spheres. These cultures tend to be territorially concentrated and based on a shared language" (76). Membership in either a nation-state or in a more or less institutionally complete "distinct society" in the sense of an ethnic or cultural nation (e.g., indigenous people or French-speaking Quebecois) is a prerequisite for leading a good life in modern societies. Only a societal culture can provide the rich cultural environment that is presupposed by the liberal idea of freedom, that is, the idea that choosing one's own direction in life (in a complete societal culture) is the greatest good.

It may be clear that Kymlicka's view will not be shared by all liberals. His notion of a societal culture is much more substantive than an "overlapping consensus" (John Rawls) or a widely shared "constitutional patriotism" (Jürgen Habermas). But given my conclusions in parts 2 and 3, it will not come as a surprise when I say that Kymlicka is right in pointing out that liberalism presupposes a much more substantive notion of culture—which encompasses both private and public spheres and values—than these authors believe. Furthermore, Kymlicka's view is strengthened by the recent literature on nationalism and cultural belonging. Indeed, Kymlicka excels in relating his normative theory to sociological, anthropological, and empirical political-theoretical findings—a rare quality indeed. This literature shows that citizens of liberal societies strongly value their cultural membership and even that modernization and "liberalization ha[ve] in fact gone hand in hand with an increased sense of nationhood" (88).

Now, instead of arguing that one complete liberal societal culture will provide all citizens of liberal societies with the conditions for leading a good life and that we therefore need a precise account of what such a societal culture should look like in detail, Kymlicka chooses another strategy. He takes cultural pluralism seriously and accepts the fact that in the real world several societal cultures may be found within one liberal-democratic nation-state. Here, he clearly starts from the Northern American experience. Indigenous people such as American and Canadian Indians, religious groups such as the Amish, and "distinct societies" such as Quebec may indeed be said to sustain more or less complete societal cultures—some of them quite liberal, others quite illiberal. Special rights to land, language, education, and limited self-government have, in some cases quite long ago, actually been accorded to these groups.

Often, such rights are called *collective rights*. But Kymlicka is unhappy with that term. It suggests that all minority rights are accorded to, and exercised by, collectivities, which is not the case. They may be accorded to individual members of a group (see, e.g., language rights for French-speaking Canadians or Frisians in the Netherlands[11]), to a group as such (e.g., hunting rights for indigenous people), or to a province or territory (e.g., rights to the promotion of national culture by Quebec and Frisian governments). In order to evade the ambiguity of the term, Kymlicka proposes to label minority rights "group-differentiated rights" (45). Such rights, he claims, do not imply the primacy of community over individual freedom. Rather, the idea is that nation-states in which several societal cultures live together cannot be considered just if they do not accord such rights to people who need them in order to have the opportunity to exercise exactly their individual freedom within one or more stable and secure societal cultures.

In order to indicate what kind of group-differentiated rights a liberal society can allow, Kymlicka differentiates between what he calls internal restrictions on the individual freedom of people that emanate from such rights and external protections that limit the impact of decisions of the larger society. Internal restrictions are what critics of group-differentiated rights are—rightly—most afraid of. They fear that special rights for national and ethnic minorities may be misused to restrict the individual freedom of their members. For instance, they may be used to discriminate against those who want to loosen their ties to the community. External protections, on the other hand, are less controversial. An indigenous people may protect its hunting grounds or its language by such measures, but this does not necessarily imply that all members of the group will be forced to stick to traditional hunting practices, hunting grounds, or their native language. In short, Kymlicka argues that liberalism cannot allow measures that are meant to justify internal restrictions, but that it can, and indeed sometimes should, allow measures that foster external protections. The main reason for this is that liberal societies cannot allow societal cultures that restrict the freedom of individuals to question substantive aspects of their societal culture (the argument against internal restrictions) while they have an obligation to provide individuals with a stable and societal culture (the argument in favor of external protections that benefit secure cultural membership).

It may be clear that the analytic distinction between internal restrictions and external protections is mostly a matter of theory. In practice, things are more complex. Kymlicka distinguishes between three kinds of group-differentiated rights and asks to what extent they may be expected to foster internal and external limitations. He differentiates between "special group representation rights," "self-government rights," and "polyethnic rights." The first category concerns special representation quotas that are meant to correct the underrepresentation of disadvantaged groups within the political institutions of larger society. They "make it less likely that a national or ethnic minority will be ignored on decisions that are made on a country-wide basis" (37). These rights, which may be understood as instating a form of affirmative action, are attractive to regionally scattered minority groups in particular. The second category of rights decentralizes political powers to smaller political units. They prevent a geographically concentrated national minority from being outvoted on important cultural issues such as education, immigration, and family law (37). Finally, the third category of rights "protect specific religious and cultural practices which might not be adequately supported" through the market or by existing legislation (38).

All of these rights clearly serve the purpose of upholding external protections. They make way for political and social practices that give members of minority groups a greater chance at protecting the political and social conditions necessary for their well-being. However, internal restrictions do not necessarily spring from these rights. A largely self-governed indigenous group need not necessarily restrict its members' ability to leave the group. And the polyethnic right of Sikh men not to wear a helmet when riding a motorcycle does not oblige all Sikh motorcyclists to wear a turban instead of a helmet. Yet, self-government and polyethnic rights can be used by groups to impose (internal) restrictions on their members. Self-government rights for indigenous people have sometimes resulted in restrictions on their members' ability to challenge cultural practices in the courts of the larger society. And something similar goes for polyethnic or for other group-based rights. The Amish, for example, have the right to withdraw their children from school before the age of sixteen. And in their relatively closed societies, internal restrictions on leaving the group are severe (41–42). Yet, Kymlicka is unwilling to discard such rights for the simple reason that they can be used to enforce internal restrictions on group members. In a pragmatic mode, he weighs the advantages and disadvantages of these rights and concludes that liberals should accept them on the premise that, on principle, they should not be used to justify internal restrictions (176ff.).

What I find most appealing about Kymlicka's way of discussing liberalism's relation to multiculturalism is that he fully acknowledges the fact that many problems cannot be solved by theoretical exercises. A thorough belief in the primacy of social and political practice is characteristic of his writing. Where there is hope, he clearly articulates it (particularly where there are questions of social integration of immigrants). And where there are problems, he openly identifies them. His views on integration are inspired by the belief that, since immigrants do not bring complete societal cultures with them and since their best chances of flourishing in their new society are given with integration, polyethnic rights should serve the purpose of integration—not that of worshiping the integrity of a lost societal culture, which may be expected to end in a "ghettoization" or "Balkanization" of multicultural societies (55ff.). Contrary to Waldron, Kymlicka clearly articulates the responsibilities that liberal societies have in providing immigrants with the goods and rights that will enable them to integrate successfully. One of the responsibilities that comes across very clearly is that liberal societies and the majority of their citizens should be willing to change their received ideas of what is just, right, and good in the light of the needs and interests of new citizens, who are, after all, citizens just like anybody else. This may seem to be a commonplace, but it is not. Many obstacles to the social integration of immigrants still spring from the culturalistic hardheadedness of governments and from members of liberal-democratic societies. As a general rule, immigrants may be expected to adjust to their new societies even though the long-term inhabitants will encounter difficulties with their new neighbors. In fact, particularly when it comes to immigrant ethnic minorities, it may well be the case that claims to the integrity of one's own culture play at least as big a role in the cultural majority's perception of immigrants as they do among immigrant groups themselves (96ff.).

Of course, many difficult cases remain. For example, Kymlicka addresses the important question—which has come up several times in the present study—whether or not liberals should impose their views on nonliberal minorities (164). Just as I have done in the previous chapters, Kymlicka argues that liberalism is based on the value of personal autonomy. Therefore, group-differentiated rights that restrict the autonomy of group members should be rejected. But this does not mean that liberals can simply impose their views on groups and individuals that adhere to illiberal values. In fact, Kymlicka convincingly shows that attempts to liberalize communities and nations by imposition often backfire. Liberalism and adherence to the value of personal autonomy should come from within. Therefore, they should be "internalized by the members of [a] self-governing society" before support from the outside stands a chance of being successful (167).

Kymlicka does not explicitly use the argument that belief in the value of personal autonomy implies respect for the capacity for personal autonomy of others. Without explicitly using the argument from autonomy, however, Kymlicka does in the end choose a similar path. Usually, he says, we will have to start from a modus vivendi. The starting point of debates on the acceptability of differing cultural frameworks will not always be the same. With respect to the Amish, for example, liberals will have to respect the group-differentiated rights that this community actually has, even if they feel that the internal restrictions this group imposes on its members are clearly unjust. Yet, liberals "have a right, and a responsibility, to speak out against such injustice" (168). Liberals within the group should try to give reasons for liberal reforms, and liberals from outside the group should welcome such reforms—even very small ones—when they occur. Through deliberation, experience, and revision of institutional arrangements, some injustices may gradually disappear from the practices of the group in question.

Of course, Kymlicka's theory can be, and has been, criticized. Three points of critique are obvious. First, one could argue that the theory mistakenly assumes that the world divides up into liberal and illiberal societal cultures, and that only the former have the right to claim that other cultures should accommodate to their principles. One could call this a critique of the supposed ethnocentricity of Kymlicka's position: in the end, only liberals may interfere in the cultural affairs of others. Kymlicka certainly is more in favor of interference than, for instance, politically liberal authors. The latter can only recognize the public autonomy of citizens, including the public autonomy of members of illiberal minority groups. They trust that this is enough to guarantee them the minimum conditions that are needed to have both a voice in public affairs and the opportunity to decide for themselves how they want to lead good lives. In theory, this may seem an attractive position. It evades normative conflicts over questions of the good and the importance of cultural membership. In practice, however, it is clear that it is not. Here, liberal ideal theories could learn a lot from the many group-differentiated rights that have been granted to various groups. The justification of such rights can only be given in terms that take claims to cultural well-being into account. Within illiberal groups, liberal sympathies may well appear as "private" matters that should not affect the public agenda. Most liberals would call this discrimination, a serious offense against the freedom of conscience and the political freedoms of individuals. In this case, they would be all too willing to make the personal political. And this is exactly what Kymlicka does, for both liberal and illiberal sympathies. Since such sympathies are crucial to the self-understandings and well-being of individuals, they have to be respected, at least in a minimal sense. Furthermore, it is only by allowing the public defense of such sympathies—through the subsidization of cultural forms among other things—that they can be controlled. For once the personal and the cultural have become politically and publicly relevant, there are grounds to engage in debates that will usually start from a modus vivendi only, but that might lead to stronger common understandings. In such debates, liberals are free to promote the value of personal autonomy—they have to if they want to instigate changes. Yet, Kymlicka makes it very clear that some liberal self-understandings might be mistaken. He explicitly stresses the fact that group-minority rights are not only directed at particular groups but also—in a less immediate sense—call for changes in the common values that underlie an order that considers itself a liberal one. Indeed, no society is ideally liberal. And as I have argued earlier it is only through an open confrontation of liberal values with values that do not seem to fit into the liberal scheme that societies—and the many groups that inhabit them—could become more liberal.

This view does not presuppose that only liberals may interfere in other cultures. Rather, it presupposes that all groups in society may enter into debates and practices that may be expected to bring about a common understanding that fits in well with actual states of affairs. Kymlicka sees liberalism not so much as a political ideology that may be expected to transcend normative conflicts. He sees it— rightly I think—as a very influential and powerful doctrine which, exactly because of its considerable influence, has a responsibility to openly confront dissenting opinions. In such confrontations, it of course draws a bottom line in terms of respect for the capacity for personal autonomy. But then again, all parties to conflicts draw bottom lines. Kymlicka looks for ways in which such bottom lines, which may seem categorical at first sight, could be changed. It is precisely because of his belief that the liberal bottom line is no less controversial to some than the latter's bottom line is to liberals, that the kind of moderate interference with cultures he professes must be considered more liberal, more humane, than the abstinence from interference that a purely political liberalism must profess.

Some might criticize Kymlicka for not developing a coherent recipe for success. His recent book is full of "I don't knows." For instance, Kymlicka does not really know which common values could hold a multicultural society together. He considers some options, shows that shared political values are not enough, but does not come up with clear answers. He even suggests that self-government rights for national minorities—rights that he has defended on several occasions—pose a considerable threat to social unity. Why defend them in the first place? His answer to such questions seems to be that there are reasons—historical and legal reasons mainly—why these rights cannot simply be taken away from groups. And since empirical research clearly shows that such blunt measures usually backfire and in fact strengthen malignant nationalist and separatist sympathies, Kymlicka has to admit that "[w]e seem caught in a Gordian knot" (186).

I find these remarks refreshing. Normative political theory is a discipline that is used to finding general answers to practically all social problems. The details of these answers, normative theorists often say, have to be worked out by means of empirical research and political effectuation. Often, this is not a bad strategy. The work of many political philosophers has played and continues to play an important role in our understanding of the concepts of justice, rights, freedom, toleration, solidarity, and so forth. But their role is a limited one. Often we hear empirical researchers and politicians say that philosophical answers are too abstract, too idealistic, and impractical. It is not surprising that such remarks are very often addressed to those philosophers who are inspired by the belief that there simply must be a reasonable answer to all social problems. Here again, we reach a point where we may have to admit that, in the end, not all ethical and cultural aspirations can be combined. If this is true, the conclusion must be that liberal-democratic societies will sometimes have to come up with justifications of policies that simply cannot be justified in terms that everybody will accept because of their reasonableness. I do not want to suggest that we should no longer search for reasonable justifications. On the contrary, we always should. But there may be a considerable amount of reasonableness in admitting that sometimes we simply do not know the answers and fear that they will never be found.

A third point of critique concerns Kymlicka's notion of a societal culture and his distinction between external protections and internal restrictions. I fear that, generally, external protections of a societal culture against the impact of decisions of the larger society are more likely to narrow the range of options that members of this culture can choose from (and promote internal restrictions) than Kymlicka is willing to admit. These terms are useful tools in assessing what liberals should and should not find problematic about claims to cultural integrity. But they represent a first step in coming to terms with such questions. A second step would be to emphasize more strongly than Kymlicka that not only internal restrictions can frustrate the personal autonomy of people, but that external protections may do so as well. Here, the problem is that the need for external protections will often be advocated by representatives of a group who do not just value a cultural structure but who voice their claims in terms of characteristics of this structure that may well be controversial within the group they represent. I do not see any easy solutions to this problem, which is one of access to cultural-political power. The best we can do is to understand Kymlicka's vocabulary as a new and not yet properly tested proposal to look at pressing problems. The value of the proposal will have to be tested in practice. For it is only in practice that we can find out whether liberal strategies work. In this case, I am moderately optimistic. But I do think that his argument for regarding cultural membership as a primary good is sound. In a Rawlsian or Waldronian world we might not need it. But in the world we are living in—a deeply pluralist world in which tragic conflicts abound—Kymlicka's strategy of looking explicitly at the needs of those whose well-being is under threat because of the prevalence of liberal institutions seems to be well taken.

Conclusions to Part 5

What conclusions follow from this investigation into liberalism's relation to multiculturalism? I think that it shows that the theoretical interpretation of liberalism I have presented could be of considerable value for the assessment of pressing social and political questions. Questions of multiculturalism can be taken seriously if we drop the understandable but ultimately mistaken search for Archimedean foundations. Liberalism is a valuable doctrine the central values of which are deeply entrenched in Western culture and, more specifically, in the institutions and practices of Western nation-states.

Adherence to liberalism should be (and ultimately always is) inspired by the value of liberal practices themselves, not by some a prioristic understanding of the deep structures of human reason or the unquestionable value of "our" way of doing things. Let me judge the three positions we have studied from a perspective that acknowledges the tragedy of liberalism.

As we have seen, Taylor's account of liberalism's relation to questions of multiculturalism is sensitive to the tragedy of liberalism. Taylor explains the tragedy of liberalism in terms of often irresolvable tensions between two notions of respect or recognition that he claims are crucial to modern life; a notion of equal respect for the dignity of human beings per se and respect for the often very different notions of the good life—including notions of cultural belonging—that different human beings adhere to. The conflicts he identifies between these notions are very similar to the various conflicts that I have called tragic conflicts. I have shown that liberalism presupposes both notions of respect and recognition, and that the tragedy of liberalism springs from tensions that may exist between them. It is because of the genuine aim of liberalism to do justice to both perspectives that some conflicts become tragic. And because of the aim to do justice to both perspectives from a firm belief in the value of personal autonomy this aim becomes liberal. It is at this point, however, that Taylor's position becomes problematic. For although he explains respect for the dignity of human beings in terms of the recognition of their potential for autonomous action, he tends to explain respect for difference too strongly in terms of respect for communities, cultures, and so on—that is, not always in terms of the value of communal and cultural belonging as a prerequisite for individual well-being. In doing so, he introduces an understanding of valuable social forms to his account that, from a liberal perspective, must appear as deeply problematic. To put my point in perhaps somewhat exaggerated but clear terms, Taylor wants liberalism to incorporate a sense of respect for culture as such, which simply is foreign to liberal values. By doing so, he overshoots the liberal mark. Even liberals who acknowledge the tragic predicament of liberalism and who understand that Taylor identifies a very real problem must reject his normative proposal, since it is not clear that it respects the capacity for personal autonomy that is characteristic of liberalism. Such liberals prefer to endure tragic conflicts of multiculturalism rather than to try to overcome them according to Taylor. For they fear that instead of enriching liberalism, Taylor's proposal seriously endangers its highest aims.

Jeremy Waldron's cosmopolitan alternative cannot be said to be sensitive to the tragic predicament of liberalism (or cosmopolitanism understood as a variation of liberalism, for that matter). On the contrary, his arguments go against the grain of much I have argued for in this study. My argument starts from the assumption that our moral and political responsibilities toward others flow primarily from those actions and beliefs that we genuinely stand for. If we stand for liberal values, then the first thing we must ask ourselves is how these values relate to the values of others. For given our social nature, it is only through a comparison of our own values, principles, and practices with others that we can come to understand their general worth. If the circumstances are right, liberalism can offer personal and public autonomy, freedom, moral pluralism, equality, and toleration. With the influence of liberal ideas on human relations throughout the world come great powers and, therefore, great responsibilities. People are not liberals by birth. They have to be brought up to be liberals. And it is for this reason that Waldron's theoretical treatment of individuals and groups who have a hard time accepting liberal values and practices is so inappropriate. Harshly put, his argument is that because it is possible to lead a good liberal life, and because liberalism is able to respond adequately to the many global interdependencies that characterize the lives of contemporary individuals, all people should become liberals. Of course, Waldron is entitled to make this claim. But as we have seen, making this claim in a responsible fashion presupposes that one reflect on the social conditions that provide individuals with genuine options. Among these conditions are provisions such as special, group-differentiated rights that may be expected to enable members of minority cultures to make responsible choices between the values they were brought up with and the values that more or less liberal cultures provide. Since Waldron is unwilling to admit that this is what the social responsibilities that come with liberalism require, his position must be rejected. It is less attractive than Taylor's position, which at least identifies serious problems that spring from the reign of liberal values and practices. Whereas Taylor expresses respect for cultural integrity in terms that liberals should be reluctant to embrace, Waldron makes a mockery of the idea of cultural integrity as such. He is not able to acknowledge the tragedy of liberalism's relation to multiculturalism because he simply discards one of the very real constituent poles of the tragic conflict at hand. The very questionableness of his account seems to provide us with an additional reason to take the tragedy of liberalism seriously.

As to Kymlicka, it is not the questionableness but rather the convincing nature of his account that provides us with such a reason. His achievement is that he takes seriously the two notions of respect that we have so frequently discussed, without neglecting the many tensions that exist between them. In many ways, Kymlicka stands for a kind of liberalism that I think is highly promising. First of all, he defends a moderately perfectionist liberalism based on a firm affirmation of the ideal of personal autonomy. Second, he does not see liberalism as a doctrine that transcends pluralism and social conflicts. Rather, he understands it as an influential party in a pluralist world that professes a normative outlook which, if defended correctly, indeed stands a good chance of winning the adherence of many. Third, and following from the second point, he makes it very clear that liberalism consists to a large extent in the willingness to endure tragic conflicts without giving up the hope that they may one day be overcome or at least mitigated

There is much modesty in this approach, a modesty that I think should characterize all positions that recognize—either implicitly or explicitly—the tragic predicament of liberalism. Such modesty must be inspired by respect for individuality, and by its social conditions, per se. For respect for individuality is the first condition that has to be met before it becomes possible to address individuals as persons who are capable of autonomous action. I strongly believe that versions of liberalism that simply take individuality—and the vulnerable nature of individuality—seriously, stand the best chance of being accepted as benign, humane doctrines. Highly worked out notions of justice, reasonableness, and toleration are essential to liberal normative theories. But as we have frequently seen, a one-sided focus on these notions tends to obscure what liberalism is really all about. By evading these simple terms of respect for individuality and by immediately diving into the theoretical depths of academic reasoning, many liberal political theories lose contact with the real problems that are at issue. I do not mean to say that from now on all political philosophers should abstain from fundamental theoretical activities and engage in low-threshold missionary work. What I do mean to say, however, is that there are serious dangers to the one-dimensional focus on purportedly neutral justificatory strategies that characterizes much of liberal political philosophy. There is a strong tendency in liberal thought to get lost in the puzzles that come with the unquestioned assumption that human reason must in principle be able to provide a reasonable and neutral solution to all normative conflicts. Of course, the benign intentions that inspire these theories are beyond doubt. But as we have seen, some of the practical conclusions that follow from them cannot be reconciled with a perspective that puts respect for individuality and for the pluralist nature of our social world above obligations to rigid and nonresponsive notions of neutrality and reasonableness. A perspective that takes the tragic predicament of liberalism seriously is one that tries to mediate between respect for individuality and pluralism and the notions of reasonableness that we need in order to respond to them. Of course, the aim for such a mediation characterizes the work of most liberal theorists I have discussed. It has been the aim of this study to show that their arguments would become more convincing if they were to take seriously the perspective that I have tried to develop and defend here.

Notes

Part 1: Liberalism, Pluralism, Tragedy

Introduction

1. For similar formulations, see Will Kymlicka, *Liberalism, Community, and Culture* (Oxford: Clarendon Press, 1989), 13; and Andrew Kernohan, *Liberalism, Equality, and Cultural Oppression* (Cambridge: Cambridge University Press, 1998), 2. Of course, this formulation raises the question whether liberalism can pursue this aim while remaining neutral toward conceptions of the good life. Throughout this study, I will argue that liberalism should be understood as a moderately perfectionist doctrine that presupposes the validity of conceptions of the good life to which the ideals of personal autonomy and an affirmation of the value of pluralism are crucial. This does not mean, however, that a perfectionist liberal politics is allowed straightforwardly to coerce citizens into accepting these controversial ideals.

Chapter 1: Liberalism and Moral Pluralism

1. Richard Bellamy, *Liberalism and Modern Society. An Historical Argument* (Cambridge: Polity Press, 1992), 1.

2. A "just" society is one in which questions of distributive justice have been answered in a way that reasonable citizens could on principle agree to. A "good" society is not only just in this sense, but is also understood by its members to be a well-integrated community that helps foster their personal as well as their collective conceptions of a good life. Both notions are ideal notions. I have elaborated on the two concepts in "Die anständige,

die gerechte und die gute Gesellschaft," *Deutsche Zeitschrift für Philosophie* 47 (1999): 271–89.

3. Reflections on the role of the market fall outside the scope of this study. I firmly believe that people are first and foremost self-interpreting ethical beings; beings who live and act in the world from partly pregiven and partly self-defined frameworks of value that help them define what is right and what is wrong, what is good and what is bad, and who primarily find their fulfillment by shaping the social and natural world they inhabit in ways that reflect these frameworks. Of course, the market often plays an important role in this, but neither the market nor the primarily instrumentalist, calculative type of rationality it thrives on should be considered fundamental in attempts to come to terms with ideas of social, legal, and political order and legitimacy in liberal thought. For such approaches see Axel Honneth, *The Struggle for Recognition: The Moral Grammar of Social Conflicts*, transl. by Joel Anderson (Cambridge: Polity Press, 1995); Alasdair MacIntyre, *After Virtue: A Study in Moral Theory* (Notre Dame: University of Notre Dame Press, 1981); Philip Selznick, *The Moral Commonwealth: Social Theory and the Promise of Community* (Berkeley: University of California Press, 1992); and Charles Taylor, *Sources of the Self: The Making of the Modern Identity* (Cambridge: Cambridge University Press, 1989).

4. See Wibren van der Burg, "The Importance of Ideals," *Journal of Value Inquiry* 31 (1997): 23–37.

5. See Robert Bellah et al., *Habits of the Heart: Individualism and Commitment in American Life* (Berkeley: University of California Press, 1985); and Peter Ester, Loek Halman, and Ruud de Moor, *The Individualizing Society: Value Change in Europe and North America* (Tilburg, Netherlands: Tilburg University Press, 1993). Of course, not all citizens share the orientations mentioned here. I will come back to that many times throughout this study.

6. John Rawls, *Political Liberalism* (New York: Columbia University Press, 1993), 19.

7. For recent reconstructions of the normative core of modern societies that all in some way or other combine these two notions of freedom, see Jürgen Habermas, *Between Facts and Norms: Contributions to a Discourse Theory of Law and Democracy*, transl. by William Rehg (Cambridge: Polity Press, 1996); Honneth, *Struggle for Recognition*; Christoph Menke, *Tragödie im Sittlichen: Gerechtigkeit und Freiheit nach Hegel* (Frankfurt am Main, Germany: Suhrkamp, 1996); Rawls, *Political Liberalism*; and Taylor, *Sources of the Self*.

8. Steven Wall, *Liberalism, Perfectionism and Restraint* (Cambridge: Cambridge University Press, 1998), 128.

9. Taylor, *The Ethics of Authenticity* (Cambridge: Harvard University Press, 1993), 29.

10. Menke, *Tragödie im Sittlichen*, 196; Taylor, *Ethics of Authenticity*, 28–29.

11. See chapter 3 for a discussion of political liberalism.

12. Rawls, *Political Liberalism*, 179–80. See also Charles Larmore, *Patterns of Moral Complexity* (Cambridge: Cambridge University Press, 1987), 106.

13. The last point is made by William A. Galston, who, however, should not be taken to be a "political liberal." Galston, *Liberal Purposes: Goods, Virtues, and Diversity in the Liberal State* (Cambridge: Cambridge University Press, 1991), 253ff.

14. In chapter 4, we will see that some authors think that liberalism can and should be grounded in certain ideas of personal excellence. See my discussion of the work of Joseph Raz in that chapter.

15. Of course, many liberal authors have severely criticized the idea of neutrality characteristic of political liberalism. Still, in some way or other, neutrality in the minimum sense of fair treatment of all citizens as equals is important for all liberals. In most cases, the question at stake is not whether the liberal state should treat its citizens as equals, but at what point such treatment should start. Raz, for example, holds that liberalism is "not a doctrine of neutrality but of moral pluralism" (Raz, *The Morality of Freedom* [Oxford: Clarendon Press, 1986], 133). In chapter 4 we will see that I agree with that view. Yet, neither Raz's nor my own account of liberal perfectionism denies that, for instance, fair and impartial treatment of all citizens before the law is important.

16. Rawls is the most influential representative of the first approach. See his *Theory of Justice* (Cambridge: Harvard University Press, 1971); and *Political Liberalism*. Habermas is the most well-known representative of the second approach. See his book *Between Facts and Norms*.

17. Habermas, "Die klassische Lehre von der Politik in ihrem Verhältnis zur Sozialphilosophie," in Habermas, *Theorie und Praxis* (Frankfurt am Main, Germany: Suhrkamp, 1971), 56ff.; Jeremy Waldron, "Theoretical Foundations of Liberalism," in Waldron, *Liberal Rights: Collected Papers 1981–1991* (Cambridge: Cambridge University Press, 1993), 43ff.

18. Of course, early liberals had very narrow ideas about full membership and citizenship. For example, they often thought of women and "savages" as emotional beings who were not capable of reasonable thought and action and who should, therefore, not be granted the status of full citizenship. However, this bias, which was characteristic of their time, does not necessarily discredit the fundamental idea that all reasonable beings should

have a fair say in the generation of general principles for social life. In order
to make effective use of this fundamental idea in contemporary theory, we
have to both redefine the class of reasonable beings and ask whether we can
still accept early liberal ideas of reasonableness.

19. See Selznick, *Moral Commonwealth*, 374f.

20. For the characterizations of Robert Nozick and James Buchanan
see Amartya Sen, *Inequality Reexamined* (New York/Cambridge: Russel
Sage Foundation/Harvard University Press, 1992), 13; Buchanan, *The Limits of Liberty* (Chicago: University of Chicago Press, 1975); and Nozick, *An-
archy, State, and Utopia* (Oxford: Blackwell, 1974). For the idea of treating
people "as equals" see Ronald Dworkin, "Liberalism," in Dworkin, *A Matter
of Principle* (Cambridge: Harvard University Press, 1985), 190ff.

21. The liberal tradition is by no means characterized by any deep
agreement as to what it means to treat individuals as equals. See chapters
10 and 11, where liberal views as to the treatment of citizens with different
cultural backgrounds are discussed.

22. Often, liberalism is understood as a rights-based doctrine. See,
paradigmatically, Dworkin, *Taking Rights Seriously* (Cambridge: Harvard
University Press, 1978). Since rights are among the chief means of liberal
societies to protect and foster the freedom and equality of their citizens, this
is understandable. Especially when questions concerning (the philosophy of)
law or social policy are one's primary interest, there is much to be said for
such an understanding of liberalism. In this study, however, I am primarily
interested in frameworks of value that can help us understand why certain
rights are so important in liberal thought. Here, I team up with liberal authors who hold that the meaning of rights should primarily be explained in
terms of more basic interests they serve for rights holders, most importantly
the interests in personal freedom, political freedom, and membership of a
flourishing common culture. See Raz, "Rights and Individual Well-being," in
Raz, *Ethics in the Public Domain* (Oxford: Clarendon Press, 1994), 33ff.
Such interests, I will argue, are critical to the frameworks of value that underlie convincing liberal theories, including liberal theories of rights.

23. Taylor, "The Politics of Recognition," in *Multiculturalism*, ed. by
Amy Gutmann (Princeton: Princeton University Press, 1994), 66ff. Taylor
uses the idea of a "presumption of equal value" to elucidate questions of intercultural diversity. However, his hermeneutic point also applies to intra-
cultural diversity.

24. Bruce Ackerman, "Why Dialogue?" *The Journal of Philosophy* 86
(1989): 5–22.

25. Seyla Benhabib, "Liberal Dialogue versus a Critical Theory of Discursive Legitimation," in *Liberalism and the Moral Life*, ed. by Nancy
Rosenblum (Cambridge: Harvard University Press, 1989), 143–56.

26. Raz, *Morality of Freedom*.

27. I agree with Waldron that the ideal of freedom—most importantly that of individual freedom—is at the heart of liberalism. See Waldron, "Theoretical Foundations of Liberalism." This does not mean, however, that there can be no real conflict between, for instance, the ideal of personal freedom and that of equality of opportunity. For the ideal of freedom does not simply trump that of equality. Rather, it is likely that the conflict can be "translated" into the language of freedom—that it can be understood as a conflict between my freedom and yours.

28. Rawls, *Political Liberalism*, xxiv.

29. In the case of Rawls, it is necessary to emphasize that his *Political Liberalism* corrects many of the less convincing aspects of the theory of justice he presented in his *Theory of Justice*, at which my argument here is directed. Some readers may wonder whether it is correct to present Habermas as a liberal author. Usually, the work of Habermas and his many followers is labeled "discourse-theoretical." And sometimes it is also referred to as "critical-theoretical." What I find unfortunate about these labels is that they hide rather than stress that, as a normative political theory, Habermas's theory is a thoroughly liberal-democratic one. See part 3 for a detailed analysis of Habermas's work.

30. Galston, *Liberal Purposes*; Raz, *Morality of Freedom*; Richard Rorty, *Contingency, Irony, and Solidarity* (Cambridge: Cambridge University Press, 1989). Authors who take this position are sometimes also said to stand for a "hermeneutic" defense of liberalism. See Georgia Warnke, *Justice and Interpretation* (Cambridge: MIT Press, 1993).

31. Which is not to say that these differences will always be "morally" neutral. Think, for instance, of racist ideologies that ground their "moral" views to a considerable extent on bodily differences.

32. J. Donald Moon, *Constructing Community: Moral Pluralism and Tragic Conflicts* (Princeton: Princeton University Press, 1993), 24.

33. Ibid., 24. See also Taylor's analysis of struggles for recognition of cultural communities within liberal states in his "Politics of Recognition."

34. Habermas, "On the Pragmatic, the Ethical, and the Moral Employments of Practical Reason," in Habermas, *Justification and Application*, transl. by Ciaran Cronin (Cambridge: Polity Press, 1993), 1–17. From now on, I will use the term *ethical pluralism*—not moral pluralism—to refer to a pluralism of competing and sometimes incompatible conceptions of the good life.

35. This line of thought has strong roots in the Kantian belief that the dignity of the human subject is not bound up with particular desires, aims, purposes, and notions of the good life, but rather with the essential capac-

ity of the subject for autonomous thought and action. In later chapters we will see that liberal theories such as those presented in Rawls's *Theory of Justice* and *Political Liberalism*, and in Habermas's *Between Facts and Norms* problematically build upon this line of thought. Note that the claim is not that these authors would explicitly state that personal ideas of freedom are mere preferences, but rather that implicit in their theories is a tendency to treat these ideas as if they were mere preferences.

36. Paradigmatically, this distinction is developed by Habermas in his article "On the Pragmatic, the Ethical, and the Moral Employments of Practical Reason," in Habermas, *Justification and Application*.

37. Stephen Mulhall and Adam Swift, *Liberals & Communitarians* (Oxford: Blackwell, 1996), 197.

38. One could also call them rhetorical questions. I present them here because all are regularly being put forward by critics of what I call Archimedean liberalism. In the context of this part of the book, their sole purpose is to make it easier for me to elucidate some basic theoretical assumptions and approaches of Archimedean liberal theories in an economical, yet fair way.

39. This is the basic strategy for dealing with these issues in the work of Habermas. See chapters 5 and 6.

40. This strategy can be found in Rawls, *Political Liberalism*, particularly on 152f. See chapter 3.

Chapter 2: The Tragedy of Liberalism

1. For the conceptual connection between the notions of tragedy and loss see Susan Mendus, "Tragedy, Moral Conflict, and Liberalism," in *Philosophy and Pluralism*, Royal Institute of Philosophy supplement, ed. by David Archard (Cambridge: Cambridge University Press, 1996), 191–201.

2. Peter Szondi, *Versuch über das Tragische* (Frankfurt am Main, Germany: Insel Verlag, 1961), 65ff. In this particular reading, the theme of *Oedipus Rex* fits my understanding of the tragic in this study very well. However, I do not mean to suggest that every Greek tragedy expresses the same idea of the tragic. From a literary perspective, Greek tragedies form a genre that is characterized by formal features such as particular techniques of storytelling and an important role for the chorus, rather than by the expression of "the" tragic experience. I thank Keimpe Algra for pointing this out to me.

3. Bernard Williams, *Shame and Necessity* (Berkeley: University of California Press, 1993), 163.

4. Ibid.

5. Ibid., 164 (for the citation) and 164ff.

6. The term *value pluralism* refers to the irreducible plurality of values that can be found in the social world. "Moral pluralism" and "ethical pluralism," on the other hand, refers to a pluralism of moral and ethical doctrines within a particular society. These normative doctrines represent reactions to value pluralism. But the same goes for what we might call moral monism, which would be a doctrine that denies the moral significance of most given values and constructs one supreme and incontestable conception of what is morally permitted and what is not. Where I use the term *value pluralism*, I do so in the sense of an ontological claim. Where I use the terms *moral pluralism* and *ethical pluralism*, I refer to a plurality of moral and ethical doctrines within liberal society.

7. Isaiah Berlin sketched the contours of his tragic liberalism—which was never presented as a systematic theory—in many of his essays. Of course, his most influential statements concerning irreconcilable and sometimes tragic conflicts of value can be found in "Two Concepts of Liberty," in his *Four Essays on Liberty* (Oxford: Oxford University Press, 1969), 118–72. See Bernard Williams, *Shame and Necessity* (Berkeley: University of California Press, 1993); J. Donald Moon, *Constructing Community: Moral Pluralism and Tragic Conflicts* (Princeton: Princeton University Press, 1993); Christoph Menke, *Tragödie im Sittlichen: Gerechtigkeit und Freiheit nach Hegel* (Frankfurt am Main, Germany: Suhrkamp, 1996); and Mendus, "Tragedy, Moral Conflict, and Liberalism." In developing my thesis of the tragedy of liberalism, I have learned much from these works. Works of related interest, that have influenced me less though, are Martha Nussbaum, *The Fragility of Goodness: Luck and Ethics in Greek Tragedy and Philosophy* (Cambridge: Cambridge University Press, 1986); and J. Peter Euben, *The Tragedy of Political Theory. The Road Not Taken* (Princeton: Princeton University Press, 1990).

8. Berlin, "Two Concepts of Liberty," 169.

9. I think this appraisal of Berlin is in line with the reconstruction of his thought presented in John Gray, *Isaiah Berlin* (Princeton: Princeton University Press, 1996). A book that points in the same direction is Michael Ignatieff, *Isaiah Berlin: A Life* (London: Chatto & Windus, 1998).

10. It comes as no great surprise, then, that both Moon and Mendus seem to have learned much from communitarian and feminist critiques of liberalism.

11. Moon, *Constructing Community*, 10; my emphasis.

12. As will become clear in chapter 3, the main problem I have with Moon's account is that it ultimately grounds liberalism in a politically liberal notion of "agency-rights." In my view, this approach is far too formal and too capacity-focused to be convincing, especially in light of Moon's ear-

lier claim that liberalism is a far more substantive normative doctrine than most liberals want to admit.

13. Mendus, "Tragedy, Moral Conflict, and Liberalism," 200.

14. Williams, *Shame and Necessity*, 130.

15. Ibid.

16. Ibid., 141.

17. Some of the works that have been influential in this reorientation of the predominantly Rawlsian liberalisms of the 1970s and 1980s are William A. Galston, *Liberal Purposes: Goods, Virtues, and Diversity in the Liberal State* (Cambridge: Cambridge University Press, 1991); Will Kymlicka, *Liberalism, Community and Culture* (Oxford: Clarendon Press, 1989); Kymlicka, *Multicultural Citizenship* (Oxford: Oxford University Press, 1995); Stephen Macedo, *Liberal Virtues: Citizenship, Virtue, and Community in Liberal Constitutionalism* (Oxford: Clarendon Press, 1990); and Joseph Raz, *The Morality of Freedom* (Oxford: Clarendon Press, 1986).

18. Menke, *Tragödie im Sittlichen*, 30ff. I have benefited from Menke's discussion of metaphysical (or, in my terms: *ontological*) notions of the tragic (ibid., 36ff.). See chapter 7 for Menke's extremely helpful typology of tragic conflicts.

19. This uncontestable claim explains why so many authors understand the conflict over abortion to be a paradigmatic example of a tragic conflict that liberalism is a party to. See Mendus, "Tragedy, Moral Conflict, and Liberalism" and, especially, Moon, *Constructing Community*.

20. For instructive liberal discussions of controversies surrounding the right to abortion see Ronald Dworkin, *Life's Dominion: An Argument about Abortion, Euthanasia, and Individual Freedom* (New York: Knopf, 1993); and Andreas Kuhlmann, *Abtreibung und Selbstbestimmung: Die Intervention der Medizin* (Frankfurt am Main, Germany: Fischer, 1996).

21. I follow Moon, *Constructing Community*, 79-80, whose argument is inspired by Kristin Luker, *Abortion and the Politics of Motherhood* (Berkeley: University of California Press, 1984). Against their interpretation of the debate, the point could be raised that not all prolife positions necessarily rest on traditionalist or orthodox religious worldviews. I do not mean to deny that a secular liberal could have difficulties with abortion. Yet, the absolute rejection of abortion (even after rape, if the life or health of the mother is at stake) does in most cases seem to rest on traditionalist or orthodox religious beliefs. Therefore, I think that there is sufficient reason to follow Luker and Moon.

22. See chapter 3 for a discussion of this issue.

23. See also Mendus, "Tragedy, Moral Conflict, and Liberalism," 198.

24. The argument is Raz's. See chapter 4.

25. This idea is ascribed to Goethe, Napoleon, and Benjamin Constant. See Williams, *Shame and Necessity*, 164; and Menke, *Tragödie im Sittichen*, 9.

Part 2: Political Liberalism versus Liberal Perfectionism

Introduction

1. In part 3, we will see that some "deliberative democrats," Jürgen Habermas in particular, opt for a similar view. For systematic reasons, I will postpone my discussion of the theory of deliberative democracy until the next part of this book.

2. John Rawls, *Political Liberalism* (New York: Columbia University Press, 1993), 13. Rawls is the most influential representative of this interpretation of liberalism. I will concentrate mainly on his work. Other writers in this tradition are Bruce Ackerman, *Social Justice and the Liberal State* (New Haven: Yale University Press, 1980); Ackerman, "Why Dialogue?" *The Journal of Philosophy* 86 (1989): 5–22; Charles Larmore, *Patterns of Moral Complexity* (Cambridge: Cambridge University Press 1987); and J. Donald Moon, *Constructing Community: Moral Pluralism and Tragic Conflicts* (Princeton: Princeton University Press, 1993).

3. Rawls, *Political Liberalism*, 99.

4. Joseph Raz, *The Morality of Freedom* (Oxford: Clarendon Press, 1986), 369. I take Raz to be the most outspoken contemporary liberal perfectionist. I will discuss his work in the next chapter. Other writers who loosely stand in this tradition are William A. Galston, *Liberal Purposes: Goods, Virtues, and Diversity in the Liberal State* (Cambridge: Cambridge University Press, 1991); Andrew Kernohan, *Liberalism, Equality, and Cultural Oppression* (Cambridge: Cambridge University Press, 1998); Stephen Macedo, *Liberal Virtues: Citizenship, Virtue and Community in Liberal Constitutionalism* (Oxford: Clarendon Press, 1990); and Stephen Wall, *Liberalism, Perfectionism and Restraint* (Cambridge: Cambridge University Press, 1998).

Chapter 3: Political Liberalism: Justification through Public Reason

1. Stephen Macedo, *Liberal Virtues: Citizenship, Virtue, and Community in Liberal Constitutionalism* (Oxford: Clarendon Press, 1990), 41.

2. John Rawls, *Political Liberalism* (New York: Columbia University Press, 1993), 217. In this chapter, references to Rawls, placed in parentheses in the text, are to this work.

3. See Rawls's comments on this strategy of *A Theory of Justice* (Cambridge: Harvard University Press, 1971) in the introduction to his *Political Liberalism*, xiiff.

4. Alasdair MacIntyre, *After Virtue: A Study in Moral Theory* (Notre Dame: University of Notre Dame Press, 1981); Michael Sandel, *Liberalism and the Limits of Justice* (Cambridge: Cambridge University Press, 1982). See Stephen Mulhall and Adam Swift, *Liberals & Communitarians* (Oxford: Blackwell, 1996) for a good overview and analysis of the communitarian critique of Rawls's early theory.

5. Charles Taylor, "Cross-Purposes: The Liberal-Communitarian Debate," in *Liberalism and the Moral Life*, ed. by Nancy Rosenblum (Cambridge: Harvard University Press, 1989), 159–82; Taylor, "The Politics of Recognition," in *Multiculturalism*, ed. by Amy Gutmann (Princeton: Princeton University Press, 1994), 25–73.

6. Rawls, *Political Liberalism*, xvii n. 6.

7. Note that Rawls does not claim that people who have these capacities will necessarily be free in other, nonpolitical spheres of their lives. The claim is just that the two moral powers are a minimum prerequisite for successful citizenship understood as participation in a fair system of social ooperation

8. They are "a. Each person has an equal right to a fully adequate scheme of equal basic liberties which is compatible with a similar scheme of liberties for all. b. Social and economic inequalities are to satisfy two conditions. First, they must be attached to offices and positions open to all under conditions of fair equality of opportunity; and second, they must be to the greatest benefit of the least advantaged members of society" (291).

9. Rawls spells out the exact consequences of this idea in a recent article, "The Idea of Public Reason Revisited," *The University of Chicago Law Review* 64 (1997): 765–809. In this article, he states that the idea of public reason applies to "the discourse of judges," to "the discourse of government officials," and to "the discourse of candidates for office" (767). Furthermore, he claims that it does not apply to "the background culture with its many forms of nonpublic reason nor to media of any kind" (768). In my discussion of Rawls's theory, which focuses on *Political Liberalism*, I may sometimes seem to forget about this distinction, which was not spelled out as clearly in the book as in the later article. However, I am quite certain that Rawls has not really changed his view on the conversational constraints that not only public officials but also citizens within the wider background culture have to respect. For in this article, he keeps emphasizing that, when constitutional

essentials or matters of basic justice are at stake, "all reasonable citizens should think of themselves as if they were legislators following public reason" (771). Rawls's ideal notion of cooperation and deliberation within the "background culture" is still much more constrained than he sometimes suggests in his reactions to those who criticize his views (see, e.g., 768 n. 15, 775 n. 30).

10. They speak for themselves in the sense that liberals will not find them controversial—not in the sense that all human beings will see them as the most fundamental social goods

11. Rawls, *Political Liberalism*, 193; my emphasis.

12. Historically, the universal granting of basic civil rights preceded, in most Western countries, the granting of political rights to all or most groups in society. And the reasons had to do with social struggles and civil strife within society that had to be controlled, not primarily with democratic deliberations over fundamental questions of justice. Still, as a thought experiment in moral psychology that starts from theoretical assumptions basic to his approach, Rawls's point seems to be well taken.

13. I do not mean to suggest here that we have to accept some sort of teleological belief in the likelihood of an irreversible transition from the first to the second stage. Rawls himself does not suggest this either.

14. I largely follow Joseph Raz and Steven Wall's understanding of autonomy. See Raz, *The Morality of Freedom* (Oxford: Clarendon Press, 1986); and Wall, *Liberalism, Perfectionism and Restraint* (Cambridge: Cambridge University Press, 1998).

15. For Rawls's view on the conflict over abortion, as argued for from the second stage see *Political Liberalism*, 243 n. 32.

16. Rawls, "Idea of Public Reason Revisited," 798.

17. Bruce Ackerman, "Why Dialogue?" *The Journal of Philosophy* 86 (1989): 16.

18. Ibid., 23; cf. Charles Larmore, *Patterns of Moral Complexity* (Cambridge: Cambridge University Press, 1987), 50ff.

19. Unconstrained dialogue is a form of dialogue that does not define rigid conversational constraints concerning structural and substantive aspects of views that may (or may not) be brought into public deliberation. It holds that such constraints, should they prove necessary, can only legitimately be arrived at through public dialogue. In chapters 5 and 6 I will go further into this notion of dialogue.

20. William A. Galston, *Liberal Purposes: Goods, Virtues, and Diversity in the Liberal State* (Cambridge: Cambridge University Press, 1991), 104; J. Donald Moon, *Constructing Community: Moral Pluralism and Tragic Conflicts* (Princeton: Princeton University Press, 1993), 77f.

21. I do not mean to suggest that unconstrained, consensus-oriented public dialogue—at a roundtable conference, so to speak—is the only or even the main social force by which social movements put their interests on the public agenda. Nor are interest-based groups or "classes" easily identifiable and necessarily characterized by singularity of outlook and purpose. Rather, social movements, interest-based groups, and classes "exist" because public spokespersons lend credibility to certain reality-based interests that are associated with a designated (and thus created) group that struggles for symbolic representation in the public domain (see Pierre Bourdieu, "What Makes a Social Class: On the Theoretical and Practical Existence of Groups," *Berkeley Journal of Sociology* 32 [1987]: 1–17). Symbolic representation takes on many forms, varying from silent marches to radical publications, terrorist activity, and democratic deliberation. My focus on public deliberation serves the purpose of taking symbolic representations seriously from a liberal-democratic political perspective, from which we have to reconstruct their meanings in terms of a contribution to an open-ended conversation on the legitimacy of the social and political order to which they are directed.

22. Moon, *Constructing Community*, 11. In this section, all references to Moon, placed in parentheses, are to this work. Unfortunately, Moon does not offer a detailed conceptual account of what a tragic conflict is. He speaks of tragic conflicts as "situations in which, no matter what is done, some will experience the action that follows the decision that resolved the conflict as an imposition" (63). Since this definition stays close to what I would call a sad experience, I am not sure whether he would agree with the account in terms of the "double" collision of necessities that, following Menke, I sketched in chapter 1.

23. Seyla Benhabib, *Critique, Norm, and Utopia: A Study of the Foundations of Critical Theory* (New York: Columbia University Press, 1986); Benhabib, "The Generalized and the Concrete Other: The Kohlberg-Gilligan Controversy and Feminist Theory," *Praxis International* 5 (1986): 402–24; and Benhabib, "Liberal Dialogue versus a Critical Theory of Discursive Legitimation," in *Liberalism and the Moral Life*, ed. by Nancy Rosenblum (Cambridge: Harvard University Press, 1989), 143–56.

24. This sums up the most important positions that Moon rejects in chapters 2–4 of his book.

Chapter 4: Liberal Perfectionism: Autonomy and Pluralism

1. Joseph Raz, *The Morality of Freedom* (Oxford: Clarendon Press, 1986), 426. In this chaper, all references to Raz, placed in parentheses, are to this work.

2. For example, Stephen Macedo, *Liberal Virtues: Citizenship, Virtue and Community in Liberal Constitutionalism* (Oxford: Clarendon Press, 1990); William A. Galston, *Liberal Purposes: Goods, Virtues, and Diversity in the Liberal State* (Cambridge: Cambridge University Press, 1991); and Steven Wall, *Liberalism, Perfectionism and Restraint* (Cambridge: Cambridge University Press, 1998).

3. Raz, "Government by Consent," in Raz, *Ethics in the Public Domain* (Oxford: Clarendon Press, 1994), 349.

4. Both citations are from Raz, "Government by Consent," 349.

5. I have benefited from the discussion of Raz's work in Stephen Mulhall and Adam Swift, *Liberals & Communitarians* (Oxford: Blackwell, 1996), 309–47.

6. Raz, "Rights and Individual Well-being," in Raz, *Ethics in the Public Domain*, 29.

7. Ibid., 34, 37, 38.

8. Raz, "Facing Diversity: The Care of Epistemic Abstinence," in Raz, *Ethics in the Public Domain*, 59f., 63.

9. Raz, "Duties of Well-Being," in ibid., 23.

10. Ibid., 23, 24.

11. See also Raz, "Duties of Well-being," 4f., 24.

12. Ibid., 24.

Part 3: Deliberative Democracy as a Way Out?

Introduction

1. Other approaches in this tradition are Kenneth Baynes, "Liberal Neutrality, Pluralism, and Deliberative Politics," *Praxis International* 12 (1992): 50–69; Seyla Benhabib, *Critique, Norm, and Utopia: A Study of the Foundations of Critical Theory* (New York: Columbia University Press, 1986); James Bohman, *Public Deliberation: Pluralism, Complexity and Democracy* (Cambridge: MIT Press, 1996); Jean Cohen and Andrew Arato, *Civil Society and Political Theory* (Cambridge: MIT Press, 1991; Joshua Cohen, "Deliberation and Democratic Legitimacy," in *The Good Polity: Normative Analysis of the State*, ed. by A. Hamlin and Ph. Pettit (New York: Blackwell, 1991), 17–34; Rainer Forst, *Kontexte der Gerechtigkeit* (Frankfurt am Main, Germany: Suhrkamp, 1994); and Amy Gutmann and Dennis Thompson, *Democracy and Disagreement* (Cambridge Mass: Belknap/Harvard, 1996). With the exception of Joshua Cohen and Gutmann and Thompson's works, all these works in important ways draw on Habermas's arguments.

2. Perhaps it would be more appropriate to label Habermas's approach a "liberal-democratic" one, since it makes much of the dependence of liberal ideas of individual freedom and public autonomy on democratic freedom. Since most liberals and theorists of deliberative democracy readily admit that the similarities between their respective theories are much greater than the actual differences, it makes more sense to see the theory of deliberative democracy as providing us with an alternative interpretation concerning the same broad liberal tradition that political liberals and liberal perfectionists reflect on. See Jürgen Habermas, "Reconciliation Through the Use of Public Reason: Remarks on John Rawls's Political Liberalism," transl. by Ciaran Cronin, *The Journal of Philosophy* 92 (1995): 109–31; and Rawls, "Reply to Habermas," *The Journal of Philosophy* 92 (1995): 132–80.

Chapter 5: Discourse Theory and Moral Character

1. Michael Walzer, "The Idea of Civil Society. A Path to Social Reconstruction," *Dissent* (Spring 1991): 294ff.

2. Mark E. Warren, "The Self in Discursive Theory," in *The Cambridge Companion to Habermas*, ed. by Stephen K. White (Cambridge: Cambridge University Press, 1995), 167–200.

3. I follow Warren, ibid., 169ff.

4. See John Rawls's remarks on the relation of his notion of public reason to processes of opinion formation in civil society in "Reply to Habermas," *The Journal of Philosophy* 92 (1995): 136.

5. Kenneth Baynes, "Liberal Neutrality, Pluralism, and Deliberative Politics," *Praxis International* 12 (1992): 57ff.

6. T. H. Marshall, "Citizenship and Social Class," in Marshall and Tom Bottomore, *Citizenship and Social Class* (London: Pluto Press, 1992), 1–51; Ralf Dahrendorf, *The Modern Social Conflict: An Essay on the Politics of Liberty* (London: Weidenfeld and Nicholson, 1988).

7. As we have seen, Joseph Raz's perfectionism lacks a sufficiently worked-out account of public deliberation. For that reason, I compare the deliberatively democratic view with political liberalism only, and introduce perfectionist ideas to the idea of public deliberation where I think this is appropriate.

8. Jürgen Habermas, "Reconciliation Through the Use of Public Reason: Remarks on John Rawls's Political Liberalism," transl. by Ciaran Cronin, *The Journal of Philosophy* 92 (1995): 110.

9. All quotations are from ibid., pp. 118–19.

42. Ibid., 78–79.

43. Ibid., 80.

44. Christoph Menke, *Tragödie im Sittlichen: Gerechtigkeit und Freiheit nach Hegel* (Frankfurt am Main, Germany: Suhrkamp, 1996), 219.

Chapter 6: Law, Democracy, and Deliberation

1. In this chapter, all references to Jürgen Habermas, placed in parentheses, are to his book *Between Facts and Norms: Contributions to a Discourse Theory of Law and Democracy*, transl. by William Rehg (Cambridge: Polity Press, 1996). For a good introduction to Habermas's theory of law and democracy see Kenneth Baynes, "Democracy and the *Rechtsstaat*: Habermas's *Faktizität und Geltung*," in *The Cambridge Companion to Habermas*, ed. by Stephen K. White (Cambridge: Cambridge University Press, 1995), 201–31, from which I have greatly benefited.

2. See, for instance, the interpretation of Habermas's work in Nicholas Rescher, *Pluralism: Against the Demand for Consensus* (Oxford: Clarendon Press, 1993).

3. Baynes, "Democracy and the *Rechtsstaat*," 214.

4. See also ibid., 215f.

5. For an account of the complex relations between communicatively integrated life worlds and strategic subsystems of society, see Habermas, *The Theory of Communicative Action, vol. 2: Lifeworld and System: A Critique of Functionalist Reason*, transl. by Th. McCarthy (Boston: Beacon, 1987), 113–97.

6. Bernhard Peters, *Die Integration moderner Gesellschaften* (Frankfurt am Main, Germany: Suhrkamp, 1993).

7. See for a similar view Charles Taylor, "Die Motive einer Verfahrensethik," in *Moralität und Sittlichkeit. Das Problem Hegels und die Diskursethik*, ed. by Wolfgang Kuhlmann (Frankfurt am Main, Germany: Suhrkamp, 1986), 101–35.

8. For an excellent argument for such an advocacy strategy, which is not formulated in terms of the theory of deliberative democracy see Andrew Kernohan, *Liberalism, Equality, and Cultural Oppression* (Cambridge: Cambridge University Press, 1998).

9. Kenneth Baynes, "Liberal Neutrality, Pluralism, and Deliberative Politics," *Praxis International* 12 (1992): 56.

10. Ibid.

Chapter 7: Liberal Community and the Normative Potential of Tragic Conflicts

1. Christoph Menke, *Tragödie im Sittlichen: Gerechtigkeit und Freiheit nach Hegel* (Frankfurt am Main, Germany: Suhrkamp, 1996), 192ff.

2. Ibid., 197. This is my translation of "Eine allgemeine Bestimmung [des Guten] kann zwar den Inhalt, aber niemals den Grund des je eigenen, authentischen Guten bilden: Was für uns gut is, kann auch gut für mich sein—aber nicht *weil* es für uns alle gut ist."

3. Ibid., 193f.

4. Ibid., 270. This is my translation of: ". . . als das, was die Identität eines Individuums ausmacht, als eine Bestimmung seines Guten, seiner Authentizität."

5. Menke does not go into the theological question whether it is the sacred that lies "beyond," or rather conceptions of the sacred that constitute religious individuality. In using the term *the sacred* (*das Sakrale*), I suspect that he remains open to both possibilities. What he is interested in is not the ultimate source of religious individuality, but rather the obligations that religious convictions lay on individuals.

6. Menke, *Tragödie im Sittlichen*, 270. In our discussion of the case of abortion, we saw that the sacred—the belief in God, in unconditional respect for human life—can play a role in tragic conflicts in liberal societies. Menke looks to Australian aboriginal cultures to make the same point. In an interesting reading of Bruce Chatwin's ethnographic novel *The Songlines* (New York: Viking/Penguin, 1987), he focuses on the unavoidable clash of values on the Australian continent between traditional aboriginal mythology and the principles of the Australian constitutional state.

7. Menke, *Tragödie im Sittlichen*, 274.

8. Menke draws on an example by Thomas Nagel, *The View from Nowhere* (Oxford: Oxford University Press, 1986), 190.

9. For Menke, obligations to the sacred are not necessarily intersubjectively shared obligations. He may be right about this, but I think that it is fair to say that, in most cases (including the one he discusses), they are. For this reason, I interpret them in this sense.

10. Menke, *Tragödie im Sittlichen*, 282.

11. Ibid., 283. This is my translation of "Denn die Idee des Versuchs läßt keinen Raum für die Gewißheit, daß es *diese* Vorhaben und Wünschen sind, die für ein Individuum kategorisch oder fundamental sind; das eben soll ja im Versuchen erst herausgefunden werden."

12. Menke mentions John Stuart Mill, *On Liberty*, in Mill, *On Liberty and Other Essays*, ed. by John Gray (Oxford: Oxford University Press,

1991), 5–128; and Richard Rorty, *Contingency, Irony, and Solidarity* (Cambridge: Cambridge University Press, 1989).

13. I do not go into Menke's further development of experimental individuality in terms of "aesthetic experiments" here (see Menke, *Tragödie im Sittlichen*, 287ff.).

14. Stephen Macedo, *Liberal Virtues: Citizenship, Virtue and Community in Liberal Constitutionalism* (Oxford: Clarendon, 1990); William A. Galston, *Liberal Purposes: Goods, Virtues, and Diversity in the Liberal State* (Cambridge: Cambridge University Press, 1991); Philip Selznick, *The Moral Commonwealth: Social Theory and the Promise of Community* (Berkeley: University of California Press, 1992).

15. Alasdair MacIntyre, *After Virtue. A Study in Moral Theory* (Notre Dame: University of Notre Dame Press, 1981); MacIntyre, *Whose Justice? Which Rationality?* (Notre Dame: University of Notre Dame Press, 1988); Michael Sandel, *Liberalism and the Limits of Justice* (Cambridge: Cambridge University Press, 1982); Charles Taylor, *Sources of the Self: The Making of the Modern Identity* (Cambridge: Cambridge University Press, 1989); Taylor, "Cross-Purposes: The Liberal-Communitarian Debate," in *Liberalism and the Moral Life*, ed. by Nancy Rosenblum (Cambridge: Harvard University Press, 1989), 159–82; Michael Walzer, *Spheres of Justice: A Defense of Pluralism and Equality* (Oxford: Basil Blackwell, 1989); Walzer, "The Communitarian Critique of Liberalism," *Political Theory* 18 (1990): 6–23.

16. The liberal-communitarian debate is so well-known by now that it would be superfluous to discuss it at length in this study. I simply make use of "communitarian" arguments where I think this is necessary, and trust that the reader will be able to judge whether or not the argument is sound and can be defended from a liberal point of view (see Sean Sayers, "Communitarianism and Moral Realism," in *The Problematic Reality of Values*, ed. by Jan Bransen and Marc Slors [Assen, Netherlands: Van Gorcum, 1996], 121–36); and my comments on Sayers, "Some Thoughts on Communitarianism and Moral Realism," in *The Problematic Reality of Values*, ed. by Jan Bransen and Marc Slors (Assen, Netherlands: Van Gorcum, 1996), 137–41. For critical overviews and reconstructions of the liberal-communitarian debate see Daniel Bell, *Communitarianism and Its Critics* (Oxford: Clarendon Press, 1993); Rainer Forst, *Kontexte der Gerechtigkeit: Politische Philosophie jenseits von Liberalismus und Kommunitarismus* (Frankfurt am Main, Germany: Suhrkamp, 1994); and Stephen Mulhall and Adam Swift, *Liberals & Communitarians* (Oxford: Blackwell, 1996).

17. For a critical overview of earlier communitarian critiques of liberal thought see Walzer, "Communitarian Critique of Liberalism."

18. To my knowledge, the only influential author (whom many critics consider to be a communitarian) who sees practically no value in the liberal tradition is MacIntyre, *After Virtue. A Study in Moral Theory* (Notre Dame: University of Notre Dame Press, 1981).

19. Will Kymlicka and Wayne Norman, "Return of the Citizen: A Survey of Recent Work on Citizenship Theory," *Ethics* 104 (1994): 353.

20. I follow Selznick, *Moral Commonwealth*, 361ff.

21. For the role of social "imagination" in the construction of a historic identity see Benedict Anderson, *Imagined Communities* (London and New York: Verso, 1991).

22. Think of the role of experiences from past wars in defense politics and the recollection of past periods of immigration in assessing contemporary questions of immigration. For historicity and the reproduction and sustainment of shared traditions see Selznick, *Moral Commonwealth*, 361; Jürgen Habermas, *The Theory of Communicative Action, vol. 2: Lifeworld and System: A Critique of Functionalist Reason*, transl. by Th. McCarthy (Boston: Beacon, 1987); MacIntyre, *Whose Justice?*; and Charles Taylor, *Sources of the Self. The Making of the Modern Identity* (Cambridge: Cambridge University Press, 1989).

23. But see Ronald Dworkin, "Liberal Community," *California Law Review* 77 (1989): 474–520; Will Kymlicka, *Liberalism, Community, and Culture* (Oxford: Clarendon Press, 1989); Galston, *Liberal Purposes*; and the work of Joseph Raz as discussed in chapter 4 for firm liberal acknowledgments of the value of community.

24. Selznick, *Moral Commonwealth*, 362.

25. Ibid., 363.

26. Ibid.

27. Ibid., 363f.

28. Ibid., 364.

29. This view has been supported by understanding the community as a traditional, hierarchically structured means of social organization that has, in the course of modernity, gradually been replaced by society understood as a posttraditional and egalitarian means of social organization. See ibid., 365ff., for a discussion of Ferdinand Tönnies's *Community and Society*, ed. and transl. by C. P. Loomis (New York: Harper, 1963). Tönnies's book seems to have encouraged this way of viewing things.

30. This way of viewing the issue is reinforced by the many debates on citizenship and social cohesion that have dominated both academic and public debates over the last few years. In these debates, the importance of a work ethic, social solidarity, cultural belonging, and the importance of microcommunities such as neighborhoods has often been emphasized. Richard Dagger, *Civic Virtues: Rights, Citizenship, and Republican Liberalism* (Oxford: Oxford University Press, 1997); Robert D. Putnam (with Robert Leonardi and Raffaela Y. Nanetti), *Making Democracy Work: Civic Tradi-*

tions in Modern Italy (Princeton: Princeton University Press, 1993); Herman van Gunsteren, *A Theory of Citizenship: Organizing Plurality in Contemporary Democracies* (Boulder, CO: Westview Press, 1998).

31. Wibren van der Burg, "The Importance of Ideals," *Journal of Value Inquiry* 31 (1997): 23–37.

32. Galston, *Liberal Purposes*; Stephen Macedo, *Liberal Virtues: Citizenship, Virtue, and Community in Liberal Constitutionalism* (Oxford: Clarendon Press, 1990); Selznick, *Moral Commonwealth*.

33. Taylor, "Self-Interpreting Animals," in Taylor, *Human Agency and Language: Philosophical Papers, vol. 1* (Cambridge: Cambridge University Press, 1985), 53.

34. Ibid.

35. Ibid., 58.

36. Ibid.

37. Ibid., 63–64.

38. Taylor, *Sources of the Self*, 35.

39. Ibid., 32, 39.

Chapter 8: Struggles for Recognition and Tragic Conflicts

1. Recent examples are Axel Honneth, *The Struggle for Recognition: The Moral Grammar of Social Conflicts*, transl. by Joel Anderson (Cambridge: Polity Press, 1995); Avishai Margalit, *The Decent Society* (Cambridge: Harvard University Press, 1996); and Judith Shklar, *The Faces of Injustice* (New Haven: Yale University Press, 1990).

2. In this chapter, all references to Honneth, placed in parentheses, are to his *Struggle for Recognition*.

3. See also Anderson, "Translator's Introduction," in ibid., xiv.

4. As I have argued earlier, the idea that liberal rights presuppose an affirmation of specific social forms and understandings of moral character does not imply that individuals who do not live up to the expectations that come with them should not be respected as rights holders. In practice, liberal rights aim to protect individuality per se, not a narrowly circumscribed conception of personhood.

5. T. H. Marshall, "Citizenship and Social Class," in Marshall and Tom Bottomore, *Citizenship and Social Class* (London: Pluto Press, 1992), 1–51. See also Albert O. Hirschman, *The Rhetoric of Reaction: Perversity, Futility, Jeopardy* (Cambridge: Belknap/Harvard University Press, 1991).

6. Marshall's historical reconstruction of the subsequent struggles for, and granting of, civil, political, and social rights in England does not apply to all societies. However, this is not a real problem for Honneth's understanding of (struggles for) legal recognition. His basic claim is that the legal status of citizenship and the social opportunities it creates has such a normative-practical force that it is bound to be understood as highly desirable by marginalized citizens, who will try to attain and further develop it. This claim can be made without maintaining that struggles for legal recognition will necessarily follow the route they took in England.

7. See also Michael Walzer, *Spheres of Justice: A Defense of Pluralism and Equality* (Oxford: Basil Blackwell, 1989), 272ff.

8. For the case of slavery see Orlando Patterson, *Slavery and Social Death* (Cambridge: Harvard University Press), 1982. For the case of illegal immigrants (although not in terms of "social death"), see Chris de Stoop, *Haal de was maar binnen. Aziza of een verhaal van deportatie in europa* (Amsterdam: Bezige Bij, 1996).

9. Honneth draws on John Dewey, "The Theory of Emotion I," *Psychological Review* (1895): 553ff., and Dewey, "The Theory of Emotion II," *Psychological Review* (1886): 13ff.

10. For this point see Nancy Fraser, "From Redistribution to Recognition? Dilemmas of Justice in a "Postsocialist" Age," in Fraser, *Justice Interruptus: Critical Reflections on the "Postsocialist" Condition* (New York and London: Routledge, 1997), 11–39.

11. Barrington Moore, *Injustice: The Social Bases of Obedience and Revolt* (White Plains, NY: M. E. Sharp, 1978); E. P. Thompson, *The Making of the English Working Class* (London: Gollancz, 1963).

12. Of course, nationalism can take on benign and malignant forms. The aim of what I call benign state nationalism here has been to overcome the fragmentation of society along lines of language, religion, and ethnicity (see Ernest Gellner, *Nations and Nationalism* [Oxford: Blackwell, 1983] and, in normative theory, Will Kymlicka, *Multicultural Citizenship* [Oxford: Oxford University Press, 1995], 76–77). The nationalist groups mentioned in the text contest, for various reasons, this integrationist and unifying form of state nationalism. Even though some of their claims may be justified, the terrorist means by which they are sometimes accompanied must be rejected from a liberal perspective. This is not to say, however, that the state nationalism of Great Britain and Spain in these matters can always be justified from a liberal perspective.

13. Not all authors would agree with this view. Lon L. Fuller, for example, states that "In the whole field of human purpose . . . we find a pervasive refutation for the notion that we cannot know what is unsuited to an end [or what our duties are] without knowing what is perfectly suited to

achieve it [live up to them]." Fuller, *The Morality of Duty* (New Haven: Yale University Press, 1977), 11. Although this remark is directed more to the means to achieve an end than to the intelligibility of the end itself, it still suggests that we do not need specific knowledge of where we are heading in order to determine whether claims to justice are valid. Honneth would agree to this, though not without remarking that the cognitive components implicit in experiences of injustice open us on to conceptions (knowledge) of what a just world would be like and how we could achieve it.

14. Contrary to Rawls, Honneth and Habermas derive their ideas concerning the "objective-intentional" path from an account of the socio-ontological constitution of people. Therefore, their theories appear to be more comprehensive and controversial than Rawls's. Yet, as we have seen in our discussion of Rawls's "two-stage path" to an overlapping consensus, Rawls also relies on a notion of human action or reasonableness that is taken to represent the most adequate reaction to a pluralist and posttraditional society. In this sense, his expectations are more similar to Habermas and Honneth's than they initially appear to be.

Chapter 9: Vulnerability an Responsibilities of Liberal Citizenship

1. See Robert E. Goodin, *Protecting the Vulnerable: A Reanalysis of Our Social Responsibilities* (Chicago: University of Chicago Press, 1985).

2. John Stuart Mill, *On Liberty*, in Mill, *On Liberty and Other Essays*, ed. by John Gray (Oxford: Oxford University Press, 1991), 14.

3. For all three points see ibid., 16–17.

4. Ibid., 15.

5. Joseph Raz, *The Morality of Freedom* (Oxford: Clarendon Press, 1986), 414.

6. Of course, these outcomes will not be reached overnight. It may take years or much longer before the social struggle that sparks the conflict result in an identifiable "outcome." For reasons of clarity, I disregard this sociological fact here.

7. The Right Hon. Robert Lowe MP, *Speeches and Letters on Reform* (London: Bush, 1867), 170. Quoted in Albert O. Hirschman, *The Rhetoric of Reaction: Perversity, Futility, Jeopardy* (Cambridge: Belknap/Harvard University Press, 1991), 94.

8. I do not have a ready-made answer to the question as to whether representatives of extremist right-wing parties who claim that they will respect the limits democratic institutions lay on them should be allowed to run

for Parliament. In many European countries, such as Germany, Belgium, the Netherlands, and France, they are. In the Netherlands and in Germany, the pragmatic strategy to allow this in order to prevent them from going "underground" (where their activities cannot easily be controlled) has on occasion been successful. In Belgium and France, however, the situation is more problematic: Le front national (France) and the Vlaams Blok (Belgium) have recently succeeded in becoming "respectable" political forces in these countries.

9. I thank Axel Honneth for urging me to stress this point here.

10. William A. Galston, *Liberal Purposes: Goods, Virtues, and Diversity in the Liberal State* (Cambridge: Cambridge University Press, 1991), 216; Claus Offe, "Bindung, Fessel und Bremse: Moralische und institutionelle Aspekte 'intelligenter Selbstbeschränkung,'" in *Zwischenbetrachtungen im Prozeß der Aufklärung: Jürgen Habermas zum 60. Geburtstag*, ed. by Axel Honneth, Thomas McCarthy, Claus Offe, and Albrecht Wellmer (Frankfurt am Main, Germany: Suhrkamp, 1989), 739–74.

11. Kenneth Baynes, "Democracy and the *Rechtsstaat*: Habermas's *Faktizität und Geltung*," in *The Cambridge Companion to Habermas*, ed. by Stephen K. White (Cambridge: Cambridge University Press, 1995), 223; Ulrich Rödel, Günter Frankenberg, and Helmut Dubiel, *Die demokratische Frage* (Frankfurt am Main, Germany: Suhrkamp, 1989), 166ff.

12. Stephen Macedo, *Liberal Virtues: Citizenship, Virtue, and Community in Liberal Constitutionalism* (Oxford: Clarendon Press, 1990), 275.

13. Amy Gutmann and Dennis Thompson, "Moral Conflict and Political Consensus," *Ethics* 100 (1990): 76ff.

14. Macedo, *Liberal Virtues*, 275–76.

15. Ibid., 276f.

16. See Christoph Menke, *Tragödie im Sittlichen: Gerechtigkeit und Freiheit nach Hegel* (Frankfurt am Main, Germany: Suhrkamp, 1996), 307ff., for an account of the free, sovereign subject in terms of her ability to have mercy and to make sacrifices.

Part 5: Liberalism and Multiculturalism

Introduction

1. For questions of social policy and the welfare state see Gotfried Engbersen and Robert van der Veen, "De tragiek van de verzorgingsstaat," in *De verdeelde samenleving: Een inleiding in de ontwikkeling van de Nederlandse verzorgingsstaat*, ed. by Kees Schuyt and Robert van der Veen (Leiden, Netherlands: Stenfert Kroese, 1986), 195–207; and J. Donald

Moon, *Constructing Community: Moral Pluralism and Tragic Conflicts* (Princeton: Princeton University Press, 1993), 121–45. For tragic tensions of the liberal market see Susan Mendus, "Tragedy, Moral Conflict, Liberalism," in *Philosophy and Pluralism*, Royal Institute of Philosophy supplement, ed. by David Archard (Cambridge: Cambridge University Press, 1996), 191–201. For the application of law to individual cases see Titia Loenen, "Recht en het onvervulbare verlangen naar individuele gerechtigheid," *Rechtsgeleerd Magazine Themis* 4 (1996): 123–36. For feminist theory and a tragic view of liberalism see Moon, *Constructing Community*, 146–62.

2. But for discussions of liberal views on the rights of minorities in the nineteenth and early twentieth century see Will Kymlicka, *Liberalism, Community, and Culture* (Oxford: Clarendon Press, 1989), 206ff.; and Kymlicka, *Multicultural Citizenship* (Oxford: Oxford University Press, 1995), 49ff.

Chapter 10: Multiculturalism and Cultural Authenticity

1. Wibren van der Burg, "Reflections on Collective Rights and State Sovereignty," in *Nation, State and the Coexistence of Different Communities*, ed. by T. van Willigenburg, F. R. Heeger, and van der Burg (Kampen: Kok Pharos, 1995), 221–46; Marlies Galenkamp, *Individualism and Collectivism: The Concept of Collective Rights* (Rotterdam, Netherlands: Rotterdamse Filosofische Studies, 1993); and Galenkamp, "Special Rights for Minorities. The Muddy Waters of Collective Rights," in *Nation, State and the Coexistence of Different Communities*, ed. by Willigenburg, T. van, F. R. Heeger, and W. van der Burg (Kampen: Kok Pharos, 1995), 165–84; Will Kymlicka, *Liberalism, Community, and Culture* (Oxford: Clarendon Press, 1989); Kymlicka, *Multicultural Citizenship* (Oxford: Oxford University Press, 1995).

2. George Silberbauer, "Ethics in Small-scale Societies," in *A Companion to Ethics*, ed. by Peter Singer (Oxford: Basil Blackwell, 1993), 15.

3. I have benefited from discussions with Sasja Tempelman of Leiden University, Netherlands.

4. Clifford Geertz, *The Interpretation of Cultures* (London: Fontana Press, 1993), 52.

5. Kymlicka, *Multicultural Citizenship*, 18.

6. Which is not to say that every aspect of cultures has been fabricated by people with clearly defined goals in mind. It is just to say that, in practice, cultural meanings generally have certain identifiable functions in the lives of individuals and groups.

7. I use the term here in ironic quotation marks in order to relativize the uniqueness of the current meaning of the term (as I introduce it in the next paragraph). But as the frequent use of the term *culture* in these paragraphs shows, the avoidance of unclarity alone is a good enough reason to argue against the devaluation of the term *culture*. What I call multicultural here, is far better described as functionally differentiated.

8. Kymlicka, *Multicultural Citizenship*, 18.

9. Ibid.

10. K. Anthony Appiah, "Identity, Authenticity, Survival: Multicultural Societies and Social Reproduction," in *Multiculturalism*, ed. by Amy Gutmann (Princeton: Princeton University Press, 1994), 149–63.

11. Vernon Van Dyke, "The Individual, the State and Ethnic Communities in Political Theory," in *The Rights of Minority Cultures*, ed. by Will Kymlicka (Oxford: Oxford University Press, 1995), 32; emphasis added.

12. Self-ascription is most important from a normative point of view that is interested in the question as to what extent an individual wholeheartedly identifies with her presumed ethnic or national identity. Of course, it is much less suited to explain the many factors that empirically play a role in the construction of personal and collective identity. For in such constructions, third-party construction often plays a role that is partly beyond the control of individuals.

13. In chapter 11, I discuss Kymlicka's influential arguments in favor of recognizing cultural membership as a primary good.

14. Charles Taylor, "The Politics of Recognition," in *Multiculturalism*, ed. by Amy Gutmann (Princeton: Princeton University Press, 1994), 25–73. In this chapter, all references to Taylor, placed in parentheses, are to this work.

15. After all, political philosophy and popular art should both be considered genres through which aspects of the human condition are expressed.

16. It is at least remarkable that at this concluding stage of his argument Taylor does not mention the problematic case of education that he referred to alongside the case of commercial signs in earlier parts of his essay. To me, it seems to be more problematic than the case of signs, because it may be expected to have a much more pervasive influence on people's lives.

17. Jürgen Habermas, "Struggles for Recognition in the Democratic Constitutional State," transl. by Shierry Weber Nicholson, in *Multiculturalism*, ed. by Gutmann (Princeton: Princeton University Press, 1994), 109.

18. Ibid., 123–24.

19. Ibid., 129.

20. Ibid., 128.

Chapter 11: Two Liberal Views of Multiculturalism

1. Jeremy Waldron, "Minority Cultures and the Cosmopolitian Alternative," in *Nation, State and the Coexistence of Different Communities*, ed. by T. van Willigenburg, F. R. Heeger, and W. van der Burg (Kampen: Kok Pharos, 1995), 105–51. In this chapter, all references to Waldron, placed in parentheses, are to this work. In a recent lecture, "Cultural Identity and Civic Responsibility" presented at Toronto, Otago (New Zealand), and Tilburg (Netherlands), Waldron is much more perceptive to seemingly irreconcilable conflicts over cultural authencity. Unfortunately, I have not been able to adjust my critique of Waldron's position in light of this new paper. The paper will appear in *Citizenship in Diverse Societies*, ed. by Will Kymlicka and Wayne Norman (Oxford: Oxford University Press, forthcoming).

2. International Covenant on Civil and Political Rights, adopted 19 December, 1966, Article 27, 999 UNTS, 172, 179. Quoted in Waldron, "Minority Cultures and the Cosmopolitan Alternative," 110.

3. Benedict Anderson, *Imagined Communities* (London and New York: Verso, 1991). Anderson sees imagined national communities as a means to transform "fatality into continuity, contingency into meaning" (11). In the context of the passage I quote here, he talks about the emergence of modern nationalism from the eighteenth century onward. However, there seem to be good reasons to understand the ethnic nationalism of immigrant groups in these terms as well.

4. Will Kymlicka, *Liberalism, Community, and Culture* (Oxford: Clarendon Press, 1989), 163. For the following, ibid., 163–66.

5. Ibid., 165.

6. Ibid.

7. It is this sixth point that is crucial in Kymlicka's argument. He convincingly shows that Rawls and Dworkin, the liberals he disagrees with, implicitly and wrongly assume that liberal communities are culturally homogeneous. Because they do, there is no real need for them to reflect on special cultural rights for some groups. For them (at least in their work from the 1970s that Kymlicka discusses here), cultural structure is not something that will stimulate discussions over the fair access that citizens have to it. Consequently, they do not see it as a matter that is relevant to questions of distributive justice. If we drop this assumption, which I think we must, Kymlicka's argument appears to be sound.

8. Kymlicka, *Liberalism, Community, and Culture*, 170.

9. Ibid.

10. Kymlicka, *Multicultural Citizenship* (Oxford: Oxford University Press, 1995). In this chaper, all references to Kymlicka, placed in parentheses, are to this work.

11. Wibren van der Burg, "Reflections on Collective Rights and State Sovereignty," in *Nation, State and the Coexistence of Different Communities,* ed. by T. van Willigenburg, F. R. Heeger, and van der Burg (Kampen, Netherlands: Kok Pharos, 1995), 234.

References

Ackerman, Bruce. *Social Justice and the Liberal State*. New Haven: Yale University Press, 1980.

———. "Why Dialogue?" *The Journal of Philosophy* 86 (1989): 5–22.

Anderson, Benedict. *Imagined Communities*. London and New York: Verso, 1991.

Anderson, Joel. "Translator's Introduction." In Axel Honneth, *The Struggle for Recognition. The Moral Grammar of Social Conflicts*, transl. by Joel Anderson, x–xxi. Cambridge: Polity Press 1995.

Appiah, K. Anthony. "Identity, Authenticity, Survival: Multicultural Societies and Social Reproduction." In *Multiculturalism*, ed. by Amy Gutmann, 149–63. Princeton: Princeton University Press, 1994.

Baynes, Kenneth. "Liberal Neutrality, Pluralism, and Deliberative Politics." *Praxis International* 12 (1992): 50–69.

———. "Democracy and the *Rechtsstaat*: Habermas's *Faktizität und Geltung*." In *The Cambridge Companion to Habermas*, ed. by Stephen K. White, 201–31. Cambridge: Cambridge University Press, 1995.

Bell, Daniel. *Communitarianism and Its Critics*. Oxford: Clarendon Press, 1993.

Bellah, Robert, et al. *Habits of the Heart. Individualism and Commitment in American Life*. Berkeley: University of California Press, 1985.

Bellamy, Richard. *Liberalism and Modern Society. An Historical Argument*. Cambridge: Polity Press, 1992.

Benhabib, Seyla. "The Methodological Illusions of Modern Political Theory: The Case of Rawls and Habermas." *Neue Hefte für Philosophie* 21 (1982): 47–74.

———. *Critique, Norm, and Utopia: A Study of the Foundations of Critical Theory.* New York: Columbia University Press, 1986.

———. "The Generalized and the Concrete Other: The Kohlberg-Gilligan Controversy and Feminist Theory." *Praxis International* 5 (1986): 402–24.

———. "Liberal Dialogue versus a Critical Theory of Discursive Legitimation." In *Liberalism and the Moral Life*, ed. by Nancy Rosenblum, 143–56. Cambridge: Harvard University Press, 1989.

Berlin, Isaiah. "Two Concepts of Liberty." In Isaiah Berlin, *Four Essays on Liberty*, 118–72. Oxford: Oxford University Press, 1969.

Bohman, James. *Public Deliberation: Pluralism, Complexity, and Democracy.* Cambridge: MIT Press, 1996.

Bourdieu, Pierre. "What Makes a Social Class. On the Theoretical and Practical Existence of Groups." *Berkeley Journal of Sociology* 32 (1987): 1–17.

Cohen, Jean and Andrew Arato. *Civil Society and Political Theory.* Cambridge: MIT Press, 1991.

Cohen, Joshua. "Deliberation and Democratic Legitimacy." In *The Good Polity: Normative Analysis of the State*, ed. by A. Hamlin, and Ph. Pettit, 17–34. New York: Blackwell, 1991.

Dagger, Richard. *Civic Virtues: Rights, Citizenship, and Republican Liberalism.* Oxford: Oxford University Press, 1997.

Dahrendorf, Ralf. *The Modern Social Conflict: An Essay on the Politics of Liberty.* London: Weidenfeld and Nicholson, 1988.

De Stoop, Chris. *Haal de was maar binnen: Aziza of een verhaal van deportatie in europa.* Amsterdam: Bezige Bij, 1996.

Dewey, John. "The Theory of Emotion I." *Psychological Review* (1895): 553ff.

———. "The Theory of Emotion II." *Psychological Review* (1896): 13ff.

Dworkin, Ronald. *Taking Rights Seriously.* Cambridge: Harvard University Press, 1978.

———. "Liberalism." In Ronald Dworkin, *A Matter of Principle*, 181–204. Cambridge: Harvard University Press, 1985.

———. "Why Liberals Should Care About Equality." In Ronald Dworkin, *A Matter of Principle*, 205–13. Cambridge: Harvard University Press, 1985.

————. "Liberal Community." *California Law Review* 77 (1989): 474–520.

————. *Life's Dominion: An Argument about Abortion, Euthanasia, and Individual Freedom.* New York: Knopf, 1993.

Engbersen, Godfried and Robert van der Veen. "De tragiek van de verzorgingsstaat." In *De verdeelde samenleving: Een inleiding in de ontwikkeling van de Nederlandse verzorgingsstaat,* ed. by Kees Schuyt and Robert van der Veen, 195–207. Leiden, Netherlands: Stenfert Kroese, 1986.

Ester, Peter, Loek Halman, and Ruud de Moor. *The Individualizing Society: Value Change in Europe and North America.* Tilburg, Netherlands: Tilburg University Press, 1993.

Euben, J. Peter. *The Tragedy of Political Theory: The Road Not Taken.* Princeton: Princeton University Press, 1990.

Fraser, Nancy. "From Redistribution to Recognition? Dilemmas of Justice in a "Postsocialist" Age." In Nancy Fraser, *Justice Interruptus: Critical Reflections on the "Postsocialist" Condition,* 11–39. New York and London: Routledge, 1997.

Forst, Rainer. *Kontexte der Gerechtigkeit: Politische Philosophie jenseits von Liberalismus und Kommunitarismus.* Frankfurt am Main, Germany: Suhrkamp, 1994.

Fuller, Lon L. *The Morality of Duty.* New Haven: Yale University Press, 1977.

Galenkamp, Marlies. *Individualism and Collectivism: The Concept of Collective Rights.* Rotterdam, Netherlands: Rotterdamse Filosofische Studies, 1993.

————. "Special Rights for Minorities. The Muddy Waters of Collective Rights." In *Nation, State and the Coexistence of Different Communities,* ed. by T. van Willigenburg, F. R. Heeger, and W. van der Burg, 165–84. Kampen: Kok Pharos, 1995.

Galston, William A. *Liberal Purposes: Goods, Virtues, and Diversity in the Liberal State.* Cambridge: Cambridge University Press, 1991.

Geertz, Clifford. *The Interpretation of Cultures.* London: Fontana Press, 1993.

Gellner, Ernest. *Nations and Nationalism.* Oxford: Blackwell, 1983.

Goodin, Robert E. *Protecting the Vulnerable: A Reanalysis of Our Social Responsibilities.* Chicago: University of Chicago Press, 1985.

Gray, John. *Isaiah Berlin.* Princeton: Princeton University Press, 1996.

Gutmann, Amy and Dennis Thompson. "Moral Conflict and Political Consensus." *Ethics* 100 (1990): 64–88.

———. *Democracy and Disagreement.* Cambridge: Belknap/Harvard, 1996.

Habermas, Jürgen. "Die klassische Lehre von der Politik in ihrem Verhältnis zur Sozialphilosophie." In Jürgen Habermas, *Theorie und Praxis*, 48–88. Frankfurt am Main, Germany: Suhrkamp, 1971.

———. *The Theory of Communicative Action, vol. 1: Reason and the Rationalization of Society.* Transl. by Th. McCarthy. Boston: Beacon, 1984.

———. *The Theory of Communicative Action, vol. 2: Lifeworld and System: A Critique of Functionalist Reason.* Transl. by Th. McCarthy. Boston: Beacon, 1987.

———. *The Structural Transformation of the Public Sphere: An Inquiry into a Category of Bourgeois Society.* Transl. by Thomas Burger. Cambridge Mass: MIT Press, 1989.

———. "Morality and Ethical Life: Does Hegel's Critique of Kant Apply to Discourse Ethics?" In Jürgen Habermas, *Moral Consciousness and Communicative Action*, transl. by Christian Lenhardt and Shierry Weber Nicholson, 195–215. Cambridge: Polity Press, 1990.

———. "Discourse Ethics: Notes on a Program of Philosophical Justification." In Jürgen Habermas, *Moral Consciousness and Communicative Action*, transl. by Christian Lenhardt and Shierry Weber Nicholson, 43–115. Cambridge: Polity Press, 1990.

———. "On the Pragmatic, the Ethical, and the Moral Employments of Practical Reason." In Jürgen Habermas, *Justification and Application*, transl. by Ciaran Cronin, 1–17. Cambridge: Polity Press, 1993.

———. "Struggles for Recognition in the Democratic Constitutional State," transl. by Shierry Weber Nicholson. In *Multiculturalism*, ed. by Amy Gutmann, 107–48. Princeton: Princeton University Press, 1994.

———. "Reconciliation Through the Use of Public Reason: Remarks on John Rawls's Political Liberalism," transl. by Ciaran Cronin. *The Journal of Philosophy* 92 (1995): 109–31.

———. *Between Facts and Norms: Contributions to a Discourse Theory of Law and Democracy.* Transl. by William Rehg. Cambridge: Polity Press, 1996.

Hirschman, Albert O. *The Rhetoric of Reaction: Perversity, Futility, Jeopardy.* Cambridge: Belknap/Harvard University Press, 1991.

Honneth, Axel. *The Struggle for Recognition: The Moral Grammar of Social Conflicts.* Transl. by Joel Anderson. Cambridge: Polity Press, 1995.

Ignatieff, Michael. *Isaiah Berlin: A Life.* London: Chatto & Windus, 1998.

Kernohan, Andrew. *Liberalism, Equality, and Cultural Oppression.* Cambridge: Cambridge University Press, 1998.

Kuhlmann, Andreas. *Abtreibung und Selbstbestimmung: Die Intervention der Medizin*. Frankfurt am Main, Germany: Fischer, 1996.

Kymlicka, Will. *Liberalism, Community, and Culture*. Oxford: Clarendon Press, 1989.

———. *Multicultural Citizenship*. Oxford: Oxford University Press, 1995.

——— and Wayne Norman. "Return of the Citizen: A Survey of Recent Work on Citizenship Theory." *Ethics* 104 (1994): 352–81.

Larmore, Charles. *Patterns of Moral Complexity*. Cambridge: Cambridge University Press, 1987.

Loenen, Titia. "Recht en het onvervulbare verlangen naar individuele gerechtigheid." *Rechtsgeleerd Magazine Themis* 4 (1996): 123–36.

Luker, Kristin. *Abortion and the Politics of Motherhood*. Berkeley: University of California Press, 1984.

Macedo, Stephen. *Liberal Virtues: Citizenship, Virtue, and Community in Liberal Constitutionalism*. Oxford: Clarendon Press, 1990.

MacIntyre, Alasdair. *After Virtue: A Study in Moral Theory*. Notre Dame: University of Notre Dame Press, 1981.

———. *Whose Justice? Which Rationality?* Notre Dame: University of Notre Dame Press, 1988.

Margalit, Avishai. *The Decent Society*. Cambridge: Harvard University Press, 1996.

Marshall, T. H. "Citizenship and Social Class." In T. H. Marshall and Tom Bottomore, *Citizenship and Social Class*, 1–51. London: Pluto Press, 1992.

Mendus, Susan. "Tragedy, Moral Conflict, and Liberalism." In *Philosophy and Pluralism*, Royal Institute of Philosophy supplement, ed. by David Archard, 191–201. Cambridge: Cambridge University Press, 1996.

Menke, Christoph. *Tragödie im Sittlichen: Gerechtigkeit und Freiheit nach Hegel*. Frankfurt am Main, Germany: Suhrkamp, 1996.

Mill, John Stuart. *On Liberty*. In John Stuart Mill, *On Liberty and Other Essays*, ed. by John Gray, 5–128. Oxford: Oxford University Press, 1991.

Moon, J. Donald. *Constructing Community. Moral Pluralism and Tragic Conflicts*. Princeton: Princeton University Press, 1993.

Moore, Barrington. *Injustice: The Social Bases of Obedience and Revolt*. White Plains, NY: M. E. Sharp, 1978.

Mulhall, Stephen and Adam Swift. *Liberals & Communitarians*. Oxford: Blackwell, 1996.

Nagel, Thomas. *The View from Nowhere*. Oxford: Oxford University Press, 1986.

Nussbaum, Martha. *The Fragility of Goodness: Luck and Ethics in Greek Tragedy and Philosophy*. Cambridge: Cambridge University Press, 1986.

Offe, Claus. "Bindung, Fessel und Bremse: Moralische und institutionelle Aspekte 'intelligenter Selbstbeschränkung.'" In *Zwischenbetrachtungen im Prozeß der Aufklärung: Jürgen Habermas zum 60. Geburtstag*, ed. by Axel Honneth, Thomas McCarthy, Claus Offe, and Albrecht Wellmer, 739–74. Frankfurt am Main, Germany: Suhrkamp, 1989.

Patterson, Orlando. *Slavery and Social Death*. Cambridge: Harvard University Press, 1982.

Peters, Bernhard. *Die Integration moderner Gesellschaften*. Frankfurt am Main, Germany: Suhrkamp, 1993.

Putnam, Robert D. (with Robert Leonardi and Raffaela Y. Nanetti). *Making Democracy Work: Civic Traditions in Modern Italy*. Princeton: Princeton University Press, 1993.

Rawls, John. *A Theory of Justice*. Cambridge: Harvard University Press, 1971.

———. *Political Liberalism*. New York: Columbia University Press, 1993.

———. "Reply to Habermas." *The Journal of Philosophy* 92 (1995): 132–80.

———. "The Idea of Public Reason Revisited." *The University of Chicago Law Review* 64 (1997): 765–809.

Raz, Joseph. *The Morality of Freedom*. Oxford: Clarendon Press, 1986.

———. "Government by Consent." In Joseph Raz, *Ethics in the Public Domain*, 339–53. Oxford: Clarendon Press, 1994.

———. "Rights and Individual Well-being." In Joseph Raz, *Ethics in the Public Domain*, 29–44. Oxford: Clarendon Press, 1994.

———. "Facing Diversity: The Case of Epistemic Abstinence." In Joseph Raz, *Ethics in the Public Domain*, 45–81. Oxford: Clarendon Press, 1994.

———. "Duties of Well-being." In Joseph Raz, *Ethics in the Public Domain*, 3–28. Oxford: Clarendon Press, 1994.

———. "Multiculturalism: A Liberal Perspective." In Joseph Raz, *Ethics in the Public Domain*, 155–76. Oxford: Clarendon Press, 1994.

Rescher, Nicholas. *Pluralism: Against the Demand for Consensus*. Oxford: Clarendon Press, 1993.

Rödel, Ulrich, Günter Frankenberg, and Helmut Dubiel. *Die demokratische Frage*. Frankfurt am Main, Germany: Suhrkamp, 1989.

Rorty, Richard. *Contingency, Irony, Solidarity*. Cambridge: Cambridge University Press, 1989.

Sandel, Michael. *Liberalism and the Limits of Justice*. Cambridge: Cambridge University Press, 1982.

Sayers, Sean. "Communitarianism and Moral Realism." In *The Problematic Reality of Values*, ed. by Jan Bransen and Marc Slors, 121–36. Assen: Van Gorcum, 1996.

Scarry, Elaine. *The Body in Pain: The Making and Unmaking of the World*. Oxford: Oxford University Press, 1985.

Selznick, Philip. *The Moral Commonwealth: Social Theory and the Promise of Community*. Berkeley: University of California Press, 1992.

Sen, Amartya. *Inequality Reexamined*. New York/Cambridge: Russel Sage Foundation/Harvard University Press, 1992.

Shklar, Judith. *The Faces of Injustice*. New Haven: Yale University Press, 1990.

Silberbauer, George. "Ethics in Small-scale Societies." In *A Companion to Ethics*, ed. by Peter Singer, 14–28. Oxford: Basil Blackwell, 1993.

Szondi, Peter. *Versuch über das Tragische*. Frankfurt am Main, Germany: Insel Verlag, 1961.

Taylor, Charles. "What is Human Agency?" In Charles Taylor, *Human Agency and Language: Philosophical Papers, vol. 1*, 15–44. Cambridge: Cambridge University Press, 1985.

———. "Self-Interpreting Animals" In Charles Taylor, *Human Agency and Language: Philosophical Papers, vol. 1*, 45–76. Cambridge: Cambridge University Press, 1985.

———. "Die Motive einer Verfahrensethik." In *Moralität und Sittlichkeit: Das Problem Hegels und die Diskursethik*, ed. by Wolfgang Kuhlmann, 101–35. Frankfurt am Main, Germany: Suhrkamp, 1986.

———. *Sources of the Self. The Making of the Modern Identity*. Cambridge: Cambridge University Press, 1989.

———. "Cross-Purposes: The Liberal-Communitarian Debate." In *Liberalism and the Moral Life*, ed. by Nancy Rosenblum, 159–82. Cambridge: Harvard University Press, 1989.

———. *The Ethics of Authenticity*. Cambridge: Harvard University Press, 1993.

———. "The Politics of Recognition." In *Multiculturalism*, ed. by Amy Gutmann, 25–73. Princeton: Princeton University Press, 1994.

Thompson, E. P. *The Making of the English Working Class*. London: Gollancz, 1963.

Tönnies, Ferdinand. *Community and Society*. Ed. and transl. by C. P. Loomis. New York: Harper, 1963.

Van den Brink, Bert. "Some Thoughts on Communitarianism and Moral Realism." In *The Problematic Reality of Values*, ed. by Jan Bransen and Marc Slors, 137–41. Assen, Netherlands: Van Gorcum, 1996.

———. "Die anständige, die gerechte und die gute Gesellschaft." *Deutsche Zeitschrift für Philosophie* 47 (1999): 271–89.

Van der Burg, Wibren. "Reflections on Collective Rights and State Sovereignty." In *Nation, State and the Coexistence of Different Communities*, ed. by T. van Willigenburg, F. R. Heeger, and W. van der Burg, 221–46. Kampen: Kok Pharos, 1995.

———. "The Importance of Ideals." *Journal of Value Inquiry* 31 (1997): 23–37.

Van Dyke, Vernon. "The Individual, the State and Ethnic Communities in Political Theory." In *The Rights of Minority Cultures*, ed. by Will Kymlicka, 31–56. Oxford: Oxford University Press, 1995.

Van Gunsteren, Herman. *A Theory of Citizenship: Organizing Plurality in Contemporary Democracies*. Boulder, CO: Westview Press, 1998.

Waldron, Jeremy. "Theoretical Foundations of Liberalism." In Jeremy Waldron, *Liberal Rights: Collected Papers 1981–1991*, 35–62. Cambridge: Cambridge University Press, 1993.

———. "Minority Cultures and the Cosmopolitan Alternative." In *Nation, State and the Coexistence of Different Communities*, ed. by T. van Willigenburg, F. R. Heeger, and W. van der Burg, 105–51. Kampen: Kok Pharos, 1995.

Wall, Steven. *Liberalism, Perfectionism and Restraint*. Cambridge: Cambridge University Press, 1998.

Walzer, Michael. *Spheres of Justice. A Defense of Pluralism and Equality*. Oxford: Basil Blackwell, 1989.

———. "The Communitarian Critique of Liberalism." *Political Theory* 18 (1990): 6–23.

———. "The Idea of Civil Society. A Path to Social Reconstruction." *Dissent* (Spring 1991): 293–304.

Warnke, Georgia. *Justice and Interpretation*. Cambridge: MIT Press, 1993.

Warren, Mark E. "The Self in Discursive Democracy." In *The Cambridge Companion to Habermas*, ed. by Stephen K. White, 167–200. Cambridge: Cambridge University Press, 1995.

Williams, Bernard. *Shame and Necessity*. Berkeley: University of California Press, 1993.

Index

Entries such as "liberalism" and "tragedy" have been reduced to essentials. "Tragedy" appears as a subentry in many of the entries. "Liberalism" can be further tracked in many of the entries and subentries. Subjects and names from the footnotes have been included only if they are of immediate importance to an argument in the main text.

Smith, Adam, 205
social evaluation and expectation:
and character, 133; and citizenship virtue, 172; and liberal community, 138, 142–43; and
recognition, 128, 150, 152–53,
161, 163, 165
solidarity. *See* justice (anticipated
end state), and recognition
Sophocles, 27
Szondi, Peter: on tragedy, 27

Taylor, Charles: collective rights in,
192, 196; on community, 140–42;
cultural authenticity in, 192–93;
cultural survival in, 195–97,
201–2; on difference, 192–94, 220;
on dignity, 193–94, 220; on individual experience, 140–42, 153;
liberal-communitarianism in,
136, 192–202; on liberal rights,
192–93, 195–97, 200; on multiculturalism, 192–204, 210–11; on political self-determination, 192–93,
197; and primary social goods,
196; on Quebec debate, 183,
195–201; on self-realization,
193–94; and tragedy, 195, 220–21
Thompson, Dennis, 102–4, 121
Thompson, E.P., 154
toleration: and autonomy, 77–78,
163; and citizenship virtue,
171–74; and conceptions of the
good, 15–16; of extremist right-
wing claims, 167–68, 247–48n;
Habermas on, 94, 97, 101–2, 118;
as key concept of liberal thought,
76, 78, 163, 221; militant or active, 94, 96, 121, 172; and racism,
169; Rawls on, 46, 50, 53–55; Raz
on, 64, 74, 120; and recognition,
151; and tragedy, 81, 159; and
vulnerability, 165–66
tragedy: and conflict, 5–6, 27–38;
and culture, 28, 33; defined, 27;
discussed, 5–6, 15, 27–38; Greek,

230n; and harmony, 28; and inescapability, 27, 32, 79; and internal critique of liberalism, 31; and
justice, 30–31; and liberal aim, 6,
15, 38; and loss, 5–6, 16, 27, 38;
and necessity, 27, 32, 38; ontological account of, 29–30; and pluralism, 27–38; and private-public
distinction, 33–37; and purposiveness of social structure, 32, 38;
and reconciliation, 16, 28; and religion, 28, 30, 33, 36. *See also*
tragedy of liberalism, and *other
major entries (subentry "tragedy")*
tragedy of liberalism: discussed, 5–6,
15, 27–38, 79–83, 85, 123–25,
175–79, 219–23; heuristic or normative potential of, 127–43, 154,
176, 178; and liberal aim, 6, 15,
38, 40, 76, 79–83, 102, 123–25,
142–43, 169, 177–79, 199, 225n;
from both a liberal and a nonliberal perspective, 81, 123–24; and
loss, 5–6, 16, 27, 38, 159, 160, 175;
and necessity, 27, 32, 38, 79, 81;
and purposiveness of social structure, 32, 38, 79–81, 123, 134, 177;
and sacrifice, 158–59; two views of
28–32; and universalistic ideals, 1,
125; and working hypotheses, 38,
79–83, 123–25, 175–79. *See also*
tragedy, and *other major entries
(subentry "tragedy")*

virtue: and liberal community, 140;
of mutual respect, 116. *See also*
citizenship virtue
vulnerability: and autonomy, 165;
and conflict, 169–71; and harm,
128, 163–71, 176; and justice,
165; and pluralism, 165; and public reason, 165; and responsibility,
163–71; and toleration, 165–66

Waldron, Jeremy: on communitarianism, 205; cosmopolitanism in,